The Editor's Companion

A S THE KNOWLEDGE ECONOMY takes shape, editors face many challenges: technology is transforming publishing, text is losing out to graphics, and writing is distorted by cliché, hype and spin. More than ever, editors are needed to add value to information and to rescue readers from boredom and confusion.

The Editor's Companion explains the traditional skills of editing for publication and how to adapt them for digital production. It describes the editorial tasks for all kinds of print and screen publications—from fantasy novels, academic texts and oral history to web pages, government documents and corporate reports. It provides advice on operating a freelance business and includes the *Australian Standards for Editing Practice* as an appendix. It is an essential tool not only for professional editors but also for media and publications officers, self-publishers and writers editing their own work.

With its broad coverage of editorial concerns *The Editor's Companion* is the 21st-century replacement for the friendly guidance of in-house mentors and colleagues.

Janet Mackenzie is a freelance editor with more than 30 years' experience in the profession and has conducted many training workshops on editing. She is an honorary life member of the Society of Editors (Victoria) and convenes the national working group on accreditation for the Council of Australian Societies of Editors.

The Editor's Companion

JANET MACKENZIE

CAMBRIDGE
UNIVERSITY PRESS

PUBLISHED BY THE PRESS SYNDICATE OF THE UNIVERSITY OF CAMBRIDGE
The Pitt Building, Trumpington Street, Cambridge, United Kingdom

CAMBRIDGE UNIVERSITY PRESS
The Edinburgh Building, Cambridge CB2 2RU, UK
40 West 20th Street, New York, NY 10011–4211, USA
477 Williamstown Road, Port Melbourne, VIC 3207, Australia
Ruiz de Alarcón 13, 28014 Madrid, Spain
Dock House, The Waterfront, Cape Town 8001, South Africa

http://www.cambridge.org

First published by Cambridge University Press 2004
Reprinted 2004

Printed in Australia by Ligare Pty Ltd

Typeface StempelGaramond (*Adobe*) 10.5/13 pt *System* QuarkXPress®

A catalogue record for this book is available from the British Library

National Library of Australia Cataloguing in Publication data

Mackenzie, Janet.
The editor's companion.
Bibliography.
Includes index.
ISBN 0 521 60569 5.
1. Editing. I. Title.
808.027

ISBN 0 521 60569 5 paperback

Contents

Illustrations

Preface

THE PROFESSION OF EDITING for publication is at a crossroads. Either editors go forward to a bright future, with greater status and remuneration than we have ever had; or we slip into oblivion along with other casualties of a rapidly changing world, like Latin teachers and shorthand typists.

Text is being displaced in the dissemination of information—largely because it is often clumsy and ineffective. Editors add value to raw text; we transform information into knowledge. But editorial skills, properly applied, do not draw attention to themselves, and therefore they are overlooked and undervalued. Editing is crucial to the effective presentation of information and the lucid discussion of ideas. The editor knows how to make a product that is functional and fit for its purpose. We conceptualise the kind of publication that will best do the job for the given resources—whether it is a marketing brochure, a website, a textbook or a novel—and we bring it into being.

The emerging national consciousness of the profession is a sign of hope. In 2001 editors nationwide adopted *Australian Standards for Editing Practice*, which are reproduced in the appendix to this book. The *Standards* codify the knowledge that editors bring to the job. Admirably succinct, they are statements of principles with wide ramifications that need to be unpacked. The *Standards* can be regarded as beacons on a rocky shore; *The Editor's Companion* takes them as its reference points for a detailed chart of the coastline.

The role of the editor in the production process is expanding beyond traditional copyediting. Editors now undertake concept development and information design at one end and typesetting and page layout at the other, with a bit of publicity and marketing on the side. Screen publications require editors to adapt their expertise to a new medium and learn new jargon and technical skills. As amateur publishing expands, editors are asked to assemble the publishing team and manage the whole project. *The Companion* marks out traditional editorial skills amid the fluid job descriptions of the knowledge economy.

I have taught editing at every level from primary school to postgraduate master classes and in-service training, and I am grateful to the participants for their insights. I know that editors need advice on applying the *Standards* to their work, on systematic methods of working, on adapting to screen work, and on making a success of freelancing. *The Companion* answers their questions.

Since 1966 Australian editors have relied on the government *Style Manual*, now in a splendid sixth edition by Snooks & Co. (John Wiley & Sons Australia, 2002), and I have not attempted to duplicate its thorough coverage of writing, typography and reproduction. *The Companion* translates the *Style Manual*'s recommendations into practical editing tasks and provides advice on the puzzles that arise in daily work. As in-house training declines and more editors freelance, editing can be a lonely business. *The Companion* replaces, to some extent, the friendly guidance and reassurance that were once provided by mentors and colleagues.

I am grateful to my mentors, Camilla Raab, Peter Jones and Peter Ryan at Melbourne University Press, who launched me on my editing career.

Thanks are due to the Council of Australian Societies of Editors for permission to reproduce *Australian Standards for Editing Practice*; and to the members of CASE and its working groups on standards and accreditation for pleasurable collaboration. For permission to reproduce copyright material I am grateful to John Bangsund, Mike Crooke, Peter Donoughue, Susan Hawthorne, Pamela Hewitt and Janet Salisbury.

I am indebted to many colleagues for encouragement, advice and critical reading: Trischa Baker, Robert Byrne, Amanda Curtin, Cathie Dunsford, Catherine Gray, Pamela Hewitt, Ed Highley, James Kelly, Brett Lockwood, Sam Mackenzie, Helen Bethune Moore, Robert Moore, Sharon Nevile, Ray O'Farrell, Renée Otmar, Janet Salisbury, Nick Walker, Lan Wang, Andrew Watson. For specific expertise I thank Jill Henry, Susan Keogh and the staff at Cambridge University Press, and the freelances: Jean Dunn, editor; Lauren Statham, designer; and Max McMaster, indexer. The mistakes that remain are all mine.

As always, deep gratitude to Al Rozefsky, the enabling factor.

Janet Mackenzie
March 2004

The editor in context

EDITING FOR PUBLICATION is a little-known occupation. The common impression is that it consists of correcting grammar and punctuation, which it does, but the job has many other aspects that make it endlessly absorbing. If you are suited to it, editing is the best fun you can have at a desk.

What makes a good editor? Editors share a defining characteristic: they love ideas and words and books. In a world of increasing specialisation, most are generalists. Reflecting the female domination of the book industry, almost all of them are women.

Two contradictory stereotypes prevail. One is the Jackie Onassis type, who has languorous lunches with celebrity authors and swans about with the literati at the best parties. The other is the eagle-eyed, anal-retentive, obsessive frump who flays inoffensive manuscripts with her punitive pencil. In fact, editors who fit either of these stereotypes don't get far. Editors have been compared to midwives, surgeons and even chameleons, but the most apt simile is inorganic: 'Good editors may be likened to those crystal-clear prisms which form a vital part of a pair of binoculars. They are not there to alter the view or change the scene, but to make it clearer and closer.'[1]

Editorial skills

The profession of editing rejects all but paragons with an extraordinary array of virtues:

- *Communication skills:* Editors are articulate and communicate lucidly in writing; they can write in various registers and styles and take on the voice of an author.
- *Social skills:* Editors are tactful, patient, flexible, good at negotiating and have respect for others' views.

- *Cognitive skills:* Editors are good at abstract, inductive, critical thinking; they quickly identify the essence of a piece of writing and grasp underlying concepts and themes.
- *Reading skills:* Editors use many strategies to gain meaning from text, such as skimming, skipping and parsing.
- *Imagination and initiative:* Editors perceive how to transform raw text into an effective publication by imagining the reader's needs. They are resourceful in solving problems and finding information.
- *Concentration, perseverance, attention to detail:* Editors engage with complex written material for days or weeks at a time. They are methodical and meticulous, performing tedious, repetitive tasks with painstaking care.
- *Managerial and administrative skills:* Editors are good at organising, prioritising, and meeting deadlines. They keep track of numerous multi-stage projects over extended periods.
- *Team players:* Editors collaborate well, and they expect the author or the publishing team to take credit for their work.

To some extent editing is a state of mind, poised between attachment and detachment. On the one hand, you care enough about the work to want to do it well. On the other, you usually have little control over the project—purpose, design, resources—so you must let go of it and not feel that any defects or failures diminish you personally. On some jobs, all you can do is turn garbage into mediocrity; to put it another way, you can't polish a turd. The editor's position is summed up in the old saying 'All care and no responsibility': you do your work diligently, but the overall responsibility for the outcome belongs to the publishing team.

Some editors are so self-effacing that they claim their work is invisible. It is true that non-experts might not see how the effect is achieved, but the appeal of a well-edited publication is as evident as that of a well-tended garden or a well-prepared meal.

Applying editorial skills

Editorial practice is not confined to professional editors. Many job descriptions require 'effective written communication skills'. Our highly literate society rewards those who can use language well to explain, instruct, persuade or entertain.

Every writer is to some extent an editor and needs to understand the principles explained here, whether the output is a fantasy novel or a letter to the newspaper. The same applies to communications that are not publications in the traditional sense. Teachers preparing handouts and business people giving presentations must consider structure and language, integrate words with artwork, and tailor their material to the needs of the audience.

Enlightened executives and officials know that errors in details such as spelling will diminish their organisation's credibility and enrage some of their customers. Moreover, clear writing can deliver enormous savings in time and money.

In Britain, the Campaign for Plain English estimates that 'sloppy letter-writing alone costs ... about £6000 million a year, as a result of mistakes, inefficiency and lost business'.[2]

The chapters that follow draw most of their examples from books, but the principles can—indeed, should—be applied to any print or screen publication, small or large. Editing adds value by providing clarity and precision in:

- media releases
- newspaper and magazine articles
- pamphlets and brochures
- research papers
- technical reports
- submissions
- tenders
- instruction manuals
- catalogues
- legal documents
- parliamentary statutes
- government regulations
- forms and questionnaires
- publicity and advertising
- product information
- prospectuses
- annual reports
- proposals and evaluations
- business letters and memos
- fact sheets
- menus
- résumés
- learning materials
- family history.

The book industry

Although editors work in many sectors, the book industry is the origin and the core of the profession, so we will survey it briefly.

In Australia today, the publishing world is in a state of commercial and technological upheaval that bewilders those who try to earn their living in it. In circumstances of chaos, the long view is often calming. Hindsight shows us that the trends in publishing that disturb us today—the commercialisation of mass culture, the rat race of galloping technology, the increasing domination of multinational conglomerates—are merely the latest chapters in a long-running thriller.[3] We can confidently say, however, that books are changing and the trade isn't what it used to be.

The Australian book industry has long been dominated by overseas-owned firms: once British, now multinational. The pattern is for small local houses to emerge and make their mark, and then be taken over by the giants. Mergers and acquisitions follow each other rapidly in a remorseless game of musical chairs. The book world grieved to see the venerable Angus & Robertson fall to HarperCollins and become a blip on the bottom line of News Corporation. But the news is not all bad. Compared to the late 1960s, when wholly Australian-owned publishers were hard to find, there are many small independent houses.

Sydney is home to most of the major commercial and educational publishers, including McGraw–Hill, Simon & Schuster and Hodder Headline, as well as the major independent Australian trade house, Allen & Unwin, and smaller firms like Duffy & Snellgrove and Hale & Iremonger. According to the Australian Bureau of Statistics, Sydney accounts for half of industry turnover.[4] Melbourne is the headquarters for several large houses, including Penguin, Macmillan Education, Harcourt and Pearson, and several university presses, including Melbourne, Oxford and Cambridge. Melbourne also has ABC Books, the publishing arm of the national broadcaster, and many small and specialist publishers, such as Lothian Books, Text Publishing, Scribe Publications, Spinifex Press and Lonely Planet. Melbourne-based publishers produce 40 per cent of turnover, which leaves 10 per cent distributed over the rest of the country. In Brisbane is the University of Queensland Press, which publishes poetry and fiction as well as scholarly books, and John Wiley & Sons. Perth has the University of Western Australia Press and some commercial publishing. Small publishers like Fremantle Arts Centre Press, Wakefield Press (Adelaide), Magabala Books (Broome), Institute of Aboriginal Development Press (Alice Springs) and Aboriginal Studies Press (Canberra), though economically negligible, are culturally significant.

A female industry

Unlike most Australian industries, book publishing is women's business. It employs about 5000 people, of whom almost two-thirds are female. Among editors, the ratio is nearer nine to one. As is usually the case, though, men are over-represented in decision-making positions. The role of women in Australian publishing has been overlooked. As one researcher points out: 'despite some notable exceptions, the history of the book in Australia largely omits women. This has resulted in significant gender biases and distortions in the mainstream history of Australian print culture.'[5]

It is said that the majority of readers, especially of fiction, are female.

The position of authors

Australian authors feel fragile, besieged by the bean counters and neglected by an ignorant public. It is true that publishers have abdicated their role of fostering authors' skills, but there have been compensating developments. Government patronage of writers has increased in recent decades, with the establishment of the Australia Council and the Public Lending Right. More than a dozen writers' centres, together with literary competitions, awards, grants and writers' festivals, offer support and exposure, and creative writing courses flourish in adult education, universities and TAFE. Most of our major authors of both fiction and educational books are Australian residents and some of them make a reasonable living from their work, though authors who achieve international success are often lost to local publishers.

Trends

If we take the long view, some trends in publishing are positive. Domination by overseas interests has not impoverished our culture or diminished the national conversation: we are reading a lot more Australian books than we were three decades ago. More than 9000 new titles were published in 2001/02, and the total number of books sold increased by one-quarter over the previous year to 130 million. The proportion of Australian titles has climbed from one in ten in 1969 to well over half. The value of local educational, fiction and non-fiction titles exceeds imports—in the case of non-fiction, by 179 per cent. We lag, however, in children's books: two-thirds (by value) are imported. The global nature of English-language publishing cuts both ways, with some local publishers producing primarily for foreign markets. The value of exports amounted to 14 per cent of total book sales. Publishers' profits have steadied after a plunge in 2000/01, which probably reflected the imposition of the first tax on books.

Although sales of Australian titles have skyrocketed, some see this vigour as unhealthy. They would prefer to see fewer books of better quality, arguing that good books get lost among the dross. Certainly many books are undercooked or even half-baked, but we have to maintain perspective: in the Victorian era, for instance, people read a lot of trash as well as Darwin and Dickens. (You should see the books my grandparents received as school prizes in the 1890s.)

Publishers make about 90 per cent of their profits from book sales rather than sales of rights. Add to this the news that in 2001/02 printed books earned $800 million in contrast to electronic and audio book sales of $12 million, and we can see that the traditional wood-pulp format is far from obsolete. Although electronic publishing is touted as the coming thing, no one seems to have figured out a way to make money from it. Major publishers are reviewing their investments, and problems in the world's largest media corporation, Time Warner (formerly AOL Time Warner), suggest that bigger is not necessarily more profitable. Even apparently secure niche publishers can suffer from global events, as Lonely Planet found when sales of travel books plunged after September 11, 2001.

In a new trend, the Australian publishing industry is becoming reflective and undergoing academic scrutiny. 'A recently completed bibliography itemises sixty-three Australian-originated higher degree theses on book publishing, the book trade and related topics, together with twelve higher degree research projects currently in progress in Australia.'[6]

There are many pressures on Australian book publishing—changes in intellectual property rights, the digital transformation of knowledge, shifts in reading habits and methods. So far the industry has proved vigorous and resilient. It's encouraging to hear that young readers are keen: 'Many Australian children's publishers say the local industry is basking in a golden age, prompted by "book-hungry kids" and hard-won recognition that children's books are worthy cultural investments.'[7]

Who's who in publishing

The job description 'editor' arose in the book industry, but editorial skills are in demand for all kinds of written communication. Once upon a time, stenographers routinely corrected their bosses' grammar and improved their expression. Now that everyone does their own typing, many corporate and government bodies are employing editors to add value to information and ensure that their communications are literate and effective.

Editors' workplaces are so varied that it is difficult to generalise about the personnel, but it is usually possible to distinguish a triad of editor, author and publisher.[8]

Editor

In many situations the editor manages the publication project, doing everything from drawing up the project plan to organising the launch. Large publishing houses usually split the editorial role, and although the job titles are confusing the division is usually much the same. The commissioning editor (acquisitions editor, managing editor, publisher) takes the management role: developing the concept with the author, negotiating the contract, writing the publishing proposal, drawing up the budget, assembling the publishing team and supervising production. The editor (copyeditor, line editor, desk editor) does the grunt work, as described in the following chapters.

Author

The author of a publication may be one person, or several people, or a committee of some sort. In educational, corporate and government publishing an individual may prepare a draft that is then reworked by others and approved by a committee.

Sometimes the author does very little of the actual writing. Anthologies, collections and reference works may have many contributors, and one or two individuals take overall responsibility for the content. For a historical diary or an edition of a classic literary work, the volume editor (co-ordinating editor, academic editor) plays the role of the author. Books such as celebrity autobiographies are often ghost-written, and well-known academics lend their names to textbooks on which underlings have done the bulk of the work.

In this book the term 'author' means the person who has the responsibility for authorial decisions during the publication process. However the term is defined, the editor must always respect the author's moral rights and the integrity of the work.

I have referred to the author with feminine pronouns throughout.

Publisher

The publisher is likewise difficult to characterise. The simplest case is that of editors working in house in the book industry, where the publisher is their employer; the publishing decisions are made by the commissioning editor and ratified by senior management. For freelance editors, the publisher is usually the client. In the case of self-published works, of course, the publisher is also the author. In corporate and government publishing, the media unit or the public relations department plays the publisher's role.

In essence, the publisher is the person who controls the budget and schedule, and thus determines the nature and quality of the publication.

Colleagues

The editor's colleagues are designers, typesetters, indexers and proofreaders, and for some publications there may also be picture researchers, permissions editors, photographers, illustrators and cartographers. The job descriptions are slippery: on some projects the editor not only edits but also does the proofreading, page layout and indexing, or a desktop publisher may do both the design and the typesetting. Publishing houses usually outsource most of these tasks, and even in-house editors may regularly work with colleagues they have never laid eyes on.

The reader

Lurking unseen among these various characters is the most important of all, the whole purpose of the publication—the reader. The editor holds the image of the target readers constantly in mind and shapes the content and form of the publication to fit their needs.

I have referred to the reader with masculine pronouns throughout.

Portrait of a profession

The doctrine of economic rationalism has dominated all business enterprises for some time, but publishers are beginning to realise what they have lost in sacrificing editorial standards to the bottom line. Peter Donoughue, managing director of John Wiley & Sons Australia, sounds a warning:

> At a time when celebrities can't write, corporations lie, actors can't sing, journalists run agendas, politicians deceive, and institutions are cowed, we need editors with high standards to produce text readers can trust. At a time of insecurity, a time characterised by the misuse of language, those of us professionally engaged

in the business of information need courage to confront misinformation, hype, cant, cliché and spin.

More than ever, we need editors committed to quality and excellence. Such editors have always been underrated in the publishing industry. Large and critically important parts of the editorial function have been outsourced for decades. We publishers have decided we don't own that function, just as we don't own the composition or printing functions. But it has always seemed to me that we are an impoverished industry because of it. Our standards, as publishers, have been lowered. Our regard for quality, for the quality of the text itself, is off our radar screen. The less we pay for editing the better. That's all we care about. The hope for quality therefore rests with editors themselves.[9]

Over the last few years, editors have taken up this challenge.

The Council of Australian Societies of Editors

The editing profession in Australia is organised on a federal basis. Each state and territory has its own independent society of editors, the oldest of which, the Victorian society, was founded in 1970. These societies came together to form the Council of Australian Societies of Editors in 1998. The council consists of the presidents of the societies or their nominees. They meet in person only once a year or so, and the rest of the time the council exists in cyberspace, operating by email and teleconference.

Despite its ethereal nature, CASE has achieved some solid gains, undertaking projects to promote editing and editors on a national basis. A national magazine, *The Australian Editor*, foundered after only two issues. More successful were the development of *Australian Standards for Editing Practice*, described below, and the first national conference of editors in Brisbane in July 2003.[10] Plans for a national accreditation scheme are well advanced.[11]

It is not easy to create a national focus for the profession. Each society has its own peculiarities—in Canberra and Tasmania, for instance, many editors work for government agencies—so there are particular interests to consider. Editors should cultivate the national dimensions of the profession. All the societies except the Northern Territory's have websites (listed at the end of the Appendix), and most of them make their newsletters, with many articles of interest, available online.

Australian Standards for Editing Practice

The *Standards*, which are reproduced in the Appendix, are innovative—in fact, a world first—as a comprehensive statement of the power of editing to add value to information and to clarify communication. By codifying traditional editorial skills, they mark the frontiers of the editor's territory in the flux of the knowledge economy. And the territory needs to be defended. 'After all, no one is pressing graphic designers to improve their proofreading skills or typesetters to brush up on structural editing.'[12]

I was fortunate to be the Victorian delegate on the working group set up by CASE to draw up the *Standards*. The group, comprising one delegate from each society, had diverse editorial backgrounds, from learned journals to electronic educational publishing. If you can imagine editors editing a document about editing, you will know that this was a thorough job.

The working group convened early in 1999 and agreed that the *Standards* would:

- be completely separate from any accreditation process that may or may not follow
- codify the core capabilities expected of professional editors, both in-house and freelance, in Australia
- cover editing for publication in both print and electronic media
- aim primarily at informing editors, with secondary audiences of editors' clients and educators.

Furthermore, we determined to make the *Standards*:

- generic and timeless: not establishing preferences for specific resources, such as dictionaries, referencing systems or technologies
- universal: not tailored to particular areas of specialisation, such as scientific editing, or roles such as commissioning or managing editors
- applicable at all levels: not graded, for instance, into experienced and junior editing capabilities
- statements about knowledge, not about tasks or who does them—we did not want to produce a checklist for commissioning a particular project.

The decision to call the document 'Standards' has aroused comment. Kathie Stove, convenor of the working group, explains the rationale:

> We used *The Macquarie Dictionary*'s first and most general definition of the noun 'standard': 'anything taken by general consent as a basis of comparison; an approved model'... Australian Standards produced by the organisation Standards Australia have a very specific definition and purpose which is not the same as ours. Standards Australia holds the copyright for the standards its committees develop, and charges for copies. Buying into this system would run counter to our need to disseminate these standards as widely as possible. Standards Australia has said there is no problem with the societies of editors calling their document 'Australian Standards for Editing Practice'.[13]

The working group began with standards prepared by the Editors' Association of Canada and a checklist prepared by Loma Snooks for the Canberra Society of Editors. We followed their traditional distinction of editing into substantive editing, copyediting, proofreading, and tried to subdivide these categories. But the subheadings highlighted the considerable overlaps in editorial tasks: where do you draw the line between copyediting and proofreading, or between substantive editing and copyediting, or between substantive editing and ghost writing?

Following this revelation, we changed the categories to:

- A, The Publishing Process, Conventions and Industry Practice
- B, Management and Liaison
- C, Substance and Structure
- D, Language and Illustrations
- E, Completeness and Consistency.

This required us to reconceptualise the editor's role. Suddenly the managerial skills of editors came into focus—monitoring, prioritising, liaising, managing documents, maintaining schedules, foreseeing and preventing problems. We realised that proficiency in these areas is just as essential as knowledge of spelling, grammar and typography.

After receiving comments on the resulting draft from workshops in each state and territory, the working group drew up a final proposal which was put to the members of the societies of editors and received overwhelming support. *Australian Standards for Editing Practice* was officially launched at the national conference of editors and indexers in Canberra in April 2001.

An academic assessment of the *Standards* against comparable documents from Canada and Britain concludes that the Australian approach is 'the most appropriate', given the current changes in reading, publishing and technology:

> [The *Standards*] see the editor as both freelance and in-house, working centrally but not exclusively with language, with a varied, versatile and up-to-date understanding of new technologies and publication forms. . . . The real challenge lies in the receptivity of the profession towards new competences. [The acceptance of the *Standards*] must partially reflect the changing nature of the editor's range of skills: no longer a departmentalised editor following tightly observed work flows and rigid structures but a skill-integrated, unboundaried editor as much at home with a copy of *HTML Web Pages* or *The Elements of Design* as with a style manual.[14]

Trade union

In the 1970s the Australian Journalists' Association negotiated a book editors' award through the Arbitration Commission. The AJA has since become part of the Media, Entertainment and Arts Alliance, a union that also covers actors, cinema attendants and circus workers. The organisation probably benefits from economies of scale but does not pay much attention to its book editors.

The current (2001) version of the award applies to editors working in Queensland, New South Wales, Victoria and the Australian Capital Territory. It provides for a 38-hour week, four weeks' annual leave with a 17½ per cent loading, and eight days' sick leave each year; it also covers part-time and casual work.

It divides the occupation into three levels, each with several grades: trainee editor, book editor and senior editor. Weekly rates of pay range from $532.60 for a trainee editor on commencement to $922.60 for a top-grade senior editor. In 2003 the union recommended rates for freelances of $169 per hour or $673 per day, but these are double or even triple what freelances in the book industry can realistically expect.[15] For more on hourly rates, see Chapter 11 under Cash Flows.

Union dues vary with income; they may amount to several hundred dollars a year, and they are fully tax deductible. The union's workshops on freelancing, tax and so on are aimed at journalists but have some relevance for editors.

Trade press

The *Weekly Book Newsletter*, commonly known as the *Blue News*, carries general news of the industry, lists of best-selling and prize-winning books and excerpts from the overseas trade press. Back copies are on the website of the publisher, Bowker Thorpe, which also publishes the monthly trade magazine *Australian Bookseller and Publisher*.[16] The Electric Editors website carries news of the book industry in Britain and the United States, through which you can access the trade press in those countries.[17]

The monthly *Australian Book Review* is the longest-running journal of its type and has essays, poetry and features as well as book reviews. The broadsheet newspapers review books in their weekend literary sections.

Publishing in New Zealand

The New Zealand book industry is vigorous, producing scholarly, trade and educational books for local, Pacific and global markets. According to Statistics New Zealand, about 4800 titles were published in 1999. Educational publishing accounts for about 20 per cent of sales by volume.[18] A vibrant local writing scene, with some government support, includes festivals, awards and summer schools.

Publishing is dominated by branches of multinationals such as Penguin and Random House, but the university presses—Victoria (Wellington), Auckland and Canterbury (Christchurch)—also produce a wide range of titles. Small independent firms, including Tandem Press and Horizon Press, provide strong support for fiction writers. Dunsford Publishing Consultants runs a development program that has brought more than 170 New Zealand and Pacific authors into print. Firms such as Huia Press publish Maori-language works with some government sponsorship.

Editors in New Zealand are not organised on a national basis, but they participate in the Local Publishers Forum and informal networks. Book industry organisations can be accessed through the New Zealand Book Council.[19] Booksellers New Zealand publishes a newsletter, and the *Dominion Post* and the *New Zealand Herald* review books.

Editors described

Before we look at the characteristics of editors, some reflections on the way we used to be will provide historical perspective on the transformation of the profession. I edited my first book in 1969, and even though I've lived through the changes I sometimes find it hard to believe how far we've come.

Ghosts of editors past

In the 1960s there was no training for editors, no pay scale, no career structure, no security. In fact, there was no general recognition, even in the book industry, of editing as a worthwhile or necessary task, let alone as a profession. If you did come across a trained editor, he was likely to be British and male, except for the pioneers Beatrice Davis and Barbara Ramsden who were already becoming legends. Despite these two remarkable women, editing wasn't a career that one chose; for a 'girl' who was 'brainy', it was a congenial way to occupy her time until she got married.

Editors were isolated. All of us had fallen into the job by chance. If we were lucky, we had two or three colleagues in the same firm, but beyond that there was no contact between editors, no knowledge that other editors even existed. Not only were we isolated but our jobs were ill defined.

How was editing different then? Authors, of course, were much the same—in all their rich variety—but the workplace was authoritarian and sexist in ways we find unimaginable today. As for the technology, it was primitive. Let me take you back. This is a guided meditation to summon the ghosts of editors past.

Make yourself comfortable and visualise your desk. Now obliterate the computer, the printer, the fax and the modem, and replace all that with a manual typewriter. The receptionist in the front office has a state-of-the-art electric typewriter with a golf-ball, but that's not for the likes of editors.

Correspondence has to be typed in three copies, and there's no photocopier down the corridor. You'd better add some carbon paper. You're not a very good typist, so you'll need a typewriter rubber—a disk of hard rubber with a hole through the middle, which is attached to your typewriter with string. When you make a typing error, you have to correct it on all three copies, without removing the sheets from the typewriter—otherwise the copies get out of alignment. When you rub out on the top copy, it smudges the copies underneath. If you make too many mistakes, of course, you'll have to retype the whole letter.

Before you turn to the manuscript on your desk, you'd better go and wash your hands. They're dirty from handling the carbon paper.

Now, the desk. Get rid of the highlighter pens, the sticky tags, the correction fluid. Clear them away, along with the felt-tip pens and the hi-tech ballpoints and the plastic eraser and the coloured paper clips. In their place, put the following:

- a fountain pen
- a bottle of Washable Blue ink
- blotting paper

- a lead pencil
- a pencil sharpener
- a wooden ruler, marked in inches
- a hard rubber for ink and a soft rubber for pencil
- a bottle of Milton's bleach and a glass rod.

You can add an ashtray if you like, because this is not a smoke-free work environment. You'll need scissors and a bottle of glue, because cut and paste means just that.

Now look at the manuscript. The first thing you notice is that it's not on A4 paper. It's typed on either quarto or foolscap, or possibly both. It might have been typed on several different typewriters, and some of it might be single-spaced, but it's too expensive to get it retyped. Thus the page size, the font size and the spacing all vary. There is no way of doing a wordcount except by actually counting the words, so you can see that estimates of extent are mostly guess-work. The second thing you notice about the manuscript is that it's not a clean copy. There's no chance of a revised printout. An author reading through the 'final' typed copy invariably makes a few little handwritten alterations—just adds a paragraph here and there.

Pick up your fountain pen and begin work on the manuscript. Oh no! I should have warned you, the ink takes a few moments to dry. Now you've smudged it. You should have used the blotting paper. You'd better go and wash your hands again, you've got inky fingers. That's one reason why it's so important to use Washable Blue.

As you work on the manuscript, sooner or later, you will find that you want to move or alter some of the handwritten corrections—either your own or the author's. That's the other reason for using Washable Blue. If you need to remove handwriting, you can bleach out the ink with Milton's. Take the glass rod, dip it in the bottle, and dab it on the ink marks. The writing slowly fades, leaving a faint brown stain on very wet paper.

Sometimes, of course, authors ignore your instructions about ink. Some of them fill their fountain pens with Permanent Black, and some of them use the new-fangled ballpoints. Such ink is beyond the power of Milton's. In this situation, you reach for the hard rubber. You scrub at the paper, removing the surface layer along with the ink. Now the surface is rough, so that when you write over it, the ink bleeds. If you subsequently change your mind and have to use Milton's on that spot, the whole thing turns into a soggy mess and your nib makes holes in the paper.

The technology is different now, but the frustration factor is much the same.

Editors today

Editors have upgraded their skills in response to the revolution in information technology; they are proficient in word processing and electronic file management, and some of them have mastered layout and graphic design programs as well.

Although the book industry is geographically skewed towards Sydney and Melbourne, editors are more evenly distributed. Judging by the membership of the societies of editors, New South Wales and Victoria are equal at roughly 30 per cent each, with Queensland a little over half that; Canberra and the small states together account for almost one-quarter. There is an increasing trend for freelances to telecommute from regional and rural areas. Some editors specialise in a genre or subject—children's books, law, mathematics, chemistry—but most are generalists.

It seems that the typical Australian editor is 'a forty-ish, highly qualified, highly experienced woman with her own business'.[20] Surveys and the freelance registers published by the societies of editors confirm this assessment. In a survey of editors attending the Partnerships in Knowledge conference in Canberra in 2001, Pam Hewitt found that most respondents had a postgraduate qualification, and most had also undertaken short professional courses, with just over half having completed four or more. Many reported relevant experience, the most common being as researcher, teacher or trainer, author or writer, librarian and journalist. Professions that respondents had followed before turning to editing included university lecturer, management consultant, technical writer, policy document writer, publisher, professor of English, tutor, Hansard subeditor and public relations consultant. Respondents described themselves as copyeditors, substantive editors and project managers, with a few opting for all three categories; a couple called themselves trainers, and one claimed the title of corporate identity adviser. A survey of members of the NSW society of editors found that almost half of the respondents worked outside the book industry.[21]

How do you become an editor?

First, are you sure you want to? Aspiring editors have an uphill battle. The profession has acquired more profile and formal training in recent years, but there is still no recognised pathway into it. Many editors still enter by the traditional route: falling into the job, discovering an aptitude, and learning by doing. The book industry operates mostly on personal relationships and word of mouth. (The connection between high levels of trust and female dominance in the industry would make an interesting research topic.)

It's catch-22: you can't get a job until you've got experience and you can't get experience until you've got a job. In fact, it is so hard to get into publishing that the Australian Publishers Association recommends 'killing an editorial assistant and assuming their identity'.[22] But seriously, it's a good tactic to find a job in a publishing house in any capacity, so that you are well placed to move into editing when a position becomes available. Book publishers occasionally advertise entry-level positions for editorial assistants or trainees, and for allied jobs such as permissions and picture research. Experience in editing any kind of publication, even a club newsletter, will improve your skills and your chances of employment. Some training courses provide work placements, which may lead to a job.

If you're in the job market, check the *Blue News*, and also the professional employment sections of newspapers and job websites under *editor*, *media* and *publishing*. Some of the societies of editors have email lists for their members that carry job advertisements.

Training

A study of editors' training needs has observed:

> much of the knowledge and skill in editing comes from people's natural instinct for and love of words and books ('You have to be a wordy sort of person') and from their highly developed reading skills. ... to a large degree, people have trained themselves in the core skill before they even begin work in the field.[23]

In Australia, courses in editing are offered at every level from TAFE certificates to postgraduate degrees; some are highly regarded. At the lowest level, some courses with 'editing' in their names teach grammar rather than the skills of editing for publication; at the highest level, some concentrate on publishing rather than editing. At the time of writing, no course is specifically based on *Australian Standards for Editing Practice*. The societies of editors in each state and territory fill this gap with workshops and seminars on a wide range of topics such as proofreading, freelancing and on-screen editing; check their websites for current offerings.[24] In New Zealand, Whitireia Polytechnic offers a publishing diploma, and the universities and other organisations run short courses and workshops.[25] For self-directed learning, see Chapter 11 under Professional Development.

CREATE Australia provides advice to government at a national level on education and training for the cultural industries. CASE was represented on the CREATE committee that supervised a study of training needs in journalism, publishing and writing. The resulting report examines key issues in these industries, identifying them as: the impact of technology on work contexts and practices; the democratisation of writing; changes in the way information is presented and received; and the increasingly freelance nature of the industries.[26] Work on a national training package, as recommended by the report, is expected to begin in 2004.

Commercial reality

Publishing takes place where ideas intersect with the marketplace, which gives it a peculiar satisfaction. As an editor you're working with something nebulous—information, concepts, public discourse—but you also have an end to the project, a physical product to hold in your hand. Thus you're up against commercial reality.

Editors should always keep the dollar in mind. Don't kid yourself that you're a dedicated literary artist with a soul too refined for sordid commerce. If your books don't sell, you're out of a job.

Now this raises a problem. A good editor is obsessive: you really care whether the comma is before or after the bracket, you worry about the hyphen in *on-going*. In the scale of human concerns these are minor matters, and they certainly don't carry weight in the marketplace. The most common complaint about editors is that they're pedantic, they're too focused on trivia, they lack a sense of their role in the whole publishing project.

One of the main aims of copyediting is to save costs by finding and solving any problems before the book is typeset. It's satisfying for an obsessive to get the footnotes perfect, with all the information present and correct and all the commas and brackets in the right place, but it won't add a single dollar to sales. Most readers don't look at the footnotes, and those who do won't notice the odd full stop out of place. They *will* notice if the information isn't complete, so that's worth spending time on. Editors can be self-indulgent, dwelling on the merits of a comma. Basic copyediting—correcting spelling and grammar and checking for inaccuracies and inconsistencies—is always required, but the level of intervention in other aspects, especially language editing, varies. You have to distinguish the crucial editorial tasks, which have to do with meaning and content, from the frills, the perfection that isn't always achievable. You need to know which corners can be cut.

As you work, keep a sense of the value of each task, its rank in terms of the overall project. And remember that not every publication is a Rolls Royce: most of them are Commodores. And sometimes you're asked to produce a Commodore out of the textual equivalent of a ride-on mower. So keep in mind the purpose of the publication. If it's an *Oxford Companion* or another volume of the *Australian Dictionary of Biography*, it's going to be in print for years, closely read by many scholars. But if it's a product manual or a topical book on a current issue, it will be out of print after a year or two and forgotten. Sometimes you have to get it right; sometimes near enough is good enough. On some publications, you can't do your best work. The publisher won't thank you for it, and in the end the reader won't pay you for it.

In my whole career, I've only worked on two titles where money was no object. One was the memoirs of a man who'd made an enormous amount of money in a tropical country—I didn't enquire too closely. His hobby was collecting country houses, of which he had six, on several continents. He was footing the bills, so production costs didn't matter. The other job was the history of a prestigious private boys' school. The publication committee wanted to include a lot of photos and lists of school captains, footy teams and so on. When I started to murmur about the extent and the costs, I was put firmly in my place. They would add five or ten dollars to the price, I was told, and the Old Boys would buy it just the same. I was given to understand that a sixty-dollar book was something that *their* Old Boys could well afford.

Such jobs don't come along often. Generally you have to be disciplined. You're always racing against time, either to meet an unrealistic schedule or to make a decent hourly rate. You have to be aware of the editor's part, the editor's dollar value, in terms of the whole project.

For instance, I had a book that was running very late. The publication date was an anniversary central to the book's content, and the whole marketing campaign was based on it. The schedule was so tight that the publisher had ordered some copies bound by hand in order to have them at the launch. And when I came to collate the proofs, I found that the proofreader had done a less than perfect job. I spotted several minor typos and inconsistencies that he had missed—which was understandable because he'd worked in a rush. The important thing was, he turned in a reasonable job and he kept the deadline. For this project, he'd done exactly the right thing. The conflicting imperatives are Get the Book Right and Get the Book Out, and in some cases the latter has to take precedence.

Help to sell your books

Marketing and sales are a crucial part of the publishing project, and the editor can make a unique contribution. You are probably the only person in the publishing team who knows about the author's extensive use of rare documents or that curious anecdote in Chapter 5. Make a note of phrases and examples that can be used for the blurb or quoted on the back cover. Draft a blurb for each project, even if the editorial brief does not require you to. Compare your effort with the published blurb to see where yours fell short.

One of my jobs was a book of essays on the work of the controversial historian Geoffrey Blainey. In production it had the boring title of *The Blainey View and Views of Blainey*. Fortunately this was replaced by a real gem, *The Fuss that Never Ended*, a play on one of Blainey's own titles, *The Rush that Never Ended*. I wish I'd thought of that. If you can come up with a memorable title or an angle for the publicity campaign, you'll be adding to the sales. Because you know the book, you are in a unique position to promote its strengths.

On some jobs your creativity can be brought into play. One project of mine was *The Little Aussie Fact Book*, aimed at tourists. The content was solid facts and figures, but the book was to be illustrated with cartoons and had a light-hearted, zippy feel to it. The manuscript needed structural editing to impose shape on a lot of disparate information about history, government, economic production, famous people, books and poems, wildlife, slang, even recipes. As I was editing the chapter headings, it occurred to me that alliteration would add unity and be in keeping with the mood of the book, so I invented headings such as Past, Profile, Place, Powers, People, Performances, Perceptions, Palate. The publishing team must have done something right on that one, for it has gone through several editions and is still in print nearly twenty years later.

After your books are published, follow what happens to them. Read the reviews; browse in bookshops. Find out what's selling, what's been reprinted, what's been remaindered. Talk to the sales and marketing department and ask what they think the reasons are (but don't believe them if they say it's all due to the cover). Editing is only part of the publishing process; you depend on your colleagues to sell the book, just as they depend on you to make a book that will sell.

The publishing process

IN CONSIDERING TYPES of publication we begin with the book, since that sets the standard and working editors learnt their skills on it.

The book

The printed book is arguably the most successful, durable and significant invention of the last two thousand years. For much of that period it has been the most efficient means for storing and distributing information. Until the advent of electronic communication, there were few alternatives. Broadsheets and songs provided entertainment, public lectures spread knowledge and botanic gardens codified it, but their reach was limited; the book reigned.

The book predates printing. Even if you discount its Chinese antecedents, the Romans were using the codex, or manuscript book, more than fifteen hundred years ago. The church, in the form of monasteries and universities, dominated the early publishing scene; the language was Latin and the content mostly theological. As a literate middle class emerged in the late Middle Ages, demand arose for new types of books: popular works for recreation and technical instruction, generally in a vernacular language. Such books were being commercially published by the fourteenth century. Then Gutenberg introduced moveable type to Europe in the mid-fifteenth century, and the printed book was launched.

The book has been the vehicle for Western thought and civilisation. Authors' names have become shorthand for systems of thought and whole worldviews: Rabelaisian, Macchiavellian, Dickensian, Freudian, Marxist, Orwellian. The best minds have shaped the book, refined and improved it. Long ago some genius thought of dividing text into paragraphs, and others created the conventions of the title page, contents list, appendixes, footnotes and index. The book became a tool—or rather, a toolkit.

Electronic technology is so dazzling in its potential that it distracts us from the virtues of print. Books can present information with subtlety and sophistication. In an edition of a classical text, for instance, each page may contain the original, a translation, a commentary and footnotes. A textbook on law or economics may go the whole hog, with half a dozen grades of headings as well as tables, diagrams, boxed text, marginal notes, case studies, exercises, chapter summaries, footnotes, reference list, glossary and index. Print is a more reliable archive than electronic copy: digitised information only a couple of decades old is unreadable on today's equipment. And, of course, books pleasure the senses of touch, sight and smell. As Kurt Vonnegut says: 'because of their weight and texture, and because of their sweetly token resistance to manipulation, [books] involve our hands and eyes, and then our minds and souls, in a spiritual adventure'.[1]

Figure 2.1 borrows the digital hype and applies it to the old technology.

Major Technological Breakthrough!

Announcing the BOOK— Beneficial Organised Operational Knowledge.

◆ Compact and portable!

◆ Works in ambient light—no batteries, wires or circuits!

◆ Boots up instantly—just lift the cover!

◆ Easy to operate—even a small child can use it!

◆ Browse forward or back with a flip of your thumb!

◆ Many fast-find features lead you straight to the information you want!

◆ Add annotations and comments with a user-friendly stylus!

◆ Insert multiple bookmarks and tag important points for instant reference!

◆ Millions of content creators have committed to the platform!

◆ Elegant presentation makes this not just an information tool but a work of art!

FIGURE 2.1   Hype for the printed book

Reading

Historically, reading for pleasure was an upper-class pursuit. It was not until the nineteenth century in Western countries that working people had the skill to read books or money to buy them. Since then in the West, literacy has become almost universal, governments have provided free education and free libraries, and electronic technology has made publication cheap and simple, opening the world of books to most people.

It's easy to find information on teaching beginners, but it's harder to find out what goes on in the mind of a fluent reader. Words trigger meanings because readers have learned what words look like; they perceive each word as a whole configuration, a gestalt, in the same way that they recognise faces and coins. Skilled readers sweep their eyes rhythmically over each line, noting typographical cues such as capitals, punctuation and paragraph breaks to interpret meaning.

Because fluent readers recognise words as shapes, relying particularly on beginnings and endings, the randomising of letters in the middle of words has little or no effect on their ability to understand the text. This is easy to denmtrasote. You can ramdinose all the letetrs in logner words, keipeng the first two and last two the same, and reibadailty is haldry aftcfeed. We only reuiqre the first and last two letetrs to spot chganes in meniang. This has implications for editors in the use of capitals and alternative spellings, and for proofreaders in the detection of typos.

Reading serves many purposes and there are many methods and levels of reading. Whether we realise it or not, we vary our technique according to the type of publication. When we pick up a newspaper we read selectively, making use of headlines and other signposts to pluck out what interests us. For a novel we prefer full immersion, entering into the flow of the narrative in a creative collaboration with the author. In contrast, some legal documents are so dense and formal that we have to reread each phrase several times, applying all our comprehension skills to puzzle out their meaning.

Editors apply several reading strategies to each manuscript, depending on their purpose at the time. In the appraisal stage you skim and hop to get the gist of the text. At least once during copyediting you go through the whole document, immersing yourself in order to follow the meaning. At times you scan parts of the text to locate specific information in order to crosscheck the consistency of facts, spelling and terminology. Towards the end of the copyediting process you might skim through the whole text to ensure that the division into paragraphs suits the flow of the meaning.

A method of reading for editing specialist material is described in Chapter 9 under Language Editing. The *Style Manual*, Chapter 3, explains how readers absorb information from both print and screen.

The book industry

Chapter 1 surveyed the industry; now we'll see what it produces. Print books are published in five broad categories:

- *Scholarly:* These books expand the body of knowledge on, or contribute to the debate about, a particular subject. Mostly published by university presses, they may be reworked PhD theses with extensive notes and references. They require the highest standard of editorial work, although the print runs are often tiny.
- *Educational:* Textbooks account for just over half of Australian publishing. They are usually written to fit a particular curriculum and may be subject to writing and format guidelines. The author may be one of a team that includes lesson designers, picture researchers and illustrators. The book may be part of a kit that includes CD-ROMs, teachers' manuals and learning materials.
- *Fiction:* Novels, novellas, short stories, plays and poetry have a high profile in the book trade in relation to their share of turnover. They require special respect for the author and sensitive editing (Chapter 4).
- *Specialist:* The list of specialties is long: law, gardening, art, travel, play scripts, children's books, technical books, reference books and so on.
- *General:* So-called trade publishing covers much of the above and all the rest. Trade books include fiction, scholarly books of general interest, history, biography, politics and current affairs, popular science, and children's, cooking, gardening and how-to books.

This list covers the offerings of commercial publishers, but there are other publishers who produce other kinds of publications.

Amateur publishing

The term 'amateur publisher' implies no disrespect: it denotes an organisation whose primary purpose is other than publishing. As production becomes cheaper and more accessible, more organisations are contributing to the world of books. Some instances are:

- *schools, parishes, sporting clubs:* histories, recipe books
- *local government:* information sheets, documents for community consultation, histories, tourist material
- *environment groups:* surveys of flora and fauna, alternative technology handbooks, educational material
- *charities and non-government organisations:* manuals for workers and volunteers, research reports
- *art galleries and museums:* catalogues, monographs
- *genealogical and historical societies:* family and local histories, memoirs, autobiographies.

Many of these publications, like many self-published books, too obviously lack the attention of an editor. Editors can play an important role in amateur publishing, explaining norms and jargon to the client, controlling quality, and in some cases managing the whole project. Although such clients may be ignorant about the process of producing a book, the editor should respect their expertise in their own field and not patronise or mystify them.

E-books

E-books are electronic files that can be read on a dedicated device, a handheld computer or a mobile phone. E-books have yet to establish themselves in the market, but they will transform both the publishing industry and the book. They will redefine notions of ownership, authorship and copyright, and create new rights and revenues. They promise to increase the reading public.

When the printing press liberated knowledge from the domination of the church, a vast increase in recreational reading followed. The lifting of restrictions resulted in a surge in creation and dissemination as new suppliers and consumers emerged, and one result was an entirely new genre, the novel. (It took several centuries, but time moved more slowly then.) As e-books liberate content from the monopoly of print, we can expect a similar explosion in publishing. E-books promise to reshape the relationship between author and reader; they will supply niche markets that are at present neglected and create new markets for genres yet unguessed.

E-books were hyped in the late 1990s, but major publishing houses have withdrawn their investments. Some are considering re-entry, but at present no reading device competes with printed books for comfort, clarity, durability, portability and price. Once a cheap, powerful reader emerges, e-books will take off.

E-books offer opportunities to editors. Whatever form the e-book takes, it will need the editor's skills to present content effectively to the intended reader and produce a publication that functions well.

Other publications

Editors are finding employment in many fields beyond traditional book publishing.

Newspapers

Occupational terminology in the Australian newspaper industry differs from the book trade. In newspapers the *editor* takes the role of a book publisher; a *subeditor* corresponds to an editor, *subbing* to copyediting, and an *issue* to an edition.

The two professions differ in speed and in scale. Compared to book publishing, newspaper work is fast and tiny. Subeditors' deadlines are measured in hours. Even lengthy feature articles are rarely more than a few thousand words, so subeditors do not need the sustained concentration of book editors or the sense of connections and inter-relationships that make a good book.

Subeditors start off as journalists and they are expected to have news sense as well as knowledge of grammar, spelling, house style and typography and expertise in dedicated layout software. They decide on the placement and treatment of each story and write headlines, so they have to assess newsworthiness in the context of daily events and their target readership. They have a much freer hand than book editors, with licence to drastically rewrite and cut. Subeditors work on material prepared by journalists, which needs less correction than a manuscript written by an amateur author who has only basic literacy skills. Nevertheless, because of the tight schedules and the ephemeral nature of newspapers, the standard of writing is often lower than in books. Traditionally, newspapers ignored typographical refinements like italics and en rules, but as technology improves they are adopting them.

Government publishing

State and federal governments and their agencies produce many sorts of documents of varying formality. Official publications include *Parliamentary Debates* (Hansard) and *Parliamentary Papers*, but governments undertake all kinds of publishing, both print and screen. Much of it is now expected to recover its costs, so some of these publications compete with commercial ones.

Most government departments follow the *Style Manual*, but some types of publications have their own established format and style. Editors working on official regulations may be subject to stringent language guidelines that discriminate, for instance, between *shall*, *should* and *must*. Budget papers require meticulous proofreading as well as a sense of perspective that transcends detail; one editor reports having to add the word *million* to tables of expenditure in order to clarify their meaning. Questions about who can approve editorial changes may assume particular importance in government work. The editor must adapt to the rules and procedures of the departmental publication unit.

Corporate publishing

Increasingly companies and non-government organisations are recognising the value of skilled editing for their image and credibility. When the handsomely produced brochure of a mortgage company informs us that the property market is rising in the Melbourne suburb of 'Cue', the reader wonders whether the company's arithmetic on its loans is any better than its spelling. Many firms have created a position called publications or media officer, which blends journalism, public relations, editing, graphic design, desktop publishing and web publishing. In such a multi-skilled job, the editorial tasks are likely to be neglected in favour of more showy aspects.

In the corporate world, editors work on documents such as research reports, policy papers, annual reports, presentations, product information, letters to customers and marketing literature. Editors also provide services to professionals such as engineers, scientists and stockbrokers who often lack the writing skills to make their meaning readily accessible to their clients and the public. This aspect of editing merges into business communication and technical writing.

There are many differences between the book industry and corporate publishing. The major one for editors is that corporate publishing tends to pay much higher rates. The management often do not understand the role of the editor or the stages of the production process, but they are likely to be more innovative and adventurous.

Corporate publishing suits an editor who is prepared to take responsibility for managing projects and to move beyond the core skills into areas like ghost writing and knowledge management. To enjoy the work you must be flexible and adaptable. Cultivate a pragmatic approach to language use because you may be asked to 'synergise a customer-directed, client-focused, principle-centred risk management paradigm',[2] but be sceptical about the need for such jargon and translate it into plain English if circumstances permit. The essential copyediting tasks always have to be done, but you may spend most of your time planning and defining projects, obtaining information, compiling content, combining and repurposing documents. (See Chapter 4 under Single-source Publishing.)

The sequential production process of the book industry, outlined in Figure 2.2 below, is rarely followed in corporate publishing, and the number of corrections may increase, rather than decrease, with each iteration. A document may go the rounds to everyone in the company who is 'good with words'; perhaps the finance director does crosswords and the sales rep's aunt writes children's books. Just when the project is ready to go to the printer, the managing director may have second thoughts.

Corporate editors take a broad approach and are creative in identifying and meeting the company's publishing needs. They show initiative and work without rigid procedures or supervision. And, of course, they dress the part.

Periodicals and ephemera

Periodicals range from specialist scholarly journals to popular magazines and club newsletters. On magazines, the editor usually has a background in journalism and skills akin to those of newspaper subeditors.

Librarians use the term 'ephemera' to describe material such as pamphlets, brochures, fact sheets, forms. These publications often receive little editorial attention because they are not seen as important or enduring. As with corporate reports, there is a tendency for design to take over at the expense of text. These publications should be prepared with the same concern for the reader's needs that applies to books.

World Wide Web, CD-ROMs, multimedia

The skill set required for editing screen publications is an adaptation of traditional editorial knowledge. The structuring of the screen page may be different, with information cut up into smaller chunks and navigation achieved by different means, but the aim remains the same: ease of reading.

Electronic publications have several advantages over print. They can incorporate sound and moving images. The search feature provides more precision than a print index, and the cross-references are more direct—it's easier to click on a highlighted phrase than to follow the instruction 'see Chapter 3'. Screen publications can assemble information in a three-dimensional hierarchy, rather than the two-dimensional hierarchy of print, and promote non-linear movement through it.

Many screen publications fall far short of this potential. The reader often encounters such defects as confused structure, counter-intuitive navigation, insufficient signposting, dense, dull text, and links that don't work. This area of publishing is in desperate need of traditional editorial skills to improve the presentation of information, making it functional and fit for its purpose and smoothing the reader's path. Editing for the screen is discussed in Chapter 4.

Signs

Cities are full of print messages, many of them poorly conceived and wrongly spelt. When two or three editors are gathered together, the conversation frequently turns to the so-called greengrocer's apostrophe in phrases such as *alway's fresh*. It has been suggested that the government should enforce literacy standards in public spaces by appointing editing inspectors with power to order corrections to in-your-face text such as billboards, posters, shop signs, chalkboard menus and graffiti. Unfortunately this worthy initiative has not yet found official support. Private enterprise may fill the gap: one editor reports receiving a discount at a garden supplies store in exchange for correcting the spelling on their signs.

The production process: overview

The process of book production varies in its details. Figure 2.2 shows a bare outline for a typical book, and to emphasise the editorial role it shows the sequence as it appears to the freelance editor. The following chapters explain the requirements and working methods for each stage, and the *Style Manual*, Chapters 24–5, has more detail about production methods.

The steps in Figure 2.2 are the essential ones for a straightforward editorial project, if there is ever such a thing. In practice, there are many variations in the timeframe, in the scope of editorial work, and in the path it follows. For instance:

- There may be several meetings with the author and the publisher.
- Other tasks like picture research and obtaining permissions may have to be fitted in.
- The manuscript may arrive in batches.
- The author may supply corrections and new material during the editing stage.
- The proofs may be read by a specialist proofreader rather than the editor.
- There may be several rounds of proofs.

We will briefly characterise the items in Figure 2.2, focusing on the freelance editor; in-house processes are slightly different but the pattern is similar.

Approach

You get a phone call or an email offering a job. If it's from an amateur publisher, you need to find out what the job consists of and what role they want you to take. With a book publisher you can make some basic assumptions about the extent of editorial involvement, the expectations of quality, and so on. At this stage you need to establish, very roughly, three things: the size of the job, the schedule, and the budget. If the job sounds interesting and fits your schedule and expectations for payment, you agree to proceed to the next stage.

Appraisal

The manuscript arrives by email, post or courier, and you examine it. Even when the client has provided a detailed editorial brief, you will have to clarify some points of style and confirm the requirements of the production process—how much can be left to the typesetter? You may find particular problems in the manuscript that the client hasn't noticed, which will affect the budget and schedule (Chapter 4).

Agreement

If you have an established relationship with the client, a phone call is usually enough to answer your queries, agree on money and dates, and get the go-ahead. But what you have now achieved would not please a lawyer; if any dispute arises, it will be messy (Chapter 11 under Contracts). Although the Australian book industry tends to work by means of personal relationships, you are in a much stronger position if you wait to begin work until you have formalised the agreement in writing.

Editing

You now contact the author and proceed to substantive and copyediting, as required. On a typical book, this will occupy you full-time for a week or more. At the end of it there may be a lengthy wait until the author responds to your queries. When the author replies, you make the necessary alterations, do a final check, complete the documentation, and send off the edited manuscript and the invoice (Chapter 9 under Despatch or Handover, Chapter 11). If you are not responsible for author liaison, at this point you list your queries or mark them on the hard copy or the e-copy, and return them with the edited manuscript and your invoice.

Proofs and index

Sometimes the various proof stages are handled in house, but often the freelance editor is responsible for the first proofs and the index (Chapters 7, 8). Educational titles commonly go through two rounds of proofs—or more, in desperate cases. Freelances rarely see the last stage of proofs: dyelines or 'blues'.

Completion

When you have received your complimentary copy, the project is complete. Evaluate the publication and the project: what could you have done better, what can you learn from the process? You can now display the finished product on your bookshelf and archive the related electronic and paper files.

Item	Received from:	Editor's task	Allow roughly:	When finished:	Followed by delay of:
Approach (accompanied by part MS, draft MS, or MS ready for editing)	client	define the project: appraise the MS, prepare an estimate	½ day	hold	nil to several weeks, until agreement is reached
Agreement	client, or supply your own	ensure all items listed in Standard B2.4 are covered (see Appendix)	½ hour	sign, retain copy, send copy to client	nil to several weeks, until complete MS arrives
MS ready for editing	client	edit the MS to author-query stage	1–2 weeks	send to author	2 weeks to several months, until author answers queries
Author's corrections	author	incorporate the author's corrections into the MS and finalise the job	1–6 days	send to client	4–8 weeks, until typesetting is completed
Proofs	client, or direct from typesetter	proofread the proofs against the manuscript	2–4 days	hold	2–4 weeks, until author returns proofs
Author's corrected proofs	author	review all corrections and collate on to one set of proofs	1–3 days	hold	nil to several weeks, until the index is ready
Index	author or indexer	edit the index	½ day	send to client	8–12 weeks or more, until complimentary copy arrives

FIGURE 2.2 The production process from the freelance editor's point of view

Legal concerns

A comprehensive discussion of legal restrictions on publishing would occupy a book in itself. This account only tickles the edges of the subject; further reading is recommended.

Copyright

Intellectual property includes trademarks, designs and patents, but the editor's main interest is in copyright. The laws relating to intellectual property are under pressure from technological developments. These challenges are being played out in genetics, pharmaceuticals and the music industry rather than in book publishing, but the situation is volatile. Be aware of the debate and note that this area of law is changing fast.

In Australia the relevant legislation is the federal Copyright Act, and the provisions of the New Zealand Copyright Act are broadly similar. The lawyers have their own language, assigning particular meanings to vernacular words like *work* and *publish*. The Australian Act applies to works that are first published in Australia, or whose publisher is an Australian citizen or resident. International treaties provide protection for most foreign works published here and for Australian works published in most other countries.

Copyright law has some odd quirks:

- Copyright protects the expression of an idea, not the idea itself—two novelists might devise a similar plot, or two biographers write about the same person, without any infringement.
- Copyright is personal property and can be assigned or bequeathed to others.
- Copyright extends beyond common notions of literary and artistic material; it has been held to cover such 'works' as a pawnbroker's pledge ticket, a football betting coupon and a computer program.
- Ownership of the copyright in correspondence remains with the writer, even though someone else may have possession of the actual letters.

Copyright does not depend on registration; it arises automatically when the work takes physical expression. There is no need to use the © symbol to protect copyright in Australia or New Zealand. The duration of copyright varies according to the nature of the work. Broadly in Australia it is fifty years from the date of the author's death or from the date of first publication, with many exceptions. The so-called free trade agreement with the United States proposes to extend this to seventy years.

There are two aspects to copyright law: ownership of the copyright to a work, and reproduction of copyright material. Generally matters of assigning or licensing copyright do not concern the editor,[3] but you need to understand how copyright material can be used.

Permissions

Permission must be obtained from the copyright holder to reproduce copyright material: acknowledging the source is not enough. Finding the copyright holder is sometimes a puzzle. Where a person creates original work in the course of their employment, such as a journalist or photographer working for a newspaper, the employer usually holds the copyright. Publishers who cannot locate the copyright holder sometimes decide to reproduce the material anyway. This is a commercial judgement. Commonly publishers insert a disclaimer in the book stating that they are willing to pay a reasonable fee to the copyright holder, but this does not provide protection at law.

Permission is always required to reproduce a whole work—a cartoon, drawing, song, poem, screen dump, letter, recipe or short story. In an anthology of previously published works the labour and fees for obtaining permissions may constitute a major part of the production process and the budget.

If you want to use part of a work, complicated rules apply. The quality of the part is more important than the proportion or amount. For short works such as a song or a poem, the quotation of a single line may infringe copyright. Your purpose in reproducing the material may be relevant; for instance, an infringement is likely to be regarded more seriously if you are producing a book in direct competition to the copyright work. Paraphrasing may infringe copyright if it reproduces an important part of the work.

The good news is that most short prose quotations and extracts are regarded as *fair dealing* for *criticism* or *review* or by way of *news report* and therefore do not need permission. The bad news is that fair dealing in quotations is not defined in the Copyright Act; it is determined on the nature and extent of the quotation in each case.[4]

Generally the author's contract with the publisher requires the author to obtain permissions for use of copyright material and pay any fees that apply. Most authors and amateur publishers do not understand the provisions of copyright law and need advice from the editor on what requires permission. Letters requesting permission should give details about the book such as author's name, title, print run and price. Mention the market if it's relevant; sometimes fees are waived for works with an educational or charitable purpose. You might state the maximum sum you can afford for permission so the holder can take it or leave it. Enclose a photocopy or exact description of the material that you want to reproduce.

You should stay up to date in your knowledge of this subject and be alert in your editing for anything that may infringe copyright. Both the Australian Copyright Council and the Copyright Council of New Zealand have excellent websites with updates on legislation, fact sheets and publications.[5]

Defamation

It is widely argued that current Australian defamation laws unduly constrain the ability of the media to report and comment on matters of public interest, and favour plaintiffs at the expense of free expression. While we wait for law reform, the editor must be alert for defamation because a lawsuit can be expensive for the publisher. A high-profile trial gains publicity for a book, but it may be paid for in legal costs, damages, and the pulping of an entire edition.

Defamation law in Australia varies from state to state because so far the attorneys-general haven't got their Act together, although federal legislation was foreshadowed in late 2003. In New Zealand the 1992 Defamation Act does not provide an effective definition of defamation; this situation favours the plaintiff. In view of these variations, the following remarks are broad and general.

The golden rule regarding defamation is this: if you have even a faint suspicion that a document contains defamatory material, point it out to the publisher and recommend urgent legal advice. Autobiographies, biographies and memoirs are most likely to defame someone, but even an economics textbook describing a company collapse may stray over the line.

Defamation occurs when someone's reputation is damaged in the eyes of reasonable people. You can say what you like about dead people, but if you damage the reputation of a living individual, a corporation or an identifiable group, they can sue you. For our purposes, libel is the same as defamation; some states distinguish (written) libel from (spoken) slander. Statements made in parliament and in court, and accurate reports of them, are 'privileged'—that is, outside the law of defamation.

It is usually defamatory to suggest that a person is incompetent in their profession or line of work. Take particular care where people are suspected of criminal behaviour: don't refer to anyone as a *murderer*, *child molester* or *people smuggler* unless they have been convicted of that crime in a court of law. This may seem elementary, but authors are sometimes oblivious to the presumption of innocence. Don't rely on adding a word like *alleged* or *suspected*; the implication may still be damaging.

An individual or corporation who is defamed need not be named: if their identity is implied, they can sue successfully. You cannot get away with saying rude things about Rupert Murdoch by referring to him as 'an Australian-born global media baron'. This provision gives rise to the risk of the unknown plaintiff—some unheard-of person bearing the same name as an unpleasant character in a novel—which causes fiction publishers to lie awake at night. The plaintiff does not have to prove that the writer intended to defame them, only that they were defamed—that people would assume that the material referred to them. The editor cannot do much to guard against this in novels that are true to life.

Defamation law, like intellectual property law, is slowly and clumsily responding to the changed circumstances created by the internet. The High Court ruled in December 2002 that Melbourne businessman Joseph Gutnick had the right to sue in Victoria for an allegedly defamatory article that had been uploaded to a website in the United States. The judges ruled that the damage to reputation occurs where the material is downloaded, and thus that is the place where the defamation is committed. This ruling is alarming: it implies that anyone posting anything on the internet should comply with all the defamation laws in every jurisdiction where the material might be downloaded. One observer claimed that the ruling 'puts the internet on ice', but it seems to have had little practical effect. Editors must stay abreast of developments.[6]

The defences to defamation vary among the states. Again, the law has its own definitions of vernacular words like *reasonable person*, *publication* and *fair comment*. You would think that truth would be an absolute defence, but some states require also that publication be in the public interest. Other defences are consent, privilege, fair comment and political comment. In New Zealand truth and honest opinion, with certain conditions, are defences. But defence is the province of the lawyer, not the editor; if you have any doubts about a passage, seek legal advice.

Contempt, moral rights, privacy

The reporting of proceedings in the Family Court and children's courts is subject to special restrictions, and other courts and tribunals may prohibit reporting of a case while it is in progress; infringements are contempt of court. These matters are relevant for publications that cover topical issues and current affairs.

Moral rights relate to creators' reputations in connection with their work. In Australia legislation that came into effect at the end of 2000 provides that the author of a literary, dramatic, musical or artistic work has a moral right to be identified as the author of the work. Indexers can claim the right to attribution under this law. The author of a work can also take action against false attribution or derogatory treatment of the work. So far there have been few court cases to test the dimensions of this legislation.

Australian legislation on indigenous communal moral rights is in preparation, under which it may be an offence, for instance, to photograph a landscape feature such as Uluru without permission. Photographs taken in a national park may breach the conditions of entry to the park.

Privacy legislation, both state and federal, applies to the collection of personal information such as names, addresses, bank account details and health records, and the use of it for benefit or advantage. Editors rarely have to think about privacy issues unless they are working on a publication that lists names and addresses. In such cases check the guidelines of the Office of the Federal Privacy Commissioner.[7]

Legal requirements relating to books

In order to preserve publications for future generations, the Copyright Act stipulates that a copy of every work published in Australia must be lodged with the National Library. 'Work' in this context includes not only books but periodicals, pamphlets, sheet music, maps, plans and charts. State legislation requires lodgement in relevant state libraries also.

By law, a publication must bear the name and address of the printer or publisher. Optional are the ISBN, or International Standard Book Number, and the ISSN, International Standard Serial Number, which are part of a worldwide cataloguing system that eases communication between publishers and booksellers. The former is a unique number assigned to each edition and format of a book, and the latter identifies serial publications. In Australia ISBNs are issued by the Australian ISBN Agency, operated by Thorpe Bibliographic Services.[8] The

National Library issues ISSNs and also Persistent Uniform Resource Locators (PURLs) for screen publications.[9] The National Library also operates a program called Cataloguing in Publication in which librarians catalogue a book during production, thus saving time and promoting uniform practice. The CIP information is printed on the verso (reverse) of the title page or on the title screen of an electronic work; it includes the ISBN, and the ISSN if needed.

In New Zealand the National Library is the legal deposit library and handles ISBNs, ISSNs and Cataloguing in Publication.[10]

Editors may have to apply for ISBNs, ISSNs or CIP data, depending on the editorial brief.

The ethics of editing

The editor has a three-way responsibility to the publisher, the author and the reader, and sometimes in balancing these conflicting needs you must make value judgements. In a book made up of transcriptions of oral history, for instance, you must weigh up the speakers' rights to authentic expression against the readers' expectations of print and need for clarity. On all projects you are constantly making a trade-off between what the publisher can afford and what the reader needs.

Sometimes editors have to work on content that they disagree with. Assuming that the manuscript has been accepted for publication, your professional obligation in this situation is to remain objective and assist the author to say what she wants to say. You may point out flaws in her facts or her argument, which may cause her to move towards your position, but this is a matter of consultation and negotiation; never distort the author's meaning or emphasis to suit your own predilections.

Gossip is unprofessional. Your relationship with the author should remain respectful, even after her book is published. No matter how exasperating she is, don't expose or mock her weaknesses to her colleagues or rivals. When recounting horror stories to your colleagues, omit any identifying details.

Freelance editors should not chat about their current projects to other clients; this information is, to use a much-abused phrase, commercial in confidence. At times you may find yourself working on books for different clients that are in direct or partial competition with each other; scrupulous discretion is required in such cases. A publisher who hears that a rival book is in production might use the information to his advantage—say, by bringing forward the publication date in order to be first in the market.

Freelance schedules are flexible or even flimsy, but editors should not tell outright lies about their ability to meet a deadline in order to secure a job. If having accepted a job you find you cannot complete it within the required time because of illness or other emergency, do not string the client along with promises of 'next week' and 'a few more days'; it is fairer to explain, apologise, and offer to step aside.

Freelances are sometimes asked to edit essays, theses and dissertations that are to be submitted for academic credit. This raises ethical concerns about the editor's contribution to the quality of the work. The Council of the Australian Society of Editors has combined with the Council of Deans and Directors of Graduate Studies, representing Australian universities, to formulate a national policy for the professional editing of research students' theses and dissertations. The policy recommends that the scope of editorial work should be restricted to matters covered in Standards D and E of *Australian Standards for Editing Practice* (see Appendix), and that any editing of substance and structure (Standard C) should be the responsibility of the student's academic supervisor. It also requires that editors work on hard copy, and that editorial assistance should be specified in the acknowledgements. Editors working on theses should observe this policy, which is on the CASE website.

Inclusiveness

Federal legislation makes it illegal to discriminate on the grounds of race, colour, national or ethnic origin, gender, marital status, age, or physical and mental capabilities. The editor must also make judgements about statements and illustrations that are potentially offensive though not actually discriminatory or defamatory. Inclusive language and cultural sensitivity have been derided as political correctness, but in fact they are a courteous recognition of the diversity of your readers. Chapter 4 of the *Style Manual* provides excellent advice, and I make only a few additional points here.

Like any human being, editors are limited by their cultural and intellectual context and by their own mental structures and strictures, but we have a duty to try to transcend our biases. Editors are not guardians of the culture or gatekeepers of the language or anything as grand as that, but occasionally we do have the power to nudge discussion towards inclusion. We must chart a course between 'the commissars of political correctness on the left and the fundamentalist sentries of morality on the right'.[11]

A report from the United States, where textbook committees are subject to intense political pressure, paints an alarming situation. Some guidelines for educational materials actually prohibit tales set in jungles, forests, mountains or by the sea (because such settings are believed to display 'a regional bias'), or mention of birthdays (because some children do not have birthday parties). Such sanitising cuts away everything that might provoke thought and replaces vivid details with bland generalities.

The over-zealous elimination of bias can falsify history. In the past, for instance, women typically worked as nurses or secretaries, and to pretend otherwise is to project the comparative gender equality of our own time onto a different world; it minimises the hurdles that women have overcome. The same applies to other marginalised groups. Editors should protest against spin and whitewash, and resist attempts to bowdlerise the past.

He or *she*

At school I learnt a grammatical rule that was coyly expressed as '*he* embraces *she*'. The move against this rule was part of the second wave of feminism in the 1970s and has been largely successful; the generic *he* now sounds old-fashioned, and publishers avoid it because they do not want to alienate half their readers.

The use of *they* as a singular neuter pronoun is widely accepted; it follows spoken usage, and it is certainly less distracting for the reader than constant repetition of *he or she*. It does, however, replace a male/female ambiguity with a singular/plural ambiguity. As one observer comments, 'The only advantage to this ploy, I suppose, is that there is/are, to my knowledge, no group(s) actively struggling for equality between singular and plural.'[12] Solving the *he or she* problem can be a fascinating challenge. In this book, for instance, I have exploited the precision of the singular by following an arbitrary convention, referring to the author and the designer as *she* and to the reader and the publisher as *he*. Does it bother you?

Be wary of the default assumption of maleness in generic terms like *Australians*, *soldiers*, *pioneers*, *farmers*. In most contexts it is demeaning to refer to adult women as *girls*. When rewriting, do not use terms like *swagpersons*. The whole point of inclusive language is that it should be the unobtrusive norm. We are all persons of gender.

Assumptions

Obviously you will query insulting descriptions and stereotypes of racial and religious groups, but exclusive or offensive assumptions can also appear in terminology. Here are some examples.

- The mainstream population in Australia is not *Anglo-Saxon* but *Anglo-Celtic*, in recognition of the numbers with Irish and Scottish heritage. Persons born in Australia or naturalised are *Australians*; when their background in another culture is relevant, they are *Anglo Australians*, *Chinese Australians*, *Lebanese Australians*, etc.
- The Vietnamese are entitled to the name of their country; don't hijack it to denote a war with phrases like *after Vietnam*.
- Although the United States is the dominant world power, its residents do not have a monopoly on *American* or even *North American*. The narrow meaning of these terms is often justified by the context, but keep in mind the claims of Central and South Americans to the first, and Canadians and Mexicans to the second. In political contexts, *American* is incorrect: use *United States* (or *US*) *Congress*, and similarly with *troops*, *citizens*, *constitution*, and so on.
- Some geographical names are burdened with centuries of hatred. The editor must be aware of the implications of, for instance, *Londonderry*, *Macedonia*, *Palestine*.

- The term *Stolen Generations* is capitalised, and it is always plural because the policy of removing Aboriginal children from their families persisted for more than half a century.
- When citing dates, use *CE (Common Era)* and *BCE (Before the Common Era)* rather than *AD* and *BC*, which belong to the Christian calendar.
- In a publication that describes countries and their dominant religions, it is incorrect to use *Catholic* and *Protestant* alongside *Sunni Muslim* and *Shi'ite Muslim*; parity requires *Catholic Christian* and *Protestant Christian*.
- The use of *Roman Catholic* rather than that church's preferred name, *Catholic*, has been described as 'a shot in a religious war'.[13]

As a guiding principle, think of all the people who might read the book and make them a part of it. Don't let the author assume that Anglo-Celtic origin is the norm for the Australian population. The claim that 'everyone' can use the internet should be tempered by awareness that the majority of the global population has never used a telephone, let alone sent an email. Similar caution should apply to claims that literacy is universal or that some consumer product is affordable.

Indigenous writing

The purpose and nature of indigenous writing vary so widely that it may be misleading to lump it all together, but its editing always requires sensitivity and openness, especially from non-indigenous editors. Cross-cultural editing is a complex maze of negotiations.[14] Indigenous writing often confounds mainstream expectations: for instance, it may not fit neatly into a literary genre and its authorship and copyright may be communal. Non-indigenous editors must be aware of their own biases, tastes and preconceptions, and in many cases mediate between the author and the publisher. As always, respect the moral rights and authentic voice of the author.

An editor who is open-minded may have a tiny part in a literary success. Keri Hulme's powerful novel *The Bone People* was initially rejected because, as one New Zealand author says, 'the publishing industry and editors did not have the breadth of knowledge or vision to recognise a book of brilliance that was beyond the depth of their cultural or gender experiences'. Hulme's courage in resisting substantive editing 'changed the face of New Zealand literature and literature globally'.[15] Once published, the book was embraced by readers and went on to win the coveted Booker Award.

Writing on Aboriginal topics should observe cultural norms such as the prohibitions on revealing certain information to the uninitiated and on naming and reproducing images of recently deceased people. If a book for the general reader breaks the latter prohibition, it is courteous to add a note in the preliminary pages to warn Aboriginal readers.

The original inhabitants of Australia and their descendants are always capitalised as *Aborigines* or *Aboriginals* and *Torres Strait Islanders*. Purists become etymologically enraged over the use of *Aborigine* as a singular, so prefer *Aboriginal* if you want to placate them. Regional terms include *Koori* in Victoria and *Nyungar* in southwest Western Australia.

Of the hundreds of Aboriginal languages that were once spoken, only about twenty are still living. Many Aborigines speak Australian English (sometimes as a second or third language), but Aboriginal English is a regional English that is due the same respect as other varieties. Chapter 5 discusses the spoken word in print, and Figure 9.3 shows an edited example of nonstandard speech.

Aboriginal names have been spelt in various ways; for instance, *Arrernte* is now preferred to *Aranda* or *Arunta*, though the latter may be found in historical contexts. Commonly used names are in general dictionaries, but editors working on Aboriginal-language materials will need specialist reference books.[16] In some contexts it may be necessary to observe local spelling variations used by particular groups; all states and territories have cultural centres that can give advice.

The original inhabitants of New Zealand and their descendants are *Maori*; the plural is the same as the singular. Many Maori words have entered New Zealand English; some, such as *Aotearoa*, *pakeha* and *kia ora*, are known to global readers, but others may need to be explained in books for external markets.[17] The website of the Maori Language Commission lists its publications, services and resources, and dictionaries are available for various levels of interest.[18]

A diacritic called a macron is used in Maori words to show a long vowel, which can determine meaning; for instance, *ana* means 'a cave', but *anā* means 'behold'. The practice of doubling the vowel to show length—*anaa*—is obsolete. In English-language writing the macron may be dropped when the word is naturalised, as in the word *Maori* itself, which is properly spelt *Māori*.

Design, typography and formatting

Editors have sophisticated verbal skills, but their spatial and visual skills may be underdeveloped. Knowledge of typography, the use of type and white space to convey meaning, is one of the core editorial skills, right up there with language and general knowledge. Typography is thoroughly covered in Chapter 18 of the *Style Manual*.

In your recreational reading, note what makes reading easier and what annoys you, and try to define why. Are the margins too small, or is the measure (the width of the line) too wide for the size of the type? Many examples of print pass through your hands every day—magazines, newspapers and brochures as well as books. Refine your appreciation of typography by paying attention to it.

The more expertise you develop in typography, the more you value the work of book designers. Liaison with designers is discussed in the next chapter, and there is more on typography in Chapter 8 under Proofreading Methods.

Technology relevant to editing practice

Word processing and email are indispensable for the editor. You should be comfortable sending and receiving files and know how to convert formats and attachments so that your system can read them. Techniques for word processing and handling electronic documents are covered in Chapter 10.

Reproduction

Editors need a general understanding of the reproduction requirements for different types of publication and delivery modes in order to choose the one that is most suitable for a given project. Each method of reproduction has implications for accessibility, costs, schedules and production processes.

Editors should understand the principles and have sufficient knowledge of the jargon to talk to other members of the publishing team: printed publications may have *bleeding edges* (pictures that extend to the edge of the page), and web pages should *degrade gracefully* (display accurately on old and rare browsers). All editors should thoroughly understand the proof stages that they handle (Chapter 8). Editors who manage publication projects need to be familiar with paper characteristics and their implications for reproduction, as well as print buying and the different binding methods. For information on all aspects of this topic see the *Style Manual*, Chapters 24–6.

Management and liaison

A T THE RISK OF IMITATING the podiatry textbook which claimed that the foot extends to the armpit, I see the editor as the pivotal figure in the production process, at the centre of a triangle. The points of the triangle are:

- *Author:* It's my book!
- *Publisher:* I'm paying the bills!
- *Reader:* Don't forget me! I'm the purpose of the whole exercise!

For the author you are an assistant; for the publisher you are a quality controller; for the reader you are an advocate. So you're always subject to a three-way stretch, balancing competing demands.

Liaison and negotiation

The aim in liaison is to work out what everyone needs to know and to tell them at the appropriate time. The editor maintains the flow of information between author, publisher, designer and typesetter, but don't flood people with detail they don't need.

Before you begin editing, find out whether the publisher or commissioning editor has informed the author of the schedule and told her what she is expected to do in the way of approving changes, obtaining illustrations and permissions, providing material for publicity, preparing the index and so on, and especially the technical requirements for these tasks. You may have to brief the author yourself.

During the project, keep the publisher informed of progress and co-ordinate your approaches to the author so she doesn't receive contradictory instructions. If you haven't heard from the author for a while, ask the publisher about the state of play. Other members of the publishing team may have been in touch with her to discuss illustrations or the marketing campaign, in which case they will know her movements and her mood. If the author cuts up rough about editorial proposals, discuss with the publisher how to handle it and who should approach her.

Negotiating strategies

In any publishing project there are many rounds of negotiation, both formal and informal. Freelance editors negotiate a formal agreement with the client at the beginning of the project, as described in Chapter 11. Negotiations with authors are described below.

Before you begin any negotiations, clarify your objectives: how would you like things to turn out? Know your extremes: how much extra can you afford to give to get a settlement, what is the smallest offer you will accept? Although you are not aiming to hit these limits, it is worth knowing what they are so that you're not pushed into exceeding them.

For freelance editors, money is not the only point on which to bargain. You can trade off the timing of the job or the amount of work—perhaps some tasks can be done by the author or in house. A book that is one of a series may be worth a small discount in exchange for a written guarantee of continuing work. Consider what is valuable to your business, not the costs. If the negotiation fails, you may end up losing something that is more valuable than money: a reliable client, or your reputation.

In order to negotiate you need confidence, which comes from knowing your business and the worth of your services. Keep the tone friendly and communicate your confidence without being cocky. Aim as high as you feel necessary in order to gain the best deal for yourself, because it's easier to retreat gracefully than to push the demand higher. Give the publisher room to move: for instance, if your realistic quote for substantive editing seems impossibly high, tell the publisher that you can also quote on a less ambitious, and cheaper, job.

Stay flexible in case the publisher decides to change the direction of the negotiations, offering different incentives or even changing the objectives. This is why you must know your limits. If you're not a quick thinker, ask for a few hours to consider. Your negotiations will be successful if you genuinely seek a compromise that suits both you and the publisher, rather than trying to bulldoze the other party into accepting your fixed plans.

Management textbooks have more information on negotiation skills; look in the business section in bookshops or under Dewey 650s in libraries.

Author

The editor translates the author's vision into practical instructions for the designer, typesetter and printer. You bring to the project your specialist knowledge of language, presentation of information, referencing, typography, and the possibilities of the genus Book. When the author wants something that's expensive or impractical, such as a large table on a foldout page, you can suggest another method of achieving the same effect.

A fruitful partnership

The editor enters into the author's purpose in order to make the best possible publication. As we have said, your aim is not to alter the view or change the scene but to make it clearer and closer. You are not a critic but the author's ally and assistant, coaching and coaxing her, enlarging her vision and saving her from pitfalls. Convince her that you have the interests of her book at heart. A creative interaction between author and editor is exhilarating for both, and it can transform an ordinary manuscript into a bestseller. A skilful editor encourages an author to scale new heights and to realise potential she didn't know she had.

Authors come in all varieties. Some are incredibly knowledgeable about economic theory, say, or the eye muscles of the ox, but they can't write a coherent sentence to save themselves. Others write like angels and then heap praise on you in their acknowledgements, although all you have done is sprinkle a few commas about. There are timid, anxious authors who need to be soothed and encouraged; high-maintenance authors who involve you in their personal lives; and opinionated, stubborn authors who fight you every step of the way. With all of these you must try to attain a rewarding collaboration of mutual admiration in which you value each other's strengths and compensate for each other's weaknesses.

Liaison with the author depends to some extent on the level of editing required. If you are involved in the early stages of a project—concept development, substantial revision of a draft document—meetings with the author are part of the job and freelance editors should cost them in. Where substantive editing or major language editing is required, it is best to talk to the author as soon as you have appraised the manuscript to discuss in general terms what changes are needed and agree on the schedule for detailed queries. Such a meeting enables you to gauge the likely responses to your editorial suggestions. In some cases, though, a personal relationship with the author can distract you from the needs of the manuscript. Remember that the reader doesn't have the opportunity to talk to the author and receive explanations before he begins reading.

Who is boss?

The editor must understand the ground rules of the relationship with the author. In educational and corporate publishing the editor takes on major responsibility for content, but in trade and scholarly books the author has the final say. It's the author's book: she gets her name on the title page, she gets the glory, and she gets the flak.

Authors are usually keen to correct errors and ambiguities when you point them out, but occasionally a difference of opinion will arise. You can suggest and reason and cajole, but if the author says no, that's it—unless there is some over-riding consideration such as costs or defamation, in which case you must ask the publisher to step in. But in general, editors subordinate their egos and accept the author's verdict.

On a title that has joint authors, try to set things up so that you deal with only one. It can be clumsy to send copies of everything to two or three people, and they may disagree on decisions. Such questions of authority and accounta-bility should be set out in the project plan, as explained below, and clearly under-stood by all the authors before editing starts. Anthologies and collections are co-ordinated by the volume editor, who passes your queries on to individual contributors, reviews their responses and makes the authorial decisions.

If you advertise your services as a freelance editor, authors will approach you. Sometimes they want you to edit their work to a standard suitable for submission to a publisher; sometimes they want you to manage the whole publishing project, including marketing and distribution; sometimes they don't know what they want. In this situation the editor must help the author to define the project and specify the editorial role, as described below. Editorial advice in the early stages of a project can be both helpful for the author and satisfying for the editor.

Attitude

On most projects the editor must be careful not to appear to take over—even if that is, in fact, what you are doing. In all aspects of the editorial process the editor must respect the integrity of the text and the author's moral rights (Chapter 2).

Be sensitive to the author's position. To you the manuscript is raw material, but to her it's a finished product. No matter how awful it is, it's the result of many months, possibly years, of hard work. Be especially diplomatic with fic-tion, autobiography and memoirs, where the text is an extension of the author's identity and she may feel exposed and vulnerable. Begin your contact with the author by congratulating her sincerely on her achievement, and find some specific points to praise. Throughout the project keep her informed about what's hap-pening in terms she can understand, without condescension; anticipate her queries, explain the production methods, and give her early warning of dates for each stage of production.

Editors have no false pride and are not afraid to ask dumb questions. Shed your inhibitions about looking stupid and be comfortable saying 'I don't under-stand' or 'I need more information on this.' If the editor, having read a passage carefully, can't understand it, the reader probably won't either.

A perennial question is 'how much editing to do?' Theoretically, editing can continue almost indefinitely. The level of intervention on a particular job is determined by the quality required in the finished publication and the resources available, as identified in the project plan. An experienced editor can judge whether a particular feature of the text is there because it is the author's consid-ered preference or because she didn't know any better. In general, never edit on a whim or to suit your own tastes; you must be able to defend every change in terms of the reader's needs and the requirements of the publication.

Tactful tactics

Phrase your remarks with consideration and respect. If the author is boss, make it clear that your changes are only suggestions and that she has the right to reject them. Do not dwell on weaknesses or errors, but suggest how to overcome them. Lighten the critical tone of your queries by including occasional positive comments like 'good point' or 'well described', and in hard copy add ticks in the margin. The author may not know what her strengths are, but when they are identified she can build on them.

Your expression should be diplomatic. A question mark at the end of a comment like 'Explain or delete' changes it from a peremptory command to a tentative suggestion. Useful phrases are 'What do you mean by . . .' and 'What do you understand by . . .'.

Be precise in your queries to the author. If you have an uneasy feeling about a part of the manuscript, analyse it until you can express it clearly. For instance, I was editing a novel in which one character switched between two extremes, being by turns fastidious and elegant, and coarse, brutal and dirty. The contrast was so marked that I wondered whether the author had inadvertently used the same name for two different people. No, she replied, she had portrayed a man whose personality was contradictory, and she was quite satisfied with him. I still wasn't happy and I felt the reader wouldn't get it. So I did a global search on the character's name and carefully reread every scene in which he appeared. I concluded that the dialogue and actions fitted the author's intention, but there were a few sentences of physical description that flatly contradicted each other. I pasted them into an email, and also suggested that the author add some early hint or clue to help the reader understand the paradoxical nature of the character. Once the problem was defined, the author agreed that it was indeed a problem and fixed it with a few deft touches.

Sometimes when editing you will have second thoughts after altering a sentence, wondering whether you have misinterpreted the meaning. But, assuming your editorial judgement is sound, the fact that you altered it indicates that there was something wrong. In this situation, an annotation saying 'Is this what you mean?' indicates to the author that the passage is ambiguous and that your emendation is tentative. It also has a practical advantage, in that you don't have to erase and reinvent the change you have already marked.

Although knowledge of typography is spreading, don't assume that the author understands specialist terms and marks. You must gauge each author's capabilities. Some are expert with a word processor; others can't type and have to be told that italic is the slanty bits. Take these matters into account in your dealings and, despite the smart remark in the last sentence, don't be patronising.

When you ask the author to do something, such as reply to queries, explain exactly how you want her to respond, taking into account her level of expertise both in language and technology. She may prefer a list of queries on paper that she can tick off, rather than annotated e-copy.

Techniques for compiling author queries, version control and electronic files are explained in Chapter 10.

Author's response

In almost all cases the author appreciates the editor's skills and is grateful, and a competent editor does not arouse hostility. Some authors, though, never really grasp what you have done. On one heroic editing job, after I had completely restructured the material, rewritten every sentence and added several diagrams and tables of my own devising, the author's response to the clean printout was 'I like the way you've set it out.'

You may encounter an author who quells your editorial preoccupations with magnificent disdain, as demonstrated by Lawrence of Arabia. Exchanges with the proofreader of *Seven Pillars of Wisdom* included:

- 'Jeddah and Jidda used impartially throughout. Intentional?'—'Rather!'
- 'Sherif Abd el Mayin becomes el Main, el Mayein, el Muein, el Mayin and el Muyein.'—'Good egg. I call this really ingenious.'

Designer

It is difficult to edit unless you can visualise the format of the publication and the layout of the printed page. Often, especially if both of you are freelance, your only communication with the designer is through the design brief. This is a lost opportunity because the designer can often suggest some device of typography or layout to solve a problem that seems intractable on the editor's desk. Sometimes, though, designers are more interested in the appearance of the publication than the content, and must be tactfully discouraged from including gratuitous design elements or GDEs.

Knowledgeable designers are a pleasure to work with. They recognise the centrality of meaning and use their skills to clarify it. 'It is important that, once a reader accesses a publication, the design refocuses them so they are not distracted away from it. The designer needs to use a visual language that attracts the target reader. The designer must understand the concept of the publication and design a "signal system" appropriate for it.'[1]

Freelance editors should ask the client for contact details and consult the designer on particular points. In a book where design is of the essence—say, a recipe book or a complicated textbook—the designer should help to develop the concept from the beginning and liaise closely with the editor throughout. The same applies to screen publications (Chapter 9). Editors and designers who build alliances can benefit, both by producing a superior product and by recommending each other's services for other projects.

The design brief is discussed below, under Project Documentation.

Project definition

Project definition is like foreplay: if it's omitted, there is little chance of a successful outcome; if it's perfunctory, the result may be unsatisfying; but if it's thorough, the experience is enhanced for everyone concerned.

The editor may enter a publication project when it is no more than a gleam in someone's eye, with not a word on paper; or there may be a draft or partial manuscript; or there may be a final manuscript, complete with format and layout, which the author will defend to the death. Commissioning editors working with authors, and freelance editors working with amateur publishers, may need to clarify the purpose of the publication. They rely on your knowledge of what is possible in order to develop the concept they have in mind.

It is best to proceed systematically and draw up a formal project plan. Here is a summary of the process.[2] Even if you are not required to prepare a plan, you should have these matters clear in your own mind.

Project plan

In any publishing project, you have to establish what the publication intends to do and work out the best way to achieve that purpose. The steps below will need close consultation and negotiation with the publisher. At the end of the process you will have all the information you need to draw up the editorial brief and the contract. The examples here are drawn from books; the same principles apply to screen publications.

1 *Define the publisher's purpose:* Why is the publisher publishing the book? What do they hope to achieve?
2 *Identify the readership:* What is the target market? Who will buy this publication and how will they use it? What knowledge does the reader bring to the text? What level of language will he be comfortable with? What specialist terminology will he want explained?
3 *Define the purpose of the publication:* List its objectives and the manner in which it will be used. This will help you decide what content you need and how to organise it to aid access. Once you know the purpose and who the readers are, the questions about format, production process and quality narrow to a few options.
4 *Evaluate the competition:* For a commercial project, research the other books on the market, their strengths and weaknesses. How does this book compare?

5 *Determine the appropriate specifications:* Length and structure, illustrations, the format (size, typography, page layout, colour, cover, binding) and the print run.

6 *Examine the manuscript:* Make a preliminary assessment to evaluate requirements, or if possible a full appraisal of the complete manuscript (Chapter 4).

7 *Determine quality, identify constraints:* The required quality of the finished product dictates the extent of editorial and design work and the quality of illustrations and printing. Identify the constraints on quality, including the budget, the timetable, the quality of the manuscript, and legal and formal requirements. Other constraints may relate to the authors, other team members, material or permissions to be acquired, review or approval processes, printing and production.

8 *Negotiate tasks and responsibilities:* Define the agreed scope of the core editing tasks and any additional services that the editor will provide—research, rewriting, desktop publishing. Establish accountability for the budget and the schedule, and for quality control and team performance. Make sure that these expectations are achievable. Agree on the schedule for all stages of production and on the budget for editing, for additional services, and for any production costs that you will negotiate and control—subcontractors, equipment, expenses, materials, printing, distribution.

9 *Formalise these decisions in an editorial brief and an agreement:* See Project Documentation, below, and Chapter 11.

Reader's report

In the book industry the editor usually does not enter the process until after a manuscript has been accepted for publication, but occasionally you will be asked to give an opinion on a draft manuscript or write a reader's report, also called an editorial review. A reader's report resembles a book review, but its central concern is whether the publishing project is worth proceeding with. Publishers often obtain several reports on a manuscript from experts on the subject matter, but a publisher who asks an editor for a reader's report does not expect specialist knowledge. Your tasks are to identify the strengths and weaknesses of the manuscript, determine what editorial work needs to be done, and suggest how the book could be marketed.

Publishers seem to think that a reader's report deserves only a token fee. But typically it takes several hours to get to know the manuscript and a couple more to write, say, a two-page report, and freelance editors should charge realistically. A major reason for undertaking a reader's report is that you will probably get the job of copyediting.

A reader's report does not require a detailed appraisal, as described in Chapter 4, but only a general understanding of the quality of the manuscript and its major defects, if any. Anyway, at the normal woeful rate of pay you do not have time to read the whole manuscript closely. Your report begins with a brief account of the manuscript, its purpose, scope and significance. Then describe its strengths and weaknesses, giving examples. Suggest, if necessary, how it could be revised to make a marketable book. Conclude with some comments on readership, competing titles and marketing.

For instance, here is part of a detailed reader's report on a half-baked manuscript which suggests imaginative solutions to the problems of the publishing project.[3]

> The book is not divided into chapters, and such headings as there are seem to have been chosen almost at random. As an urgent first stage, a framework or skeleton of the whole work should be prepared. In this the material should be divided into chapters of about 5000 words, each covering a clearly recognisable topic or period. The material within each of these chapters should itself be subdivided into smaller units, each with headings to assist the reading. ...
>
> The often fascinating insights into the significant people could be incorporated but in a much shorter form and strictly in terms of their relation to the main topic.
>
> The book should not be more than about two-thirds of the present length, and an orthodox, strictly chronological treatment should be aimed at. Nevertheless, I do not consider that the division into years only (which begins at a fairly late stage of the manuscript) is a satisfactory one. Dating events in this way has some advantages, however, so I suggest that the designer be asked to devise a page style which provides for a running head giving the date, to keep the reader in constant touch with the location in time. The discipline imposed by such a treatment would also demonstrate to the author the way in which he often skips backwards and forwards, and help him to eliminate this.

In preparing a reader's report, give your comments more force by linking them to examples in the text, as in this brief report on *Australian Standards for Editing Practice*.

> This is a ground-breaking work by an unknown author. Modest in extent, it weaves a richly imagined tapestry out of universal themes: duty, lost innocence, and the struggle for autonomy.
>
> The writing is uneven in quality. Some parts have a grand sweep, breathtaking in their implications, such as the requirement to be conversant with 'Words and their meanings' (D3.2). There are gems of polished brevity, such as 'The use of punctuation to ensure clarity of meaning and ease of reading' (D1.4). The relentless accumulation of detail is effective, but at times becomes fussy or even anxious in tone.
>
> The writing has some powerful moments, as when the postmodern fracturing of personal identity is embodied in a lugubrious cadence: 'The author may be one or more individuals. The author may or may not be the client' (D2.1). There are some striking images (widows and orphans adrift on rivers of space, E5.2),

but the author tends to show off with tedious verbal tricks such as alliteration ('Prepress, print production and proof-checking processes', A6.1).

The work has some serious flaws. The promising cast of characters introduced in the note to B1.5, 'Members of the publishing team may include . . .', is never developed. There are dramatic possibilities in the implied tension between editor and client that could be explored further. The plot is weak and predictable, and it lacks a denouement.

If published as it stands, with a targeted marketing campaign and aggressive pricing, this slim volume could have a modest success. Alternatively, if it were reworked to include humour and perhaps a love interest, blockbuster status and film rights could follow.

Estimating length

If you're in the preliminary stages of a project and want a very rough idea of length, an approximate figure for a book is 300 words per page, plus or minus 50 per cent according to the design; with small type and large pages, you might cram in 500 words.

To make a more accurate estimate, called a cast-off, you need to know the wordcount of the original document, and how many words will fit on a page of the finished publication. Don't rely on the author's wordcount; she may have omitted substantial items like appendixes, notes or solutions to exercises.

If for some reason you cannot do an electronic wordcount, you can make an estimate:

1 Select an average line and count the words.
2 Multiply by the number of lines per page.
3 Multiply by the number of pages of text.

Once you know the wordcount of the original document, you can work out the number of pages in the finished publication:

1 Divide the wordcount by the number of words on the printed page.
2 If there are illustrations and tables, count them up as full, half- and quarter-pages and add them to your total.
3 Add a small percentage to allow for headings and for space at the beginning and end of chapters.
4 Multiply to get the number of pages of text.
5 Add an appropriate number of pages for prelims and endmatter, including the index.

Selecting material for a sample setting

Books that have a complicated design often require a sample setting. The sample is usually about half a dozen double-page spreads prepared as page proofs, so that the publisher, author and marketing department can review the design and modify it as required. If you are asked to select material for a sample setting, choose a chapter opening and some pages of text that include all the elements in the book—text, all grades of heading, set-down quotations, pix and tables, boxed text, footnotes and so on. The selected pages should be consecutive if possible, but you may have to include some odd pages in order to provide examples of all the elements.

When you have chosen the pages, photocopy them and mark up the photo-copies for the designer as you would the manuscript (Chapter 8); label the result 'copy for sample setting'. Provide a list of the elements, including the colour code or Microsoft Word styles that you have used for mark-up.

Preparing an estimate

In order to estimate the editorial costs of a job, you need both the project plan and the editorial brief. The project plan, as described above, identifies the purpose of the publication, who the readers are and what quality is required, and it includes at least a rough appraisal of the manuscript. The following discussion takes the freelance editor's point of view; commissioning editors follow similar steps to work out what they are prepared to pay for a job.

Estimating time required

To estimate the price for a job, you need to know how much time it will take. The project plan and the editorial brief list the editor's responsibilities, and from them you can draw up a list of the tasks that you have to do. Figure 3.1 shows how I break up the process, as explained in Chapter 9, but there are many other ways. It's easy to overlook some areas. You must include all the tasks required for copyediting each part of the manuscript, and also the managerial and administra-tive tasks described in this chapter and any others specified in the brief.

Now comes the tricky bit: having listed every task that you are responsible for, assign an appropriate amount of time to each one, according to the length and quality of the manuscript. The estimation of time is something that you learn with experience, but there are some shortcuts. If you have done a sample edit as part of the appraisal of the manuscript (Chapter 4), you can extrapolate from it an approximate time for editing the text. If you have kept careful records, the hours spent and payment received on similar jobs will provide a guide. But of course the particulars of the job are the determining factor.

After you've made a rough allocation, review the subtotals you have arrived at to ensure they accord with the importance of each group of tasks—manage-ment and liaison can account for as much as a quarter of the available hours, but obviously you want to spend most of your time on editing. The number of hours goes up according to the degree of difficulty—allow extra time for poor-quality writing, extensive references, multiple authorship and so on. Additional tasks beyond copyediting, such as picture research, collating proofs or editing the index, also need extra time.

Task	Estimated time (hours)	Subtotal
Appraisal and estimate		
Author and client liaison		
Rough Edit:		
text		
references		
pix and captions		
prelims, check text headings		
Smooth Edit:		
text		
references		
pix and captions		
prelims		
Compile author queries		
Incorporate author corrections		
Compile documentation, final check all		
Print and check edited manuscript		
Proofread and correct printout		
Invoice, package and despatch		
Total		

FIGURE 3.1   Allocating time for copyediting

A price for the job

One method of preparing an estimate is to calculate the hours of work needed, as shown in Figure 3.1, and multiply by your hourly rate (Chapter 11). You don't yet have a price for the job, though.

- Some freelances regard expenses—telephone calls, internet time, paper, postage and courier fees—as overheads covered by the hourly rate, but if you cost them separately, add them in.
- Add a loading if you are working on screen because you are using additional skills—journalists get a 6 per cent allowance for this—as well as providing equipment that has to be maintained and saving your client keyboarding costs.
- Add a small percentage—known technically as 'the fudge factor'—to allow for unforeseen problems. Because of the nature of unforeseen problems you can't say exactly what form they'll take, but believe me they'll be there.

The first estimate that you arrive at generally causes you to go and lie down for a while, because you have been too generous in allocating time. Go back over your hourly figures and prune them to something more realistic. Don't be too harsh, however. It's fatally easy to underquote—either you underestimate the amount of work involved, or you fear that you won't get the job. Have courage! Sometimes when you state a seemingly enormous figure in fear and trembling, you find that you're well under the client's budget and could have charged more. Always estimate on the high side of what you really expect; not only does this allow for cases where you underestimate, but occasionally you can promote goodwill by passing genuine savings on to the client.

When you submit your estimated price, document exactly what work it covers. In the informal relationships that prevail in the book industry, you might agree on a figure and later find that your client expects proofreading and collation for a sum that you thought covered only copyediting.

Project documentation

A publishing house or a government agency will have documentation procedures for you to follow; if you are a freelance editor whose client is the author or a corporate publisher, you will have to devise your own. Always label any documentation or separate part of the manuscript, whether paper or electronic, with the author's name and the title of the publication.

It is not necessary to prepare documentation to record editorial changes and the authority for making them, but your working processes should be clear in case any dispute arises. Progressive versions of a manuscript saved under logical file names, along with correspondence, show author's and publisher's agreement to particular proposals (see Chapter 10).

The documents that you should have before you begin editing a manuscript include:

- project plan, discussed above
- for freelances, a contract (Chapter 11).
- editorial brief
- job file.

When you send off the edited manuscript, whether in print or electronic form, you should enclose or attach:

- covering letter or handover form
- brief for designer (and for artist, illustrator, indexer if required)
- word list and style sheet
- order of book
- a timesheet (in-house editors) or an invoice (freelances).

Let's look at some of these more closely.

Editorial brief

The editorial brief should conform to the guidelines listed under Contracts in Chapter 11. Study the brief closely and make sure that you understand its implications in terms of tasks to be done. You don't want any surprises when you recheck the brief at the end of a tightly costed job.

Figure 3.2 shows a typical editorial brief from a publishing house. Such a succinct brief is suitable only where the editor and the publisher share assumptions as to definitions and quality. Editors who work for other organisations will need to clarify the publisher's expectations.

Job file

At a minimum the job file contains name and contact details for client and author, the contract between editor and client, the editorial brief, and the house style if there is one. It may also include background material like correspondence between publisher and author, the publishing proposal and reader's reports. There may be writing guidelines, a series style or a word list to follow. Sometimes there are lists of artwork, and there may be a pattern volume to follow for style or a sample setting that shows the intended layout and design.

Covering letter

If the publisher does not provide a handover form, send a covering letter with the edited manuscript. Begin with a list of what you are sending. Then state any

---

For this title, you are required to:

- ❑ edit manuscript
- ❑ submit editorial queries to author
- ❑ check revised manuscript
- ❑ appraise and integrate illustrations
- ❑ supply order of book and design brief
- ❑ complete the editorial section of the attached typesetting specification
- ❑ supply copy for running heads
- ❑ supply caption copy and list of illustrations
- ❑ supply illustration label copy
- ❑ supply draft blurb and cover copy
- ❑ collate first proofs
- ❑ edit index.

All edited files are to be delivered in electronic format.

FIGURE 3.2 Where both parties share assumptions and definitions, as in the book industry, an editorial brief may be a simple checklist

actions that the publisher must take, such as following up permissions or obtaining CIP data. Note any copy that is still to come, stating its length, position and arrival date. If there have been any changes to the project during editing that will affect costs — the wordcount has blown out or the author has added extra maps — state them in writing, even if the publisher has already agreed to them informally.

Design brief, type specification

As job descriptions blur, so does documentation. The traditional roles of designer and typesetter are often joined in the person of the desktop publisher, and the design brief and the type specification become one. You may not know how much expertise the designer-typesetter has; if you suspect she is inexperienced in bookwork, give full, clear instructions and include a list of the proof correction marks that you have used.

Editors working in house can usually talk over problems with the designer, but a written design brief is always advisable. It sets out the characteristics of the manuscript and any unusual features. Some publishers provide a form to fill in, but often you need to tell the designer more than the form allows. A freelance editor who composes a design brief should prepare it on business letterhead so the designer can make contact if she has any questions. Give it an appropriate heading and identify the job by author and title, as shown in Figure 3.3.

Start off with a statement of what the manuscript consists of. Continue under headings for each of the different components, stating generally what they comprise and drawing attention to any special points, including decisions you have made. Make sure you tell the designer everything she needs to know. If you have used colour coding, explain the system. Draw her attention to any layout problems, such as a large table or lengthy headings or quotations. List any special 'sorts' or characters that are used, such as mathematical symbols or diacritics, and indicate their frequency and location.

You can also list general instructions and global changes for the typesetter to make. In Figure 3.3, some of the global changes would normally have been made by an editor working on screen, but they are included to show the range of possibilities. Attach to the design brief the word list, the style sheet and the order of book, described below, and copy for running heads (Chapter 4).

As we have seen, the type specification overlaps with the design brief. They both list the components of the book with brief notes on their treatment, but the type spec may also include detailed guidelines for composition (such as 'close word spacing throughout') and make-up (such as 'facing pages should be the same depth'). You should be familiar with these guidelines, particularly when working on proofs, but you don't normally have to write them.

Artwork brief

The artwork brief can take various forms, from a list of photographs to detailed instructions to an illustrator or cartographer. Educational publishers often have a standard artwork brief to fill in. If you have to prepare your own, it should:

DESIGN AND TYPESETTING BRIEF

Likiardopolous & Ng, eds, *Wafer, Cone or Dixie Cup: A history of Australian ice-cream preferences*

- MS consists of prelims pp P1–P12, text pp. 1–359, two disks in Microsoft Word 2000 for PC, and 24 halftones plus table copy pp. T1-T17.
- See also word list, style sheet, order of book and artwork brief, attached.

Headings

- Part heads, chapter heads and three grades of subheads, A, B, C. See style sheet.
- Chapter heads are double-barrelled, would suit two-line treatment.
- C-heads occur only in Chapters 5 and 8.

Quotations

- Single quote marks are used throughout (but double quote marks for a quote-within-a-quote). Follow copy.
- Closing punctuation is inside final quote mark if sentence is grammatically complete, but outside final quote mark if sentence is incomplete. Follow copy.
- Quotations of more than fifty words are set down (indented). Marked with red line on hard copy, styled xBlock Quote on disk.
- Bullet list in set-down quote, MS p. 157.

Endnotes

- Notes are to appear at end of each chapter; do not move to end of book.

Special setting

- Equations containing mathematical symbols are on MS pp. 23, 47–56, 278–81, 302. See mark-up on hard copy.
- URLs (web addresses) may be broken, without a hyphen, after any dot or slash.

Tables

- Location marked in e-copy with xTable Title style.
- Use marked-up hard copy for setting.
- Tables 7.3 and 7.4, MS pp. 221, 231, are very long.

Global changes

- Delete one-line space between paras and start n.p. with an indent.
- Full out (flush left) after headings.
- Text dash is typed as spaced hyphen and as spaced en rule; replace all with close-up em rule.
- Change straight quote marks to curly quote marks.
- Replace hyphen with en rule in spans of figures.

Figure 3.3   A typical design brief: scholarly essays

- identify the pic with a number (Fig. 1.1, Plate 1, etc.)
- state the format (line drawing, b&w photo, etc.), and the electronic file name if necessary
- indicate the placement of each pic in the finished work, usually by the relevant page number in the marked-up hard copy of the manuscript.

The artwork brief may also include the captions, if there is no separate caption copy; a short description of each image; and details of sources and permissions.

If you have to give instructions for artwork, describe what is needed in words and supply sketches or photographs if necessary. Specify that the illustrator should not stereotype people or show unsafe practices. The editor has to consider whether the artwork as supplied will reproduce satisfactorily; see Chapter 6.

Word list and style sheet

The editor keeps a word list for each job, detailing the spellings, capitals and hyphens peculiar to the manuscript. Traditionally this list was known as the style sheet, but then Microsoft hijacked the word *style*. The term 'style sheet' now denotes a list of the MS Word styles used in a manuscript. When compiling the word list, think about what the proofreader needs to know; for the style sheet, think about what the typesetter needs to know. Both should be identified with the author's name and the title and attached to the design brief. For examples, see Figure 3.4; the *x* prefix in the style names denotes custom styles.

Order of book

The order of book is a list that shows the sequence of preliminary pages, text and endmatter and the pagination of the prelims, as in Figure 3.5. (For more on prelims and endmatter, see Chapter 7.) The recto pages, which have odd numbers, are shown on the right, and the verso pages, which have even numbers, are shown on the left. This layout helps you to visualise which pages face each other: page i faces the endpaper or the inside of the front cover; page ii and page iii form one spread or opening, and so on.

Don't draw up the order of book until you know what has to be included. You'll have to alter it if the author comes up with extra copy such as a note on terminology or an appendix, or you realise that something has to be added, such as measurement conversions or a chronology.

Once you have prepared the order of book, you can arrange and number the prelim pages accordingly. As always, write the author's name and the title on the top of the order of book. Write 'do not set' on it and attach it to the design brief.

Monitoring

Quite a lot of editorial time is spent gently chivvying people to produce the goods.

A freelance editor whose jobs mostly follow the straightforward path that was outlined in Figure 2.2 can keep track of them by using simple records like the diary and workplan described below, and there are many other systems of monitoring work-in-progress that you can combine and adapt to suit your role. An editor who manages a project and supervises the publishing team devises a checklist that tracks receipt and despatch of all the bits and pieces of each manuscript. An important part of monitoring your work is version control, discussed in Chapter 10.

McLeod & Antonioni: Power Politics

Word list

acronyms: no full points
Area Boards
chairman (l.c.)
Chapter 9 (cap)
coal-fired
cogeneration
co-operate, co-ordinate, etc.
County Councils (NSW)
   (caps)
CRA Ltd
Davey, Ron
Davies, Ken
diesel–battery system
   (en rule)
diesel-generated
Electricité de France
federal (l.c.)
financial years: 1980/81
general manager (l.c.)

government (l.c.; but cap for
   particular ministry)
Hazelwood power station
high-voltage (adjective)
hydro-electric, hydro-
   electricity
Inquiry (1982)
interconnection
-ise
Latrobe Valley
Minister
ministerial
North-West Shelf
offshore
open-cut mine
-our
overmanning
Pacific North-West States
   (US)

policy-making
possessives: Davies's
program
real rate of return
   (no hyphens)
return on equity
   (no hyphens)
shut-down (noun)
stand by (verb); stand-by
   (adjective)
state (l.c.)
time-of-use tariffs
United States (noun); US
   (adjective)
Upper House
user-pays (adjective)
workforce
World War II
Zeidler Committee

Style sheet

xAhead: major subheading
xBhead: minor subheading
xbibliography: entry in bibliography
xbullet point: point in a bullet list
xchapter head: chapter heading; includes chapter number
xcontent: entry in table of contents
xendnote: text of endnote
xfigure caption: includes figure number; indicates figure placement
xnumbered point: point in a numbered list
xpara: body text para, first line indented
xpara f/o: body text para, first line full out
xprelim head: heading for prelims and endmatter (Contents, Preface, Notes, Bibliography)
xquote para: set-down quote, first line indented (for second and subsequent paras)
xquote para f/o: set-down quote, first line full out (for first para)
xtable: text in body of table
xtable column head: column head in a table
xtable title: title (caption) of table; indicates table placement

FIGURE 3.4 **A typical word list and style sheet: academic economic history**

A week or two before you expect to receive material, check to make sure it is on track. Be diplomatic but persistent. An enquiry to the author in tactful phrasing like 'I wondered how you're going with the queries/proofs/index and whether I could be of any help' will promote better relations than a complaint

verso (left-hand page)	recto (right-hand page)
	i half title
ii (blank)	iii title
iv imprint	v contents
vi contents *contd*	vii list of illustrations
viii list of illustrations *contd*	ix preface
x preface *contd*	xi preface *contd*
xii (blank)	xiii acknowledgements
xiv acknowledgements *contd*	xv abbreviations
xvi (blank)	p. 1 introduction
	chs 1–12
	conclusion
	notes
	bibliography
	index

FIGURE 3.5 A typical order of book for non-fiction

after the item has failed to arrive. A freelance editor asking a client whether an expected job is on schedule may get the unwelcome reply, 'Oh sorry, didn't we tell you, we've decided to hold that title over till next year.'

It is a good practice to follow up anything you send, whether packages or email. Packages can go to a town of the right name in the wrong state, or languish for days in a university mailroom or a freight depot; email may be blocked by overzealous spam filters or simply not read. If you haven't heard anything after a few days, ask the addressee to acknowledge receipt.

Diary

Diary notes are a convenient means of recording work done and liaison with author and publisher. I begin each entry with the name of the author in capitals, so I can easily look back and see when I last worked on that job. I briefly record the contents of emails and phone conversations, especially any decisions made, and the date of despatch of packages and e-copy. I also keep a running total of hours for each job. Every so often I summarise this in the workplan.

Workplan

For a full-time editor who has a dozen or more projects in various stages of production, a workplan gives an overview of the flow of work. The one shown in

Last updated: 25 July

Publisher	Author & Title	Stage	Last Action	Next Action *= could start ** = do now	Dead-line	Quote	Hrs not billed
Dicey & Dodgy	EDWARDS Orchids for Fun and Profit	design and typesetting	sent edited manuscript 20 June	collate 1st proofs due 5 Aug	12 Aug	bill for hours spent	6.5
Camford UP	HEINZ Sociology of Sociology	waiting revised MS from author	ph BM 24 July	edit manuscript due 15 Aug	author queries 23 Sept	$4000 MS and proofs	3
Linen Press	CHAN Antimacassars in Focus	edited manuscript waiting author cxns	em author 22 July	incorporate author cxns due 9 Aug	17 Aug	$1800 MS only	22

FIGURE 3.6 Part of a typical workplan for a freelance business

Figure 3.6 is for a freelance business; employed editors can add or delete columns to suit the needs of their organisation. Consult the workplan every few days in order to keep all the balls in the air. When there has been no action on a job for some time, find out what's happening. For instance in the example shown, you haven't heard anything about the Edwards job for several weeks; you'd better make sure the proofs really are going to arrive on 5 August, because if they run late they will collide with the Chan author corrections.

Running sheet

I keep a running sheet for each job which lists the tasks that have to be done and the number of hours I expect each task to take, as in Figure 3.1. I draw it up in order to prepare the estimate, and I keep it by my side during the job to monitor my progress. Thus (according to the copyediting method described in Chapter 9) if I've estimated ten hours for the Rough Edit of the text and I'm only a quarter of the way through after five hours, I know that this job is more complicated than I thought, and I have to renegotiate the budget and schedule with my client. If I find that I'm lingering too much during the Smooth Edit—dithering or being too fussy—I can press on a bit faster, or resign myself to losing money on the job.

The *Style Manual*, Chapter 26, has advice on formal monitoring processes. For freelance schedules, see Chapter 11.

4

Substance and structure

THE TERMS 'SUBSTANTIVE EDITING' and 'structural editing' are commonly used as synonyms, but shades of meaning can be distinguished. Substantive editing, being concerned with the substance of the book—content and expression as well as structure—is the more comprehensive term. This type of editing requires close consultation with the author and publisher.

Here we examine what substance and structure mean for print and screen publications; methods for substantive editing are described in Chapter 9.

Substance

It is not possible to edit a book unless you can comprehend it. An editor should be able to deal with any publication intended for the educated general reader, but specialist or groundbreaking works might challenge the limits of your understanding. If your knowledge of the topic or your cognitive ability is less than that of the intended reader, say frankly that you're not up to the job and allow the publisher to find an editor with suitable expertise.

The substance of a publication consists of language and illustrations, which are covered in the following two chapters. Here I mention a couple of general points.

Fiction

There is a marked contrast between instrumental writing and creative writing. Generally the reader of non-fiction is a passive recipient, wanting all the information laid out in a logical arrangement with everything fully explained. Fiction readers, by contrast, are active participants: they create meaning in collaboration with the author.

By fiction I mean novels, novellas, short stories, play scripts and poetry; the same applies, to some extent, to genres such as autobiography, memoir, and even some history.

The structure of fiction may be circular or spiralling rather than linear or hierarchical. The narrative or plot may work by means of hints and clues, impressions and atmosphere. Several authorial voices may speak in turn, and the tone and pace may vary markedly from scene to scene. The vocabulary may include delightful coinages such as *uninsultable* or *scruffling*. Techniques include intentional repetition, intentional ambiguity and irony. As we will see in the next chapter, fiction may flout the rules of grammar, especially in dialogue.

In editing fiction and allied genres, you must take the stance that it is not your work but the author's; your task is not to make it over to suit your own ideas, but to assist the author to accomplish her intention. The editor must be sensitive to delicate nuances and connotations of vocabulary and syntax, both written and spoken. For instance, suppose the author has written 'She hesitated for a moment. Then she moved forward.' You might think of changing this to 'She hesitated for a moment, then moved forward.' But in the author's version, the full stop after 'moment' forces the reader to pause, thus enacting the meaning; the emendation eliminates this distinction and flattens the rhythm.

Authors of fiction invest their identity in their work, and the editor must be even more respectful and diplomatic than usual. An editorial exchange on a novel is related in Chapter 3 under Author Response.

The fiction editor should have some knowledge of current trends in literary and popular writing. You must always perform the essential tasks of copyediting and language editing (Chapter 9). Some points to watch are:

- The work must be internally consistent in its descriptions of characters and places, and facts drawn from the real world must be accurate (see below).
- Check for verisimilitude: for example, action or dialogue that takes place while the characters are engaged in boiling an egg must appear to last for a few minutes—no more, no less.
- Pay particular attention to representations of nonstandard speech, as discussed in Chapter 5 under The Spoken Word in Print.
- Don't take names for granted: sometimes an author changes the name of a character or a place while writing but accidentally leaves a few instances of the old name.
- Where appropriate, suggest adding supplementary material such as maps, genealogical charts or a glossary.

Accuracy

In most circumstances the editor is not expected to have specialist knowledge of the subject of a publication and is not responsible for the accuracy of its content—that is up to the author. The editor spot-checks facts and looks for internal inconsistencies in order to assess the author's level of accuracy. Your stance in reading non-fiction should be sceptical, almost truculent—*oh yeah? is that so? sez who?* Don't be afraid to ask naive questions. A manuscript that has serious inaccuracies will have to be returned to the author with tactful instructions to correct it; an author who makes controversial statements or unlikely claims should be asked to support them with evidence.

The editor should be alert for offences against general knowledge, as in the novel that had lovers in Sydney watching the sun set into the Pacific Ocean, a topographical impossibility.[1] By general knowledge I do not mean the trivia about celebrities' personal habits and obscure sporting records that wins points at quiz nights, but a broad understanding of geopolitics, the natural world, human history, and Western and other cultures. Applied general knowledge ranks with expertise in language and typography as a core editorial skill, and it has saved many authors from embarrassment.

Authors can make astounding mistakes. There is an apocryphal story about a historian who wrote a major work on the conscription referendums in World War I, arguing that attitudes to conscription changed markedly after a certain battle on the Western Front. In an idle moment the editor happened to check the date of the battle that was central to the argument and found that the author had it quite wrong. The book was never published; the editor's scepticism saved the author's reputation and career. The lesson from this is, don't take the author's word for it.

Sometimes authors get carried away and overstate their case. A manuscript on protective behaviour for children claimed that 'the bodies of little boys and little girls are very different'. In fact, prepubescent children are more alike (head, trunk, arms, legs) than different (ratio of hips to waist, genitalia). Another author wrote, 'The normal socialisation of Western society provides us with hundreds of formal and informal training opportunities in how to be competitive; rarely do we receive similar training in the skills and capacities of being co-operative.' This overlooks myriad daily acts of co-operation, from passing the salt to team sports and volunteer activities. Maintain your critical faculties and don't get swept up in the author's enthusiasm.

The editor is not a fact-checker; you take all care but no responsibility for accuracy of content. You are responsible, though, for internal accuracy in elements such as the table of contents and the cross-references, and this is no small task.

Structure

Structure cannot be considered in the abstract: it exists in relation to those familiar considerations, the needs of the readership, the author's intention, the available resources and the type of publication. The *Style Manual*'s Chapter 3 describes how to structure material for both print and screen publications.

There are several aspects to the structure of a publication. Standard C identifies them as form, arrangement, focus and length (see Appendix), but I prefer to cut the cake in different slices: the nature of the publication, the elements, the proportions and the arrangement.

The nature of the publication

Despite the prevalence of video and graphics in today's society, we are steeped in book culture and have absorbed its conventions. Because books are all roughly the same size and shape, we may not realise how different they are. The term *book* is a category, like *furniture* or *musical instrument*. We effortlessly distinguish a table from a chair, a flute from a banjo; similarly, the dimensions and appearance of a book, together with its title, set up certain expectations in the reader.

To uncover some of the conventions, let us imagine three books with similar titles but as different in their purpose as banjo, flute and drum.

- *Restoring the Land: A practical approach*, paperback, 210 × 280 mm, 160 pp.
- *Restoring the Land: Essays on value and knowledge*, hardback, 160 × 235 mm, 248 pp.
- *Restoring the Land: A sweeping novel of four generations*, paperback, 135 × 210 mm, 620 pp.

You can easily determine which of the following structural elements you would expect to find in each of these books: subheadings, two-column setting, dialogue, bibliography or list of further reading, diagrams, photographs, set-down (block) quotations, endnotes, case studies, species lists, genealogical charts, maps, glossary, index.

The editor's job is to see that the reader's expectations are fulfilled. Don't take anything for granted: a manuscript entitled *The Backyard Goat* may turn out to be mostly about making cheese. To identify what a book sets out to do, the reader has the title, the format, the blurb, the contents page, and often a statement of the author's intentions in a preface or introduction. The editor can use additional clues, such as the publishing proposal, conversations with the author, and the project plan described in the previous chapter.

The elements

A book can contain many elements besides solid blocks of type. There are the preliminary pages, which shape the reader's expectations as he approaches the text, and the endmatter, which supplements and authenticates the text (Chapter 7). The text may contain headings, quotations and lists, as well as text features like breakout quotes, boxed text, questions, activities, summaries and lists of key terms. Illustrations come in many forms and in some types of books take precedence over the text (Chapter 6). It is the editor's job to make all these elements work together to present the content effectively to the intended reader.

The proportions

A book should be shapely, with each division of the content given space and emphasis that accord with its importance. The breadth and depth of the coverage should match the purpose of the publication.

The structure of a book cannot be imposed in a rigid, formulaic manner: its logic emerges out of the content. For instance, suppose an autobiography has a lopsided structure, with 270 pages allocated to the period from the subject's birth to the age of twenty-one, and 50 pages to the remainder of his life to the age of eighty-two. This manuscript, you might think, is a candidate for structural editing. But be careful: editors recognise when an author has successfully broken the rules. The structure described is that of Bert Facey's *A Fortunate Life* (Fremantle Arts Centre Press, 1981)—not only a classic autobiography but also a resounding commercial success.

The arrangement

The content of the publication follows some logical arrangement, recognising the various ways that readers might use to find their way around it (Figure 4.1). The table of contents and the index provide additional methods of accessing the text, and cross-references can offer a different reading, as explained below.

What makes a book

In essence, a book consists of idiosyncratic arrangements in horizontal lines of about fifty symbols (twenty-six letters, ten digits and more than a dozen punctuation marks). But of course there is more to it than this. Figure 4.1 shows the additional means by which books present content to the reader. The author may present information in a particular way because she does not know what the alternatives are. The editor, with knowledge of these tools, can help her to find an option that suits her purpose. For instance, marginal notes are rarely used because they are expensive in production, but for some kinds of information they may be just the thing.

In considering the structure of a publication, it helps to remember that the author's knowledge of the topic is spherical, but the reader's knowledge is linear (in print, at least). The divisions, the arrangement and the connections provide paths for the reader to access the text. We will look at some of these tools in more detail.

Chunking information

Part of the editor's task is to guard the reader against indigestion. Argument, information and narrative need to be divided into sense-bites or chunks, though of course the size of the chunk differs according to the readership. In an instruction book or on a web page, it is a heading and a couple of sentences; in a scholarly book, it is a paragraph of several hundred words.

Hierarchies are not the best way to arrange human relationships, but you can't beat them as a way of organising information. The divisions of a book are the reader's guide to the relative importance of the content—the nature of the chunks. For example, if the division 'chapter' is to have any meaning, the chapters should be, very roughly, of equal length. Substantive editing often promotes or demotes material from one division to another, as explained in Chapter 9.

Hierarchy of divisions	*Principles of arrangement*	*Connections*
volumes	chronological or narrative	headings
parts	alphabetical	signposts
chapters	hierarchical	transitions
sections (with or without headings)	thematic or topical	previews
	deductive: from the particular to the general	summaries
subsections and sub-subsections, etc. (with or without headings)	inductive: from the general to the particular	cross-references
		headers and footers
paragraphs	thesis, antithesis:	text features: breakout quotes, boxed text, marginal notes, etc.
numbered and bulleted lists	• theory and practice	
sentences	• problem and solution	
	• statement and critique	
	• the case for and the case against (usually concludes with a synthesis)	
	any combination of the above	

FIGURE 4.1 What makes a book: the editor's toolkit

Remember that readers may lay a book aside for days at a time; they need to be reminded of what has already been said, or directed to it with a cross-reference. The hierarchy of divisions should reflect this. If you can reasonably expect the reader to swallow a chapter at a time, then fix on the chapter as your unit. At the first mention in each chapter of a person or institution, use the full name (*Richard Johnson* rather than *Johnson*; *Australian Bureau of Statistics* rather than *ABS*) and perhaps briefly reintroduce them: *Richard Johnson, the colony's first chaplain*.

Sections and paragraphs

A text break, usually a one- or two-line space, marks the end of a section, a division smaller than a chapter but greater than a paragraph. Text breaks may be used instead of, or as well as, headings. The first line after a text break is full out (flush left), and sometimes the first few words are in small capitals. A typographical device such as an asterisk may be used to mark text breaks that fall at the top or bottom of a printed page.

Paragraphing is an important aspect of good writing. A paragraph may be several hundred words in length, but an occasional one-sentence paragraph can make a pleasing effect. A paragraph is tied together by a single coherent idea. Often this idea is encapsulated in a topic sentence, which may be anywhere in the paragraph but is most often at the beginning (as in this paragraph). Some authors make their paragraphs far too long; in contrast, journalists tend to write very short paragraphs that suit the narrow measure of newspaper columns but are jerky to read in the pages of a book. Some readers fear that the paragraph is dying.

A new paragraph is marked either by a first-line indent or a one-line space. The trend to omit any marker for a new para, particularly in blurbs and brochures, is to be deplored; the reader needs this signal in order to make sense of the text. When marking up a manuscript, be sure to indicate the paragraphing after any interruption in the text, such as a set-down quotation or a table, by marking either *f.o.* for *full out* or *n.p.* for *new para*. Similarly, on screen apply the appropriate style to text that follows an interruption. The newspaper industry abbreviates *paragraph* as *par*.

Cross-references

Cross-references are an alternative way of organising the content of a publication; they represent the road not taken. Remember, the author's knowledge is spherical. Consider, for example, a book on the history of South-East Asia: if it is organised by nation-state, with one chapter per country, cross-references enable the reader to trace a chronological path through the text; but if it is organised chronologically, the cross-references point out the geographic or political paths. Cross-references also connect the text to items like tables, illustrations and appendixes.

The cross-references, like everything else, must suit the intended reader. In most cases they are useful, but too many can be distracting. Remember that the reader will also be able to access the text by way of the table of contents and the index, or the search facility on screen. Sometimes it is better simply to repeat the information. In an institutional history, for instance, *John Frigby (see Chapter 3)* would be better in a formal register as *John Frigby (director 1949–60)*, or more informatively as *John Frigby who was director during the first major phase of expansion in the 1950s*.

In print, cross-references can be expensive if page numbers have to be inserted in proofs—a tedious task. Chapter references are less useful to the reader than page references, but cheaper; if you cross-reference by chapter number, include chapter numbers in the running heads. A dictionary-style publication cross-references by the names of the entries (headwords). Where illustrations are mentioned in the text, the cross-reference is to the appropriate number—*Map 3, Figure 1.12*—so the numbering of the illustrations must be finalised before typesetting begins.

Signposts and transitions

Courteous authors pause occasionally to remind the reader where the text has been and where it is going. Headings are one method of doing this, but signposts can also take the form of sentences or typographical devices.

A verbal signpost may be a one-sentence summary of what has gone before or a bridging phrase that points the way ahead. They range from the succinct— *as already mentioned*; *discussed below*—to the discursive:

- *Thus there are three possibilities for action, but all of them raise problems for different levels of government.*

- *Before we examine the Victorian Act, it is necessary to understand the legislation operating in other states.*
- *These issues are dealt with at length in Chapters 8 and 9. Here I will concentrate on . . .*
- *Meanwhile, back at the ranch . . .*

Academic books sometimes overdo the signposting. The old adage is 'Tell them what you're going to tell them, then tell them, then tell them what you've just told them.' This can be illuminating if each iteration adds something fresh or leads the reader forward in some way, but when mechanically applied it makes dreary reading.

An editor who is inserting signposts and transitions must ensure that they conform to the authorial voice (Chapter 5).

Running heads (headers)

I prefer the traditional terms *running heads* and the delightful *running feet*, but they are being replaced by Microsoft Word's *headers* and *footers*. Whatever they're called, they are extremely useful for the reader both in print and on screen, enabling him to orient himself to the whole publication and determine where he is within it. In screen publications, it is helpful to repeat the main title on each page because the reader may have arrived by an indirect route. In a book, though, the title is the least useful thing you can have as a running head. The reader may be presumed to know what it is; if by any chance he's forgotten, he only has to glance at the cover.

Many readers, especially of anthologies and collections, look ahead to see how long an item is, so they can predict the likely course of the argument or narrative—how will she get out of this in two pages? The reader can turn to the contents page to find out the length of the items, but running heads are more convenient.

Novels usually don't have running heads unless the chapters have names. My recreational reading has included Kathy Lette's *Mad Cows* (Picador, Sydney, 1996), in which the running heads are the title of the book and the author's name. This is a lost opportunity, because the novel is divided into parts and chapters with titles worth thinking about, such as 'Relying on the Kindness of Passing Serial Killers'. Each chapter title appears only twice in the book, on the contents page and on the chapter opening; if they had been used as running heads, they would have been held in front of the reader as an implicit commentary on what he was reading.

Here are some guidelines for running heads, which you will temper with your knowledge of how the reader will use the book. A verso is a left-hand page, a recto a right-hand page.

- Running heads do not appear on a page that contains displayed matter, such as a part title or chapter opening; or on a blank page; or on a 'turned' or landscape page.

- The recto running head usually carries the name of the chapter or of a similar division such as a learning unit, essay or short story.
- The default option for the verso running head is the title of the book, but replace it with something more useful wherever possible: with part titles if the book is divided into parts, or with contributors' names in a book of essays or short stories.
- Conference proceedings have the number of the session or the day as the verso running head and the speakers' names on the recto.
- In dictionary-style books, the verso running head is the title of the first complete entry on the page; the recto running head is the title of the last entry on the page, whether it is complete or not.
- Prelims and endmatter are usually self-titled on both recto and verso. Thus the second and subsequent pages of the preface have the running head *Preface*, and similarly for the bibliography and index. Appendixes have *Appendix 1* etc. on the verso, and the title of the appendix, shortened if necessary, on the recto.
- In some publishers' house styles, endnotes incorporate chapter or page numbers in the running heads in a form such as *Notes to pages 00–00*. The page numbers must be inserted in page proofs.

It is the editor's responsibility to prepare copy for running heads and attach it to the design brief. Present it in two columns, headed *verso* and *recto*. A rule of thumb for the length of running heads is thirty-five characters (letters and spaces); if you're working to a series style or a sample setting you might know the exact number of characters allowed.

Figure 4.2 shows how the table of contents compares with copy for running heads and how to condense the chapter titles to fit. Here are some points to note about it:

- Part numbers may be used as verso running heads (*Part I*), but in this case contributors' names have first claim.
- Since the word *Australian* is in the book's title, it can be dropped from the running heads if space is tight.
- Chapter numbers must be included in the recto running heads if they are used in cross-references, especially to endnotes. (Designers resist this because they think the number looks ugly.)
- The running heads for the notes follow a house style.
- The typesetter or the proofreader will replace the double zeroes with page numbers in the page proofs, and the editor will check them when collating proofs.

For advice on proofreading running heads, see Chapter 8 under Reading First Proofs.

Table of contents	Copy for running heads	
	verso	*recto*
Introduction	Introduction 00	Introduction 00
Part I		
1 Australian Literature and Australian Culture *Bruce Allen*	Bruce Allen 00	1 Literature and Culture 00
2 Aboriginal Literature A: Oral *Stephen Ankers*	Stephen Ankers 00	2A Aboriginal Literature 00
B: Written *Frances Marks and Jim Comerford*	Frances Marks and Jim Comerford 00	2B Aboriginal Literature 00
3 Forms of Australian Literary History *Quentin Gardener*	Quentin Gardener 00	3 Forms of Literary History 00
Part II		
4 Perceptions of Australia before 1855 *Gary Frost*	Gary Frost 00	4 Perceptions before 1855 00
5 Writers, Printers, Readers: The Production of Australian Literature before 1855 *Elena Toritsky*	Elena Toritsky 00	5 Writers, Printers, Readers 00
6 Colonial Transformations: Writing and the Dilemma of Colonisation *Richard Morton*	Richard Morton 00	6 Colonial Transformations 00
Part III		
7 Journalism and the World of the Writer: The Production of Australian Literature, 1855–1915 *Humphrey Curtis*	Humphrey Curtis 00	7 Journalism and the Writer 00
8 Melodrama and the Melodramatic Imagination *Andrea Stewart*	Andrea Stewart 00	8 Melodrama and Imagination 00
9 Romance: An Embarrassing Subject *Mary Purcell*	Mary Purcell 00	9 Romance: Embarrassing Subject 00
Notes	Notes (Introduction) 00	Notes (Introduction— Chapter 1) 00
	Notes (Chapter 1) 00	Notes (Chapters 1–2) 00
	etc.	*etc.*
Bibliography	Bibliography 00	Bibliography 00
Index	Index 00	Index 00

FIGURE 4.2 Preparing copy for running heads: Australian literary history

Appraising a document

In an appraisal, also called an editorial report, you assess the conceptual integrity of the document, decide whether it fulfils its intended objectives, and estimate how much editorial work is required to bring it to a publishable standard. Before you begin an appraisal, you must know the purpose of the publication and the readership or target market, as described in the previous chapter.

Appraisal can occur at various levels. A basic appraisal of a book-length manuscript can be done in a few hours, but it relies on sampling; if the samples chosen are unrepresentative, the conclusions may be misleading. The more samples, the more accurate the appraisal. A detailed appraisal of a really messy manuscript is based not on samples but on a thorough examination of the whole work; for this kind of job it may take a week to make an appraisal, map out the tasks of the substantive edit, and draw up a project plan.

The account that follows seems laborious, but with practice you will quickly pick out the salient features of a document. For instance, it may only take a few minutes' examination of the illustrations to find out three crucial facts—that there are way too many for the budget, that they are not numbered or arranged in any obvious order, and that there is no caption copy.

Making a start

A great lump arrives on your desk. Where do you start?

First, separate the document itself from the papers concerning it—the editorial brief, correspondence, reader's report, sample setting, author questionnaire. Look through this material to get an idea of the project. It's important to find out, for instance, whether this is a book that emerged from a conference, or a biography the author has been working on for twenty years. Take all the 'papers concerning' and put them in a folder. This is the job file.

Then identify the preliminary pages, separate them, look through them. List any missing items, such as acknowledgements or list of illustrations. Put the prelims aside. Identify all the other non-text material—artwork, captions, endnotes, appendixes. Organise it with folders, envelopes or bulldog clips, and put it aside.

On screen, the processes are different but you arrive at the same result. First, as soon as you insert the disk into your drive or open the email attachment, run a virus scan on it. Then copy everything to your hard drive, remove the disk and store it in a safe place. This is your original copy, which you will need if disaster strikes. On your hard drive, open every file to check for compatibility and completeness. List missing items and set up folders for the job file, for the text, and for other items such as artwork and permissions (Chapter 10 under Electronic Files).

The text: overview

Having isolated the text, you are ready to form an impression of its scope, coverage, balance, coherence, consistency and accuracy. Read a bit of the introduction or first chapter to get acquainted with the author's voice. Flip or scroll through the document to consider the four aspects of structure listed above: the nature of the publication, the elements, the proportions and the arrangement. As you work, note the editorial tasks that are required.

For paper manuscripts, it's handy to separate the chapters or other divisions from one another by some physical means. I use sheets of coloured paper, but you may prefer manila folders, bulldog clips or stick-on tags. These divisions provide a physical representation of the proportions of the document, and they make it easy to find the chapter heads to compare them for content, wording and style. You cannot get a feel for proportions when working on screen with the chapters in separate files; the only way is to count words or pages for each chapter and calculate them as a percentage of the whole.

To consider the balance and structure of the whole work, make use of the table of contents and the headings, or create a guide to headings as described in Chapter 9. It's usually apparent if the document follows some coherent principle of arrangement that is suitable for its subject matter.

Review the content of the document for completeness: does it cover the topic adequately? Sometimes an author is so close to the subject that she misses a whole aspect of it. Look for subtle omissions: a book that purports to be about Australia may draw all its examples from one or two states; one that discusses current trends may rely on outdated statistics. Perhaps the reader needs something that the author has not supplied, such as a list of conversions for measurements, a chronology, a glossary, maps or a list of addresses. Conversely, is any part of the document irrelevant or superfluous? I once worked on a history of anaesthetics in Australia, which commenced with a lengthy account of Captain Cook—anaesthetics weren't even invented until Chapter 5 of the manuscript. Sometimes digressions and supplementary material need to be pruned, or moved to an appendix or an associated web page.

Examine the connections within the text, such as headings, signposts, transitions and cross-references, to see if the narrative or argument is knitted together as a coherent whole. Is the heading hierarchy consistent? Do the chapters conclude, or do they just tail off? Has the author provided cross-references or is that another item for your task list?

Determine the author's capacity for accuracy: she may be prone to obvious errors of fact, or make extravagant claims, or be careless with dates or the spelling of names. A spot-check of facts and dates (and of quotations, if you have the sources handy) will show whether she is sloppy.

Consider whether defamation is likely to be an issue. Note whether copyright material is used and whether permissions have been obtained. Add all these points to your task list.

The text: language

Having surveyed the forest, you now inspect the trees. So far you have been skipping and skimming; it's time for close reading. Assess the quality of the writing:

check for verbosity, repetition, grammatical errors, clumsy constructions, inadequate punctuation, confused terminology, poor vocabulary. Check that the language level and register are suitable for the intended reader. Form an idea of how much language editing is needed (Chapter 9).

For most jobs it's best to do a sample edit. Select a sequence of twenty to fifty typical pages; note the time and begin editing, either with pencil on paper or in a test file on screen. For this exercise don't select the first or last chapter, because they're often quite different in style from the main part of the text. Chapter 3 is a good one—the author's usually well into her stride by then. Note the time when you finish, and calculate pages per hour. From that figure you can work out roughly how long to allow for the language editing of the whole document.

Non-text material

Now you have appraised the text, turn to all those bits and pieces that you put aside—prelims, pix, references, appendixes, and so on. Examine them all for quality, relevance, completeness and, above all, suitability for the purpose of the publication. Assess the referencing and spot-check it for consistency by comparing text citations or endnotes with the bibliography. Look through the notes and bibliography to see whether they conform to house style, or to some other style, or are totally inconsistent. For illustrations, you have to consider whether the originals provided can be reproduced to the desired quality, as well as assessing their number, their copyright status and the captions. Your task list is getting quite long.

Presentation

What use has the author made of technology in preparing the document? Check for errors that are typical of the software (Chapter 10). Is the document presented in a format suitable for the proposed production method, or does it require keyboarding of text or redrawing of illustrations? Determine whether it needs a lot of mark-up or styling or global changes—are the headings consistent in style, has the author applied formatting that must be removed?

Make a final check of the whole document to ensure that you know what it *does* consist of and what it *should* consist of. You have made lists of any material that is missing and of the editorial tasks required. Having determined what work needs to be done, you can now proceed to negotiate responsibilities, budget and schedule (Chapter 3).

Multi-author works

Difficulties of appraisal arise with collections of essays and anthologies, which may have a dozen or more contributors. If you're lucky, the volume editor will have done some preliminary work to level out the standard and consistency of the various pieces, but maybe not. The only way to make a sure appraisal is to sample each piece. If you're pushed for time and can't do this, you have to take a risk:

sample a few, skim the rest, and apply a rule of thumb—out of ten pieces, two will be good, six will be okay, and two will need work.

Structure on screen

There are two types of screen publications: those that the reader will download and print, and those that will be read on screen. The former include learning materials, research reports, background papers and so on; the normal print conventions apply to their structure, as described above. The brief notes that follow are for publications that are to be read on screen, that is, websites and DVD and CD-ROMs. In preparing screen publications, the editor must work closely with designers and technicians. This discussion concentrates on the editorial role and does not go into technical details because of the pace of change. For more information see Chapter 24 of the *Style Manual*.[2]

In many ways, the editorial requirements for screen publications are no different from those for books. As always, the editor imagines the intended reader and tries to meet his needs. The basic standards of editing and graphic design have been refined over centuries, and they survive because they work well. Text, for instance, is normally presented as black or dark-coloured type on a plain, light-coloured background. This isn't because print designers are unadventurous, it's because readers find this format is the easiest to comprehend.

Screen publications have two important features that print lacks: they are dynamic and interactive. Their substance and structure must be premised on a continuing relationship with readers, providing for feedback, updates and revisions.

There are many books on web design, but most devote only a few pages to the text component and none at all to the editorial role. Screens are harder to read than print is. Readers rarely take in the material word-by-word; instead they scan the page, looking for points of interest. It follows that the screen should contain plenty of signposts or landmarks, that the main points should be prominent and the wording cogent. Not all documents are suited to this format; argument and narrative are better presented as prose and made available for printing.

A screen publication requires definition and planning, as described in Chapter 3. Having decided that the information is appropriate for screen presentation, how do you put it together?

Creating a structure

First, gather all the content—text, graphics and ancillary items. If you are converting existing print material for the screen, you will need the cover, prelims and endmatter. Appraise and analyse the content and set up the structure of the publication by storing the different parts in separate files. This is known as the architecture of the publication.

Next, work out how the reader will access the publication. If it already exists in print, the table of contents and the index provide clues. It may be better, though, to develop a different structure for the screen, providing interactive components and making use of such features as animation, video and sound. The proposed structure may be represented as a table, with successive rows showing how far the reader has to drill down to find a particular page. The structure should be tested by representative readers both to identify conceptual weaknesses and omissions and to ensure that its technical functions operate.

The lower elements of the hierarchy of divisions in Figure 4.1 apply to screen as well as print. Some of the principles of arrangement can also be followed: chronological, alphabetical, hierarchical or thematic. In addition, screen publications can be structured as a web—a group of independent pages designed to be accessed in a random or idiosyncratic sequence.

The remarks above about chunking information also apply to screen publications. Keep the sense-bites short. Consider whether to change the presentation of the information, say from text to a list or table (Chapter 9 under Changing the Presentation). If the publication is lengthy, divide it into logical sections so the reader can download the sections he wants rather than printing or saving the whole publication. Large multimedia files are slow to load online and may be better delivered on CD.

Accessibility is an intrinsic part of screen design. Unreasonable discrimination against people with a disability is illegal. The Australian government has adopted the accessibility guidelines of the World Wide Web Consortium or W3C, and editors working on screen publications should be familiar with them.[3]

Navigation

Having identified the access points, your next task is to guide the reader to them. Navigation tools are the screen equivalents of headers and footers, page numbers and cross-references. Overview and summary screens, either graphic or text-based, enable the reader to go straight to the information he seeks. Consistent and predictable navigation tools give a sense of the structure of the publication and make its logic and order visually explicit.

An important characteristic of screen pages is that they stand alone. A reader who is viewing a page needs to know how it relates to the whole publication or site. If he has accessed it online, he may be wondering what on earth he's got himself into. He needs to know the basics:

- *Who:* Name the person who has created the page and the publisher or sponsoring organisation.
- *What:* Encapsulate the page content in an informative title.
- *When:* Give the date of origin; updated or revised material requires a date or version number.
- *Where:* Enable the reader to orient himself in cyberspace by providing links to the home pages of the publication and the publisher, and state their geographical location or the country of origin.

The wording of the page title requires some thought. The title will appear in files of bookmarks or favorites; will it remind the reader of what he found interesting? The title is also the primary access point for search engines, so a well-worded title increases the chances of a hit. Aim for concise wording that states the essence of the content.

The reader should always be able to return easily to the major navigation points of the publication; these links should be consistent in appearance and position on each page. As well as a descriptive title and a home-page button, every page should display the table of contents or the main headings of the hierarchy.

Content

Content is normally prepared in a word-processing program in order to take advantage of proofing tools such as spellcheckers. As explained above, the writing style should be succinct. Compress and condense the information without dumbing it down. Lead with the main point or conclusion, as in a newspaper article. Make liberal use of headings and lists to catch the reader's eye and to break up slabs of text.

In writing for a web audience, think global. Don't use in-jokes or allusions that are specific to your geographical location or your culture, and avoid or explain local terms. As in any publication, avoid defamatory and offensive material and observe copyright law (Chapter 2).

The potential of the screen can be dizzying, but the general rule is, keep it simple. Bells and whistles can be counter-productive. It is best to make good use of a limited number of typographical features and to avoid distractions—text that blinks, graphical backgrounds, excessive colour. Every sophistication must be justified in terms of the characteristics of the information and the needs of the reader. Considerations for illustrations on screen are discussed in Chapter 6 under Pix on Screen.

After the content is approved, it must be diligently proofread and corrected before it is converted to a file type like HTML, XML or PDF for screen viewing. In preparing copy for conversion, you need to understand the technical requirements of the file type that will be used. The styles and special characters of a word-processing program may not convert well. Consult the designer or an up-to-date manual for the appropriate file type.

Links

Hyperlinks enable the reader to juxtapose two separate but related pieces of information. This seems attractive, but you have to ask whether the juxtaposition will help the reader to understand the content. Excessive or badly placed links are distracting and repellent.

Links are equivalent to cross-references and footnotes in print, and they should not draw attention to themselves. The effect of a sentence like 'Click here for more information on avoiding broken links' is to elevate function over content, distracting the reader and inviting him to go elsewhere. It is better expressed as 'Avoid problems with broken links by setting up an effective <u>maintenance system</u>'. Minor links, parentheses and footnotes can be grouped at the bottom of a page or the end of a section.

If the publication is to be credible, of course, the links must be functional, relevant and up-to-date. Information changes quickly in cyberspace, so the project plan must incorporate regular maintenance. Links must be tested frequently, both during construction and after publication.

Single-source publishing

Commonly a publication is prepared for print and then converted for the screen. A different approach is to prepare a single digital document that can be published in several versions: as a book and a website, or as a full print edition with separate booklets on particular topics, or as multiple versions of the content tailored to local needs. It suits projects where the content of the different versions overlaps significantly and the information is likely to be revised or updated frequently.

Single-source publishing eliminates duplication and thus reduces the potential for error: corrections or updates are done only once, in the source document. Electronic tags in the source document code the text and illustrations for their presence and position in the finished products, so that, for instance, a page reference appears in the print version where a hyperlink appears on screen. This is not the place for a detailed discussion; an excellent paper by Catherine Gray and Alison White, 'The Power of One', presents two case studies that show the potential of the process.[4] A set of reports for Sydney Water, for instance, appeared in three versions: a short print version with an accompanying CD; a long print version, available as bound copies and in PDF; and an HTML version for CD and web.

Single-source publishing requires detailed attention in the planning stages and close collaboration between the editor and designer throughout. The structure and internal relationships of the content must be clearly thought out. In preparing the content, the editor must keep in mind the reading styles of the different formats and tailor the language and the divisions to suit them. Both editor and designer need to understand the technical requirements of the formats for print and screen and be disciplined in their use of styles and tags.

Editors and designers are often freelances with no knowledge of each other. Publishers who want to undertake single-source projects need to match compatible freelances to build creative teams. Single-source publishing requires editors to have a sophisticated knowledge of software, but it promises to be an exciting area of work.

5

Language

LANGUAGE CREATES AND CONTROLS the world: the act of naming brings concepts into existence and imposes order on chaos. Modern English is an amazing artefact, the product of thousands of years of collaborative human effort, a communication tool that is protean, subtle, sophisticated.

English is capable of great precision because its vocabulary is rich in near-synonyms. It also has great flexibility in two dimensions. First, it relies on word order rather than inflections—*an upset win* is the opposite of *a set-up win*, and the difference between *good-looking* and *looking good* is about twenty years. Second, its parts of speech are largely interchangeable—for instance, *out* may be an adverb, a preposition, a noun or a verb. English is also succinct, as textbook publishers have found to their cost when trying to fit translations into a tight page grid.

All living languages exist in a state of tension between growth and decay. Languages change because playfulness and the desire to impress are universal human traits; they grow in response to technological innovation, cultural contact and social developments. Working against these impulses to the new are the forces of stability: inertia, the fear of being misunderstood, and the fixative effect of writing.

Chapter 9 gives examples of language editing: here we look at the principles.

Clarity and precision

A sure command of the English language is one of the core skills of editing, along with general knowledge and an understanding of typography. Editors have a natural aptitude for words, deepened by study and observation. Although they are passionate about language, they are not dogmatic. They recognise that 'One person's gaffe is another person's peccadillo.'[1]

The editor as philologist

An acquaintance with the history of English will improve your grasp of the language. Linguists use the term Modern English to describe the form of the language that came into being about 1500. Modern English as it exists today is a rich and complex structure. If we imagine it as a house, the foundations are the Germanic languages Old English and Old Norse; the ground floor is Old English mixed with Norman French; the upper storeys are Latin and Greek, with Modern French highlights; and the attics are stuffed with the gleanings of four centuries of empire. Some knowledge of these layers enables you to appreciate the nuances of related words, as shown in Figure 5.1.

If we rummage in the attics, we can find more to play with:

- *settle*, *settee* (Old English), *couch* (Old French), *divan* (Persian), *sofa* (Arabic via French)
- *destiny* (French), *fate* (Latin), *kismet* (Arabic), *karma* (Sanskrit)
- *mad* (Old English), *crazy* (Old Norse), *frenzied* (Latin via Old French), *berserk* (Icelandic), *amok* (Malay).

But a little etymology is a dangerous thing: it encourages people to be dogmatic about the few examples they know. It is true that *to decimate* originally meant 'to kill one in ten', and you would think that its obvious connection to *decimal* would preserve that meaning, but it hasn't; the first definition in *The Macquarie Dictionary* is 'to destroy a great number or proportion'.

Faced with such metamorphoses, editors must surrender gracefully. It is worth trying to preserve meaningful distinctions, like *uninterested* and *disinterested*, *reluctant* and *reticent*, but most of these rearguard actions are doomed to fail: the language moves on. It would be foolish to object to the phrase *dilapidated*

Old English	French	Latin
kingly	royal	regal
left	gauche	sinister
settled	sure	secure
share	portion	part
size	calibre	magnitude
stead	place	location
weak	frail	fragile
wet (verb)	moisten	irrigate
womanly	female	feminine

FIGURE 5.1 Threesomes, triplets and trios

armchair on the grounds that the adjective means 'with the stones falling off'. No one would insist that *quarantine* should last forty days, or that a *salary* is an allowance to buy salt, or that only the Pope can *pontificate*.

There are many entertaining books on etymology; look for them near the dictionaries in bookshops and under Dewey 420s in libraries.

Vocabulary

Part of the editor's armoury is a large vocabulary, or word-hoard to use the Old English term. A rich store of synonyms (and of syntax) enables you to rewrite in a different voice, with more or less formality, or at a higher or lower cognitive level.

A large vocabulary is easily attained: just use the dictionary whenever you come across a word you're not sure of. Make it easy by keeping a dictionary of manageable size within arm's reach while you work, and consult it for every word that seems to be used in an odd sense. You might discover that some familiar word has a whole extra dimension of meaning.

Your vocabulary must be not only large, but also up to date. Beware of neologisms and fad words, though, because they date quickly—*the information superhighway*, *the new economy* and *the new world order* appeared in the 1990s and already they sound passé. The one constant in language is change. The vocabulary of English as a global language is shaped not only by new technology and social developments, but also by commercial distortion and political spin. Words, as T. S. Eliot famously said, 'slip, slide, perish, / Decay with imprecision, will not stay in place'.[2] In the late eighteenth century, Ben Franklin fulminated against using the nouns *notice* and *advocate* as verbs; his concern now seems quaint. Not long ago, *stress* was a technical term in engineering and linguistics; *cheesy* and *flaky* were the preserve of pastry cooks; and *churning* was a purposeful activity resulting in butter. Once a *patch* was something you sewed onto your clothes: now you either stick it on your skin or download it from the web. The flux of language is tough on editors, but no one person or group can purify the dialect of the global tribe. A language that is not growing is dying.

Word-spotting is an entertaining pastime that sharpens your awareness of current language use. Here are some to look for.

- *Oxymorons:* There are three categories: the classic (*military intelligence*, *business ethics*); the whimsical (*pocket maxi*, *mini jumbo*); and the mind-boggling (*Pacific War*, *reality television*).
- *Retronyms:* These are absolute terms that have been qualified as a result of changes in what they denote: *free-to-air television* and *fixed phone* are obvious examples. Technology is a fertile source of retronyms, such as the chilling term *outdoor agriculture*, but social change also contributes its share with coinages like *birth mother* and *tough love*.
- *Compressed concepts:* A few syllables can contain an elaborate idea. Examples are 'a government appropriation, bill, or policy which supplies funds for local

improvements designed to ingratiate legislators with their constituents', and 'a problematic situation for which the only solution is denied by a circumstance inherent in the problem'. The words, of course, are *pork barrel* and *catch-22*.

Australian editors should know how American and British vocabulary differ from Australian usage, and New Zealand editors have the further complication of choosing between Australian and local. Depending on where you are on the planet, the sentence 'I'm mad about my flat' translates as 'I love my unit' or 'I'm angry about my puncture.' Australian English chooses eclectically between British and American, preferring *kerosene* to *paraffin* but *petrol* to *gasoline*.[3] Beware of what *The Oxford Guide to Style* calls the perils of cisatlantic translation, especially of such words as *knickers*, *bun*, *fanny*, *faggot* and *rubber*.

Overseas readers may not understand common Australian words such as *ute*, *arvo*, *possie*, *bingle*, *bastardry*, or even *corroboree*. As always, the editor has sufficient knowledge to consider a range of choices and decide what will suit the reader best.

Jargon and parochialisms

Inappropriate use of specialist vocabulary and parochialisms is the result of a failure of the author's imagination. She has not kept the reader's needs in mind.

The jargon of science and medicine is largely Latinate (*anterior cruciate ligament*), though law still displays the influence of Norman French (*malfeasance*, *tort*). Economics emerged as a discipline in the twentieth century and its jargon comprises ordinary words but is no less impenetrable for that (*supply-side shock*, *long strangle*). Information technology is discussed largely in initialisms, often with numbers in them (*ISP*, *GUI*, *B2B*), and text messaging is encouraging the trend (*C U L8R*).

Gardeners define a weed as a plant in the wrong place; jargon is specialist vocabulary in the wrong place. As non-specialists, editors are well placed to identify it. Jargon can crop up in unlikely places—you might find text messages in a novel, for instance. Whenever you encounter it, err on the side of too much explanation rather than too little. Extra information makes the material accessible to a wider audience; the experts can skip explanations they don't need. When technical terms must be used, consider whether the reader needs a glossary.

In editing specialist works, you may feel like an eavesdropper on a conversation between colleagues. Books on, say, auditing or physiotherapy are read only by auditors or physiotherapists—and editors. A publication aimed at a specialist readership must use the appropriate vocabulary, but don't be taken in and assume 'the other experts will understand this': make the writing clearer if you can. A method for editing specialist material, reading for syntax rather than sense, is described in Chapter 9 under Language Editing.

Many ordinary words have been adopted from technical vocabulary of one sort or another—*in the spotlight* (theatre), *feedback* (electronics), *segue* (music), *punter* (horse-racing). Often specialist words lose in the translation. The precision of medical terms like *allergic* and *trauma* is blurred in everyday use. The mathematical term *parameter* means 'a variable' but many writers confuse it with *perimeter*, which means 'a circumference or boundary'; this battle is probably lost. The commandeering of technical terms is a continuing process, and the editor needs to be alert and decide in each case which words the reader is likely to understand. The grammatical term *gender*, for instance, is now in the mainstream as a handy synonym for *sex* that carries no overtones of actual bonking.

Parochial content can damage a book's sales. If the discussion, examples, statistics, illustrations and so on do not adequately cover the target market—they omit young people, say, or Tasmania—consult the publisher at once. The manuscript may need substantial revision.

To detect parochialisms, you must stand in the reader's shoes and see what information he needs. For instance, the names of suburbs and small towns may require explanation (geographic, demographic, economic) for interstate and overseas readers. Parochial writing often assumes a false universalism and its terms need to be restricted: you may have to change *throughout the world* to *throughout the Western world*, or *the north coast* to *the north coast of New South Wales*, or *the post-war boom* to *the boom that followed World War II*. In an Australian context, it is helpful to specify *state* or *federal* when *the government* is mentioned.

Parochialisms can be temporal as well as spatial. *Recent* can mean almost any period and should be replaced with a date or a decade unless the context makes it clear. It is grandiose to invoke *the end of the millennium* or *the beginning of the century* if you are discussing a short-term trend or minor event.

English rules OK!

We've been hearing laments for the death of the English language for centuries, but the corpse is remarkably vigorous. Certainly there's a lot of bad writing around, but then there always has been. Time has a winnowing effect, and we tend to compare the chaff of the present with the sifted grain of the past. The nineteenth century, for instance, was awash with mediocre novels, badly argued political pamphlets, dull newspaper articles and ponderous official reports, just as we are today. Much of it ends up in the rubbish bin. A process akin to evolution operates on written language. Bad writing self-destructs: it's hard to understand, it's not memorable, no one voluntarily reads it. Good writing is treasured and it endures.

Editors know by heart the rules of good writing as set out in grammar textbooks and Part 2 of the *Style Manual*. They include agreement of noun and verb, agreement of tenses, no pronouns without antecedents, and so on. If English is your mother tongue, you learnt the basic rules of its grammar before you went to school.[4]

As an editor, when you correct a grammatical mistake or infelicity you must be able to explain why you have done so in the correct terminology. See the bibliography for books on usage and grammar that can help you refine your knowledge. The rules of good writing are the foundation of your editing, and you apply them in relation to the meaning and the reader's needs. Stick to first principles: the purpose of writing is communication; the purpose of editing is to improve communication by removing distractions.

Understand and respect the rules, but never forget that they can sometimes be broken to good effect. Rules are for bad writers: good writers can transcend them. Narrative, for instance, may benefit from a verbless sentence or a sudden change of tense that alters the mood. An author who follows the rules strictly will be correct, but the result may be lumbering and pedantic. Although editors do not normally transgress, they can recognise when an author has successfully done so. We saw in the last chapter that Bert Facey broke the rules relating to balance and proportion, yet because the structure of *A Fortunate Life* was dictated by its purpose he produced a satisfying book. Grammatical rules may be flouted in dialogue or to preserve a particular authorial voice.

Pedantry: editors as grammar police

There are two approaches to good usage: the prescriptive, which says how the language ought to be used, and the descriptive, which says how people actually do use it. Editors tend to favour the prescriptive. It's easier to apply rules mindlessly than to engage with each sentence, its content and context. Don't become a pedant. Rather than parading your extensive vocabulary and your knowledge of grammatical byways, use them to serve the author and the reader.

Some of the rules of English are equivocal. If you, as a fluent English speaker, are in doubt about some point, it is probably a doubtful point. When you turn to reference books for a ruling, you may find that there are as many opinions as there are experts. In these cases, it's up to you to exercise editorial judgement.

As an example of disputed usage, the word *whom* is on its way out. A century may pass before it is labelled archaic, but it's certainly obsolescent. When the mass of English speakers make up their minds, a few valiant editors cannot halt the tide. At present, the use of *whom* seems to be:

- correct in formal contexts
- optional in informal contexts; it may sound stiff
- incorrect in writing that represents contemporary informal speech.

When using *whom*, use it correctly. If you don't understand why it is wrong in a sentence like *The police caught the man whom they said was driving the car*, you need to brush up on the rules relating to grammatical subjects, relative clauses and parenthetical phrases.

Another example of idiomatic usage is the placement of *only*. The strict rule is to place it next to the word it qualifies, but in some contexts this is so correct as to be distracting. The sentence *They came only for the dancing* is more awkward than *They only came for the dancing*.

The editor has the knowledge to use grammar correctly and the sensitivity to use it appropriately. Subjunctives and gerunds can sparkle in the right context, but in some kinds of writing such refinements are absurdly out of place, like crystal at a barbecue. The editor not only knows the rules, but also knows when to boldly break them.

Author preferences

Observe whether the author has consistent preferences. An author writing on a general subject who always uses Latin plurals like *fora, formulae, appendices* is probably keen on them—or, to be more accurate, is keen on showing off her knowledge of irregular plurals. You may regard this as pedantry, arguing that *forum*, for instance, has been in the language since 1460 and is surely naturalised by now.[5] But you have to make a persuasive case to the author. Never change consistent usage to suit your own preferences without consultation, unless it is clearly wrong. (And you should know that Latin plurals are preferred in certain subjects such as mathematics and biology.)

For instance, suppose you are unsure about the possessive form of names ending in *s*. Do you write *Evans'* or *Evans's, Jesus'* or *Jesus's*? You consult several style guides and grammar books, only to find that their opinions differ, and their rules are complicated and have many exceptions. Let's further suppose you are editing a biography of Robert Menzies and need a firm answer on this point. The author has used the form *Menzies'* rather than *Menzies's* consistently throughout, which—as far as you can work out from the experts' advice—is wrong. Do you change it?

The answer is no. The change would violate two editorial imperatives:

- *Don't make work for yourself:* Adding an *s* to every instance of *Menzies'* is busywork. It doesn't materially assist the reader to understand the text; ultimately, it won't improve the sales of the book. If you're working on paper, don't even think about it. On screen, global changes are fast and thorough, but it's still an unnecessary task and may introduce new errors.
- *Don't antagonise the author:* If the usage is consistent, it's probably the result of the author's considered decision. Intervention might impose on the author an inconsistent version of a system she didn't choose. If you change it, especially without asking her, she may be annoyed. In such cases authors have been known to spit the dummy and reject all editorial suggestions.

If the author has chosen an unusual convention or a rare spelling, the reader will soon accept it providing it is consistently applied. If it's bearable, leave it.

Common errors

Many writing errors are so common that correcting them becomes routine. Here are some that cause editors' fingers to itch.

Unnecessary words

Probably the most frequent error is the use of words that aren't needed. In the famous statement by William Strunk Jr in *Elements of Style*, 'A sentence should contain no unnecessary words, a paragraph no unnecessary sentences, for the same reason that a drawing should have no unnecessary lines and a machine no unnecessary parts.'[6]

Watch for extra prepositions, as in *head up*, *beat up on*, *outside of* and *watch on* (or even *watch on at*); and superfluous nouns, as in *weather conditions, bush-fire situation, development process*. Pleonasms (phrases that say the same thing twice) are everywhere: *close proximity, significant landmark, two-way dialogue, vital lifeline, surrogate mother-figure, important milestone, personal body language*, and the splendidly otiose *pre-prepared*. If you have trouble spotting them, just try to imagine the implied opposite: *distant proximity*, for instance, or an *insignificant landmark*. Make every word tell.

Feeble verbs

Authors often fail to exploit the power of simple, active verbs. Here are some strategies:

- Prefer simple verbs to verbal phrases: *made a decision* becomes *decided*; *gave a stimulus to* becomes *stimulated*; *played an influential role in* becomes *influenced*.
- Prefer the active to the passive voice: *the trust deed may be varied by the trustee* becomes *the trustee may vary the trust deed*. The passive voice can obscure agency: sentences like *the gatepost has been damaged* and *the policy was approved* leave the reader wondering who is responsible.
- Long strings of nouns have a deadening effect, and the reader cannot see how they relate to each other until he reaches the main noun at the end. Rephrase them to include verbs and prepositions: *a service delivery improvement program* becomes *a program to improve the delivery of services*; *the Reserve Bank interest rate cut proposal* becomes *the Reserve Bank's proposal to cut interest rates*.
- Unpack adjectival gerunds and simplify them if possible: *engage in risk-taking behaviours* becomes *take risks* and *during the decision-making process* becomes *while deciding*.
- Avoid vague verbs like *involve, get, address*.

Abstract words

While editing a manuscript on literary criticism, I encountered the sentence 'This is more imagistic than narratological', which I think means 'This is more like a picture than a story.' If I were prepared to commit the error I am warning against, I would call it abstractification—an ugly name for a habit of writing that muffles thought. The stem form of a word packs more punch than derivatives that trail off in suffixes. Instead of, say, *specificity*, try to recast the sentence to use *specific*, *specify* or even *species*. Discourage authors from saying *the leadership* when they mean *the leaders*, *methodology* when they mean *methods*, *profitability* when they mean *profit*.

Qualifiers

Writing that is heavily qualified becomes hesitant and vague. Overuse of qualifiers—*very*, *rather*, *quite*, *somewhat*, *really*, *a bit*—is often a sign of poor vocabulary. Inexperienced authors write *very tired* instead of thinking whether they mean *weary*, *exhausted* or *drowsy*. In most cases the qualified phrase can be replaced with a more precise word or the qualifier can simply be deleted.

Ambiguity

Don't tolerate vocabulary that is ambiguous or misleading. For instance, *the environment* may denote *the prevailing business conditions* or *the world of nature*; in the phrase *Victorian legislation* the adjective may refer to a historical era or an Australian jurisdiction. Unless the context makes the sense absolutely plain, amplify or replace such terms.

Incomplete comparatives

A creeping trend is the use of incomplete comparatives in order to soften what may be seen as an adverse judgement. When an author writes about *the smaller states* or *the weaker students*, you're entitled to ask *smaller than what? weaker than whom?* Some forms, such as *older workers*, have become entrenched, but resist *older-fashioned*.

Syntax

All the following grammatical constructions are correct, and careful writers deploy them effectively. Because they state a vague link between two concepts, however, lazy writers tend to rely on them in order to avoid precision of thought. Where an author favours these constructions to the point of monotony, suggest rephrasing some of them.

- The fact that: *This response reflects the fact that a dialogue has been established.*
- X means that Y: *Attention to detail means that you give the customer all the necessary information.*
- Both of the above: *The fact that he has arrived means that we can start the party.*
- It is X that is Y: *It is the wombat that is the main attraction.* In the plural: *There are several methods that are suitable.*
- X is about Y: *School is about education.*

Syntax may be misleading: a sentence seems to head in one direction but then proves to be going somewhere else. This is known as 'garden-pathing the reader' and is best explained by example:

- *In short, wide latitude was left for future legislation.*
- *Southeast Asians were relatively fortunate in their secure food supplies, and they struck European and Chinese visitors as relatively healthy and long-lived.*
- *His methods have long been used by farmers and gardeners, and some of them are very old.*

Metaphors

Metaphors lie embalmed in almost every word and, as Fowler puts it, they are 'sometimes liable, under the stimulus of an affinity or a repulsion, to galvanic stirrings indistinguishable from life'.[7] Examples are:

- *Under the terms of the Antarctic Treaty it was agreed that all territorial claims south of 60 degrees South would be frozen.*
- *The impact of a fallen leader on his men was usually sufficient to cause panic and flight.*
- *Small bodies of Pidgin speakers are found all over New Guinea.*
- *She had a meteoric rise in the corridors of power until she came up against the glass ceiling.*

Voice, tone and pace

Voice and tone are overlapping concepts; they refer to the author's presence in the text and her manner of relating to the reader. Your sensitivity to these aspects helps you to tailor language to a specific readership. An editor who is amending text does not use colloquialisms like *for starters* or *a bit of a* in formal contexts, or scholarly words like *solipsistic* and *epistemological* in popular works. Chapter 4 of the *Style Manual* distinguishes three registers, or levels of formality.

Pace is a concept that belongs here also. Some authors charge straight for their destination; others meander along the scenic route. In editing a manuscript you will often find that the pace is uneven and that some sections drag. If substantive editing is approved, you can speed them up by eliminating digressions and reducing the level of detail and the number of examples. Remember that the reader's pace may not be the same as the author's. A poor reader, or one who is new to the subject, may have to read each sentence twice. Clear, spare writing encourages the reader to move swiftly, but exceptionally good writing may actually slow him down as he savours the author's skill.

Some authors take a tough attitude to their readers—*make 'em work for it* seems to be their motto. This is risky. With many other choices for recreation and information on offer, the reader who is asked to exert himself too much may toss the book aside and never buy another. Dumbing down is not the answer, but there is no harm in wooing the reader. The authorial voice can be courteous, even in a formal register.

How do voice and tone work in practice? Suppose you want to add a cross-reference to Chapter 4. Here are some possibilities:

- *impersonal and formal:* This will be discussed further in Chapter 4.
- *personal and formal:* We shall discuss this further in Chapter 4.
- *impersonal and informal:* Chapter 4 looks at this in more detail.
- *personal and informal:* We will look at this in more detail in Chapter 4.

All of them are correct; your decision depends on the author's voice. Some authors studiously avoid using *we* and *I*, and you should observe this and follow their preference. Some authors prefer *we shall*, others *we will*. This should be made consistent, especially in multi-author works.

More subtle problems of tone are presented by these sentences:

- *This was one of the seminal books of the feminist revolution.* The word *seminal*, derived from *semen*, is spectacularly inappropriate here. Similarly, it is really dumb to refer to a tourist destination as *a wine mecca*. These are examples of not-quite-dead metaphors, discussed above.
- In a biographical sketch that relates to the 1880s, *he had several children by this lady but they never married.* In nineteenth-century terms, the mother of illegitimate children was no lady.
- Of a convict plan to escape from Sydney Cove in the 1790s, *the plan was nipped in the bud before they disappeared, some of them forever, into the vast emptiness of the surrounding countryside.* The assumption that the countryside was 'empty' invokes the obsolete doctrine of *terra nullius*.

Editors are alert for dimensions of meaning that the author, intent on her subject, cannot see. For instance, a monthly magazine for women would probably not be called *Woman's Monthly*.

Spelling and punctuation

The rules for spelling and punctuation are set out in Chapters 6 and 7 of the *Style Manual* and in many grammar and usage books. Editors must know the rules thoroughly.

Spelling

Spelling is not important in itself, but it is a social marker enabling those who can spell to look down on those who can't. English spelling makes sense if you have studied the Great Vowel Shift and know the difference between Long e1 and Long e2 in Middle English, but for most people it's a damned nuisance. There is little hope of reform, though; as with the qwerty keyboard, too many people have invested too much time in learning the existing system to change now. English speakers worldwide are unlikely to agree on spelling when they cannot even agree on the alphabet (*aitch*, *haitch*; *zed*, *zee*). Reform would disadvantage groups like the Scots (who pronounce the *gh* in *night* and similar words) and speakers of other European languages who can recognise cognate words (German *Nacht*) by their spelling if not by their pronunciation. Anyway, the adoption of major spelling reform would gradually render all existing printed material meaningless except to scholars who had learned the old spellings.

As a demonstration of the mutability of orthography, consider this example from the dawn of Modern English. It is part of a letter from one John Grenville, who signs himself *Graynfyld*, to his patron Lord Lisle, written in 1533.

> Ryght honerabill and my moste especiall good Lord My dewty remembred I commend me vn to yow And to my Right honerabill good Lady praying to Jhesu longe to contenew yow in honor. plesitht hit yowre lordschypp that all your fryndis In thes partis be mery and all yowre afferes doo as well as yow woll dessyre. thanke be to Jhesu.

Editors are stuck with English as she is spelt, and you must be proficient. If you have the slightest doubt about a word, you will of course check it in a dictionary, but the trouble with spelling is that you don't know what you don't know. You may discover by accident that you have been blithely misspelling some word for years. Pay attention to corrections made by experienced proofreaders on the proofs of your jobs in order to locate your blind spots.

If regular spelling is a nuisance, alternative spellings are a pain in the neck. House style can help, dictating the publisher's preferences for a whole group of words such as the endings *-ise*, *-ize*, and *-our*, *-or*. You will have to make decisions about words that aren't listed in the house style—*acknowledgement* or *acknowledgment*, *burned* or *burnt*, *cooperate* or *co-operate*, *despatch* or *dispatch*, *egos* or *egoes*, *focused* or *focussed*—in order to achieve consistency. These decisions have little significance and are not worth arguing over. Humour authors and publishers who have a favourite spelling such as *connexion*, or who insist on fine distinctions such as *judgment* for court decisions and *judgement* for everything else. And although most alternative spellings aren't important, you should know the ones that are. Don't confuse spies with guns—*MI6*, *M-16*; or Apples with hamburgers—*Mac world*, *McWorld*.

Defying the cultural imperialism of the United States, Australians stick stubbornly to their traditional spelling. The Melbourne *Age* received a flood of congratulatory letters (and a few angry denunciations) when it decided to change its house style from *-or* to *-our*. Occasionally, though, you will work on publications that use American spelling and it can be difficult to adjust. As well as preferring *-ize*, *-or* and *-er*, American English reverses our use of double and single ell, preferring *instill* and *traveled*, and there are many other differences. Scholarly books retain American spelling and punctuation in quotations, but in informal contexts change them if they will distract the reader. Your reference library should include an American dictionary. Microsoft Word's spellchecker can be set to many regional varieties of English.

Punctuation

In an interesting demonstration of the two-way traffic between spoken and written language, punctuation marks have made their way into speech: for instance, *full stop* (as in 'We're not going, full stop!') and *quote–unquote*. Quotation marks have even become a gesture.

The rules for punctuation are set out in textbooks but like most human customs they are subject to fashion. Today we write addresses as *Queen Street*, but the nineteenth-century form was *Queen-street*. The current trend is to minimise punctuation. Where we use a colon, the old style was a colon and a dash, which compositors knew by the charming name *a full set*.

The en rule is becoming fashionable as knowledge of typography increases. It is used in spans of numbers, such as years or pages. With words it has the sense of 'from, to' or 'between': *the Melbourne–Yass–Sydney route, cost–benefit ratios, hand–eye co-ordination*. It is used to join words that retain their separate identities: *Asia–Pacific region, Commonwealth–state agreement*; and to join compound nouns to another word or particle: *Nobel Prize–winner, pre–Bronze Age tools*. Except in such phrases, word particles like *pre-, mid-* and *Anglo-* do not require an en rule; they take a hyphen. A spaced en rule is some publishers' preferred style for the text dash; others use a close-up em rule, as in this book.

The computer keyboard has encouraged overuse of the solidus or virgule, now usually called a forward slash. One proper use of it is to distinguish a financial year, *2003/04*, from a span of calendar years, *2003–04*. In text the slash is often used as a vague link between two words to disguise loose thought, but it has a precise meaning, which is 'either, or'. Don't confuse *black/white dichotomy* or *public/private separation* with *black–white dialogue* or *public–private partnership*. The slash has no place in linked words like *mother–child relationship* or *owner-occupier*, or in shortened forms like *n.a.* for *not applicable*.

You should note that certain punctuation is a matter of right or wrong, but other punctuation is optional. Some authors use more commas than others, just as some speakers pause more than others. Providing the basic rules are followed, such choices are a matter of taste, and you should not override the author's preference in your zeal to make the punctuation 'correct'.

Quotations

Quotations are appraised, like all parts of the manuscript, in terms of their suitability and relevance. Quotations should not require editing, though it is usual to normalise typographic conventions such as single or double quote marks, en or em rules, italic or roman punctuation. Refer to the author any apparent mistakes, such as misspellings, unlikely punctuation and passages that do not make sense, by marking the problem and noting 'check original'. Verify against each other any quotes that appear more than once—for instance, phrases quoted in a discussion of a longer quoted passage or an appendix.

In contexts where meaning has priority it is permissible to make minor editorial changes to quotations silently—that is, without telling the reader that you have done so. Typical changes are correcting typos, standardising spelling and adding punctuation. In scholarly books, on the other hand, the spelling and punctuation must be reproduced exactly. Watch for accidental Australian spellings in quotations from American sources. In a book such as a historical diary or a collection of letters, it is often best (in consultation with the volume editor) to standardise the spelling and punctuation and add a note in the prelims explaining what changes have been made. Editorial intervention in verbatim quotes is signalled by square brackets, but don't overdo it; *sic* should not be repeated *ad nauseam*.

One matter that editors should not neglect is the placement of end punctuation in relation to a closing quotation mark. There are various rules as to whether the full stop or comma or whatever should be inside or outside the quote mark, depending on whether the quotation does or does not constitute a grammatically complete sentence and whether the punctuation in question is or is not part of that sentence. Americans cut through the dilemma by placing all end punctuation inside the closing quote mark, and dialogue in novels also follows this practice. It doesn't matter which rule you follow; the reader will soon get used to it as long as the system has some logic and is consistently applied. If the author has adopted a consistent style that differs from the publisher's house style, ask the publisher if you can leave it. Even with global searches, alterations to this minor point can occupy more time than they're worth.

Some editors have a pernicious habit. They change the first letter of a quotation from upper to lower case or vice versa, so that the quote flows smoothly from the preceding text. So far, so good; less distraction for the reader. But then they draw attention to their good deed by enclosing the altered letter in square brackets. In these cases, if you cannot edit it silently, just leave it alone; the reader is less distracted by an unexpected capital than by puzzling out a word impaled on a square bracket.

In a quotation an ellipsis (three full stops with a word space either side) indicates that words have been omitted. A complete sentence that is followed by an ellipsis retains its own full stop, making four full stops in a row. Delete ellipses at the beginning and end of a quotation unless you want to draw attention to its incompleteness.

Quotation marks

As well as delineating quotations, quotation marks signify the first use of a technical term or an ironic usage. In the trade the term for the latter is 'scare quotes'.

Beware of authors who use quote marks for the linguistic equivalent of slumming, partaking of colloquial vocabulary and sneering at it at the same time. If the use of 'scare quotes' is 'over the top' it can put the reader 'off-side', and in the 'worst-case scenario' it's a real 'turn-off'.

Most Australian book publishers have single quotation marks as house style (with double quote marks for a quote-within-a-quote); Australian newspapers and American publications use double quote marks. When converting single quote marks to double, make sure that you don"t change the apostrophes by accident. The publisher's house style may stipulate that all quotations of more than a stated length, usually fifty words, are to be 'set down' as block quotes—without quotation marks, indented, and in smaller type than the text. Citations may be placed at the end of block quotes, either run on in square brackets or on a separate line ranged right.

Microsoft Word has complicated our lives by giving us a choice between two types of quotation marks: straight quotes and curly or smart quotes. If they are inconsistent in hard copy, instruct the typesetter. On screen you can alter them yourself with the search and replace function.

All quotations should be checked for copyright status (Chapter 2), and acknowledged according to the referencing style of the publication.

The spoken word in print

The editor encounters the spoken word in many forms—interviews, focus groups, oral history, court evidence, fictional dialogue. Transcriptions and dialogue present particular problems, especially where the speaker uses nonstandard English.

Remember that literacy is largely an accident of birth and does not confer superior wisdom or virtue. Illiterate and semi-literate people have valuable contributions to make, and the editor's job is to help them get their message across. This is a balancing act. The speakers have a right to their authentic voices, but the editor also has an obligation to the reader and the conventions of print.[8]

Many people believe that they speak as they write, but for some words the written form has only a tangential relationship to speech. Nobody pronounces the *t* in *Christmas* or the *d* in *kindness*, but we're so used to the spelling that we think we do. *The Macquarie Dictionary* informs us that Australians normally pronounce *temporary* as two syllables, *temp'ry*, but many people will declare that they make it three syllables or even four. Written language is only a rough approximation of the subtleties of speech, and a literal transcription is tedious to read. Even articulate speakers hesitate, repeat themselves, and change construction in mid-sentence.

When editing transcriptions, take into account their context and their purpose: sometimes the expression must be exactly represented, but sometimes the meaning has priority. Transcriptions of legal proceedings, such as evidence given to courts and royal commissions, must be reproduced verbatim, but with other material the editor has some latitude.

In transcriptions and dialogue the use of nonstandard spellings, like *dunno*, *gunna*, *Satdee*, often constitutes a value judgement. The pronunciations represented by these spellings are common among speakers at all levels, as you will hear if you listen carefully. Another example is the demotic usage *should of*. When it appears in print, the reader is likely to draw on his knowledge of print culture and deduce that the speaker is of a certain class or subculture. In fictional dialogue this may be the desired effect, but in some circumstances you can more truly represent the speaker's intention by silently editing the phrase to *should have*, in conformity with print conventions. See Figure 9.3 for an example of an edited transcription of nonstandard English.

Where transcriptions are reproduced, both the speaker and the transcriber have a copyright interest, which should be clarified.

Enumerations

Enumerations are a way of lifting information out of the flow of the text while keeping it below the bottom rung of the heading hierarchy.

In the text

When you're reading the text for sense, alarm bells should ring at statements such as 'there are two objections to this' or 'four methods are commonly employed'. Mark such points emphatically as a reminder to make sure that both objections, or all four methods, are discussed. When you have read to the end of the second objection, or the fourth method, go back to the start of the enumeration and consider whether it is adequately signposted for the reader. The author may get so wound up in the first objection that she goes on for pages about it, and the reader cannot be expected to hold the existence of the second objection in mind all that time. You might have to add headings, or you can jog the reader's memory with some bridging phrase when the discussion finally gets back to objection no. 2.

When enumerating items in the text, some authors prefer *firstly*, *secondly* and others *first*, *second*. Either is correct but be consistent, especially in multi-author works.

Bullet and number lists

Chapter 9 of the *Style Manual* explains the rules that apply to lists, which it calls, precisely but inelegantly, 'itemised indented material'. The editor may swap lists back and forth with the lowest grade of headings or in some cases turn them into tables; see Figure 9.7 for an example. Lists help to break up slabs of type, and they set out complex subsets in a form that the reader can assimilate easily; the syntax and typography make plain the relation of the statements to one another. Moreover, the requirement that all the points be parallel and consistent forces the author (or editor) to analyse the concepts and clarify the wording, to the benefit of the reader.

Pay attention to the lead-in to the list. Eliminate repetition within the list by moving the repeated phrase to the introductory sentence. The words *following* and *as follows* are predictable and don't add much to the meaning. Move things along by replacing *Smith presented the following list of complaints* with *Smith presented her complaints*, using a colon to introduce the list.

Additional matters to note about lists are:

- Where the points in a list are complete grammatical sentences, they each start with a capital letter and end with a full stop. Phrases start with a lower-case letter and have no end punctuation, except for the last point, which has a full stop.
- The pattern of type on the page conveys information about the relationship of the items; you don't need to repeat that information in words.
- Try to keep lists to a maximum of about seven items to assist comprehension.
- Do not use more than three levels within a list.
- If a list describes a sequence of actions, as in a recipe or an activity for students, check that the steps are all present and do follow each other.

Specialised and foreign material

You may think that you only work on 'ordinary' books, but many of them contain specialised material. You don't need in-depth knowledge of specialist fields, but you should be broadly familiar with their typographic conventions. To put it another way, you don't need to understand the theory of relativity, but you should know that $E = mc^2$ has one capital, a space either side of the equal sign, and a superscript digit. You can rely on specialist authors to some extent, but they can have extraordinary lapses. As always, the needs of the reader are paramount; explain specialist terms in books for the general reader.

History

Measurements and currency can present a problem in historical material. If there are only a few measurements they can be given in modern form, but if there are a lot it is best to leave them in the old form and provide a table of conversions in the prelims. This is partly a matter of tone. Do not convert mindlessly — a land price of *£1 per acre* is not the same as *a dollar for 2000 square metres*. Sums of money are usually better explained in terms of what they could buy — *the price of a loaf of bread* or *a year's wages for a carpenter*.

Science and mathematics

When editing scientific writing, the editor can make it easier to understand by reviewing the structure of the argument and the length, complexity and lexical density of each sentence.[9]

Even though you never tackle specialist texts, you will encounter scientific terms in books for the general reader. An editor needs a rough acquaintance with the basic concepts of science and mathematics and a working knowledge of their typographical conventions. You should be confident with these:

- The metric system (properly, Système International d'Unités or SI units), and the standard prefixes such as *kilo-*, *centi-* and *milli-*. For instance, one milli-picture is a quantity of art equivalent in value to one word.
- Conversions for different systems of measurement, such as metric and imperial, Celsius and Fahrenheit, avoirdupois and troy weight, microns, nautical miles.
- Mathematics, including symbols, ratios, equations, statistics, and roman numerals.
- Species names in botany and biology. Capitalise the genus and italicise both terms: *Homo sapiens*, *Eucalyptus regnans*. If the genus can be assumed, abbreviate it: *E. coli*.
- Geological time and conventions for expressing it, such as *BP* (before the present), *MYA* (million years ago).
- Chemistry: for instance, the digits in H_2O and CO_2 are subscripts; the measure of acidity is *pH*; the well-known herbicide is *2,4-T*.
- Common errors: *a light year* is a measure of distance, not of time; *a quantum leap* is tiny; biology does not recognise the concept of different human races.

You don't have to remember all this, but have the information handy so you can solve problems as they arise. Your reference library should include a scientific dictionary.

Law

In the matter of legal jargon, there is a move towards plain English but it has a long way to go. The attempt to reduce the complexity of legal language raises practical, professional and social issues, and some parts of the legal profession resist it. However, the emergence of plain English documents does not seem to have caused a surge in litigation.[10]

Legal citations have their own style, in which the difference between square and round brackets is crucial, and quotations from court judgements are obscurely cited as *at 154* rather than following the widely used and readily understood convention, *p. 154*. Authors who cite court cases are likely to have been trained in these details; all you need to know as an editor is not to mess them up. Law book publishers provide style guides, or you can consult similar publications to determine correct usage.

Poetry

Poems and songs find their way into a variety of works, from almanacs that include the national anthem to history, biography, social science and fiction. Conventionally the titles of songs and short poems are roman in quotation marks; the titles of long poems are italicised. Wherever a song or a poem is quoted, questions of copyright arise (Chapter 2).

Where a poetry quotation is two lines or less, run it on in the text; retain punctuation and capitals and use a spaced solidus (slash) to indicate the line break: 'Australians all, let us rejoice, / For we are young and free.' The typographic conventions for songs and traditional poetry are:

- Start each line with a capital letter.
- The indent follows the rhyme.
- Turnover lines have a hanging indent.
- Stanzas are set off with a one-line space.
- Refrains may be distinguished with italic or an extra indent.

Mark set-down poetry quotations 'line for line' so the typesetter knows not to run them on.

If you find yourself editing traditional poetry, you'll need to learn the conventions of prosody. Sonnets may need special treatment; study books of poetry published by reputable firms to determine the layout for two quatrains and a sestet, or two sestets and a couplet. Free verse must follow the author's indenting and punctuation exactly. The indents require careful mark-up for the designer and typesetter, and diligent checking in proof.

Dialogue and scripts

Dialogue in play scripts is usually set with a hanging indent; characters' names are in small capitals and stage directions in italic. Transcriptions of evidence or interviews may be treated similarly. For dialogue in a novel, authors sometimes replace quotation marks with an initial em or en rule to indicate direct speech.

Foreign words and names

Multiculturalism and globalisation are forcing Anglo-Celtic Australians to come to terms with typographic conventions in languages as diverse as Arabic and Korean. Editors need some acquaintance with foreign alphabets, such as Greek and Cyrillic, and with systems of transliteration. For instance, you should know that there are two methods for transliterating Chinese, the old-fashioned Wade–Giles and the preferred Pinyin. One gives us *Peking* and *Mao Tse-tung*; the other, *Beijing* and *Mao Zedong*. Knowledge of the accepted transliteration of Arabic names and words—*al-Qaeda*, *hijab*, *burqa*, *imam*—is increasingly necessary. For new borrowings that are not yet in the dictionaries, follow the spelling of reputable newspapers.

The more understanding you have of foreign names and words and their typographic conventions, the better. Not only do you have to know the spelling and diacritics, but you may also have to decide the alphabetical order for foreign names in a bibliography or an index. The alphabetising of Asian names may present difficulties. In some cultures the convention is to place the family name first, so in an alphabetical list the order of the name remains the same and there is no comma between family name and given name; *Kim Jong-il* appears thus, under K, without a comma. But some people of Asian heritage, particularly if they live in an English-speaking country, have adopted the Anglo order. There is no way of telling the individual's preference except by checking carefully against original sources or a library catalogue. This is the author's responsibility, but the editor should make sure that it has been done.

Explain foreign words and provide a translation of phrases and passages in foreign languages unless the context makes the meaning obvious or the target readers can be expected to know the words. If there are many foreign words, consider whether a glossary is required. Foreign words are printed in italics, but naturalised words are not. Dictionaries give guidance on whether a word is naturalised, but fine judgement is sometimes required for specialist content or for recent adoptions such as *barista* or *shtetl*. In the case of a noun, if it takes an English plural (final *s*) it can be considered naturalised and does not need italics. Dictionaries of foreign languages are helpful for checking quotations and titles, but be careful of loan words that have been anglicised in spelling, like *naivety*.[11]

You can cover your deficiencies in multicultural typography with *The Oxford Guide to Style*, which provides authoritative rulings for such abstruse details as alphabetical order in Estonian, capitals in Gaelic, italics in Chinese, diacritics in Vietnamese, and word division in Russian. It will even equip you for extinct languages such as Old English, Gothic and Aramaic.

For further information on editing specialised material, see Butcher, *Copyediting: The Cambridge handbook*, Chapter 13, and Ritter, *The Oxford Guide to Style*, Chapters 12–13.

6

Illustrations and tables

BECAUSE EDITORS TEND to focus on words, they may fail to appreciate the power of graphics to convey information. Collaboration with designers can provide an education and enlarge your view of what is possible. In heavily illustrated publications—coffee-table books, annual reports, art catalogues and even cook books—the pix take precedence over the text. Their production requires close liaison between the editor and the designer throughout the project.

The term 'illustrations' covers a wide range of material, defined in Standard D as including drawings, cartoons, diagrams, charts, graphs, maps, photographs, computer-generated graphics and moving images (see Appendix). Here we will look at the editor's tasks. For more information, see the *Style Manual*, Chapter 21.

Appraising pix

Pix appear on your desk in various physical manifestations—boxes of slides, rough sketches, printouts of scanned photographs, computer-drawn graphs. When working with photographs and drawings, use photocopies or printouts; this saves the originals from harm and also allows you to freely mark crop lines and other instructions for the designer. The edited photocopies are known as artwork roughs. Store original artwork and photographs safely and return them, carefully packaged, with the edited manuscript.

Your first task is to scrutinise the pix in the same way you do all elements of the manuscript: is this pic really necessary, is it suitable for the intended reader, does it serve the purpose? In addition, consider its visual impact and quality and imagine how it will look when reproduced, possibly at a much smaller or larger scale. You may have to ask the author or picture researcher to obtain better originals or different photographs. Authors sometimes provide more pix than can be used, and the editor is asked to decide which ones to include; the decision is based first on the pic's relevance to the text and second on its visual and technical qualities.

Once the choice of pix has been finalised in consultation with the publisher, designer and author, the editor ascertains their copyright status (Chapter 3). Do this early because obtaining permissions may take some time.

Reproduction

A major consideration in appraising pix is their technical quality, or suitability for reproduction. The editor needs a working knowledge of screens, tonal qualities, resolution, colour systems and file sizes for various formats. A photograph, for instance, should be in focus and the tones should show good gradation and adequate contrast. The better the resolution, the larger the file size. If you have any doubts about the quality of the pix or the technical requirements, consult the designer. You may have to explain to the author that her treasured photo of an empty beach will appear as a smudge surmounted by a blur.

Where the author has prepared graphs and diagrams as e-copy, the editor checks them for technical compatibility with the proposed production method. Sometimes it is easier to have them redrawn than to mess about with file conversions. Authors often get excited by the capabilities of their software and add needless complications to illustrations; consider how they will appear in the finished publication. For instance, if an author provides coloured line graphs for a book that is to be printed in one colour, you will have to mark the coloured lines to be replaced with dashed and dotted lines.

If any pix are to be redrawn, edit the roughs (as described below) at an early stage and send them off so the work can proceed while you are editing. Keep copies to refer to.

Integrating pix with text

Arrange the final selection of pix in a suitable sequence and number them. Even if the numbers do not appear in the printed captions, they identify the pix during production in the artwork list and the caption copy, and they also key the pix to their places in the manuscript. You may choose to create separate number sequences for photos, diagrams and maps, but do not subdivide unnecessarily. In this book, for instance, most of the figures are actually in tabular format, but a separate number sequence would have emphasised their form at the expense of their content.

Relationship to the text

The text and the illustrations should complement each other. If the author describes a graph or diagram in detail, check whether the text simply repeats what is in the pic. By all means draw attention to the highlights, but give the reader some credit: there's no need to say everything twice.

Next, compare the text discussion carefully with the actual illustration for discrepancies. An author may alter the text slightly but forget to alter the relevant diagram, or perhaps the text says that a photograph was taken in 1940 but the caption says 'before the war'. At worst, you may find that the pic has been misidentified or the author has sent the wrong one.

Authors often refer to pix with such phrases as 'in the photograph above' or 'as the following graph shows'. Edit such references to include the pic number — 'in Plate 3.5' or 'as Figure 2.1 shows'. If the pix are unnumbered, include a page reference such as 'in the photograph on page 00', with a marginal note to insert the page number in proof.

Placement

The editor cannot decide the exact placement of pix in the text because it depends on the final page layout. The default position for a pic is at the end of the paragraph in which it is discussed, but this is often adjusted during page make-up to place the pic at the top or the bottom of a page. For pix printed separately from the text, see Placing Wraps and Inserts, below.

When editing a manuscript on paper, always mark the left margin at the main text reference to any pic. Make the mark next to the reference in the text rather than the pic itself, which may appear half a page or more further on. If the order of the pix is in doubt, just write 'Fig.' or 'Map' or whatever, and leave room to add the pic number once the sequence and numbering have been decided. The final instruction should be in the form 'Fig. 1.1 near here', or 'Map 7 anywhere MS pp. 37–41', and circled to show that it is not to be set. On screen, caption style is a sufficient marker, and the caption usually includes the pic number.

Where colour is used selectively, the placement of particular illustrations becomes critical. In most publications, though, there is room for discretion with regard to items that apply to a whole chapter or part, such as a map or an atmospheric photo. Unless the book is heavily illustrated, try not to place a pic opposite a chapter opening. Try also for an even distribution; pix that occur in clumps may be hard to accommodate in the page layout.

After you have marked the placement of all the pix, go through the manuscript to check that the pic numbers in the margin are in correct sequence and none is omitted or repeated. If there are three sequences, go through the manuscript three times. Also check any cross-references to the pix to make sure the numbers are correct. As you are checking the sequence, write the appropriate pic numbers and MS page numbers on the artwork roughs. You can then prepare the artwork brief (Chapter 3).

Captions and sources

Authors tend to run out of puff when they get to the captions. The caption copy is often inadequate, or you may have to compose it yourself. As you know by now, the captions should suit the intended reader, include all relevant information, and conform in style with the rest of the book. For most captions, brevity is a virtue; the content of lengthy captions may be better incorporated in the text.

Captions usually appear below or beside illustrations (in contrast to table titles, which always appear above tables). Make sure that similar items have similarly worded captions. It is often helpful to include a date, especially for pix that show statistics and for photographs of people, places and events.

The sequence and numbering of the pix needs to be finalised before you compile the caption copy. Generally caption copy is prepared as e-copy and a marked-up printout; the first page has the author's name and the book title, and the pages are numbered CC1, CC2, etc. Check the end punctuation for consistency; short captions do not need full stops, but if any of the captions consist of more than one sentence, it is best to punctuate them all.

Some points to watch:

- If the captions are to be set from the e-copy of the manuscript, there is no need to prepare separate caption copy. Note in the design brief that the caption copy is in the manuscript.
- If you have compiled caption copy from the author's rough captions in the text, delete the versions in the text to prevent confusion.
- If a pic is to appear uncaptioned, note this on the caption copy.
- If the pic numbers are not to be printed, note this in the design brief and circle them on the caption copy.

The source notes and acknowledgements for pix usually appear below the caption and are included in the caption copy. Where the source is a published work, the citation may be abbreviated to conform to the style for references (either author–date or short title; see Chapter 7). Add 'After' or 'Adapted from' if the pic has been altered. Some publishers prefer to put picture credits in the list of illustrations in the prelims, and in a heavily illustrated book they may be assigned to the endmatter. Generally 'courtesy of' or just a name is sufficient acknowledgement, but in some cases the copyright holder may require particular wording, such as 'reproduced by permission of . . .'.

Labels

The term 'labels' covers any lettering on a pic, such as the place names on a map or the digits on the axes of a graph. Labels, tiny as they are, may require substantive editing and copyediting as described below (see Figure 6.1).

In general, keep pix uncluttered by minimising the labels and giving the information in the caption. Edit the labels for substance, wording, capitalisation, punctuation, and consistency with each other and with the text. Minimise the number of fonts. Mark ambiguous characters such as capital O and zero, lower-case ell and number one. Where the author has provided a rough sketch, you may have to type label copy for the illustrator.

List of illustrations

Most illustrated books are improved by a list of illustrations in the prelims, and the editor often has to prepare it. It may be divided into categories: the normal order is maps, plates, figures, tables. No list need be provided if the reader is unlikely to refer to the pix separately from the text. It may be appropriate to list some categories, such as maps and plates, but not others. If there is only one pic, such as a map, it may be listed at the end of the table of contents.

The list of illustrations follows immediately after the table of contents. The wording is based on the caption copy, but discursive captions are abbreviated or summarised to about six or eight words. Page numbers are added in proof.

Editing pix

As a separate task, turn your attention to the content of the pix. Are they suitable for the nature and level of the publication? Do they clearly illustrate the point? Diagrams and graphs can often be made clearer by rearranging the components or rewording the labels, and cropping may improve a photo. Consider also aspects such as ethnic discrimination and gender stereotyping. Photographs and drawings should show people taking any necessary precautions such as wearing protective clothing. Finished drawings and any major changes to the pix, labels or captions should be approved by the author.

Photographs

Photographs are known in printing jargon as halftones. You may receive them as glossy prints, which require careful handling; sometimes you may have custody of precious originals. Hold prints by the edges and don't let paper clips or sticky tape anywhere near them. Never write on the front or back of a print. To number prints or slides, write the number on an adhesive label and attach it.

Prints are becoming obsolete: you are more likely to work with a printout. Where the author provides scanned photos, review them for file size, resolution and compatibility. There are many types of graphic file formats, such as JPG and TIFF; consult with the designer to find out which is appropriate for the planned production method.

Editors do not normally retouch or manipulate photos on screen, but there is still some editing to be done. Marks are made on a photocopy, printout or overlay. Some points to watch:

- If a photo is to be cropped, leave it to the designer to decide the exact area as best suits the page layout; mark anything that must be omitted and anything that must be included.
- Indicate to the designer which photos are particularly important (or unimportant), so they will be reproduced in an appropriate size.

- Some photos, such as close-ups of bacteria, need to be marked to show which way is up.
- If anything is to be added—lettering, arrows, a scale—ensure that its position is accurate and clear.

Photos may be reproduced on the text pages or on coated paper. Text photos are usually treated as 'figures' and included in the pic numbering, but photos printed separately are known as plates and have their own sequence. Where the layout of photos is left to the designer, check in proof whether the sequence has altered; if it has, alter the numbering, cross-references and list of illustrations accordingly.

Placing wraps and inserts

Where pix are printed on coated paper, they may form a whole signature (a section of pages), or be wrapped around a signature or inserted in the centre of a signature. At page proof stage, you may be asked to determine their placement. Here is how to place wraps or inserts in a book with 16-page signatures.

1 Determine the number of pages of prelims.
2 Identify the last page number of the first signature. If there are 12 pages of prelims, it will end on p. 4.
3 For wraps, identify the page numbers that end the other signatures—pp. 20, 36, 52, etc. For inserts, identify the page numbers at the centre of the signatures—pp. 12, 28, 44, etc.
4 Exclude the signatures that contain prelims and endmatter.
5 In the remaining signatures, decide how the wraps or inserts can best be distributed so that the pix are near the relevant text.
6 Draw up a list that shows where each wrap or insert is to be placed.

Where the photos are printed separately from the text, the list of illustrations reads 'facing 00' or 'following 00'. Page numbers are inserted in proof.

Maps

Maps can illuminate many kinds of books, from fantasy novels and detective stories to histories and biographies. Often the author, knowing her territory, does not think to include a map; it is up to the editor to suggest it.

Every map must include a scale (or the words 'not to scale') and an orientation, normally an arrow pointing north.

As you are editing the text, compile a list of all the place names and other geographical features that are mentioned, so you know what the reader needs. You can use this list either to check the maps that the author has provided, or to brief the cartographer. If you have to type the list as label copy, set it out in groups of like names (countries, rivers, oceans, capital cities, towns) so the cartographer can assign fonts to them. Consider how much detail is required. If a map shows too many names, contours, roads and so on, it may be cluttered and hard to read. Such a map may need to be redrawn as two maps, each showing different details.

Edit the labels and captions and include the maps in the list of illustrations, as described above. Some points to watch:

- Check the spelling of place names in an up-to-date atlas or, for Australia, the postcode book. Ensure they are consistent with the text.
- Compare the maps to ensure that the style and conventions are consistent and that the scale is the same, if appropriate.
- Cartographers sometimes include a legend on a map that gives the information normally given in a caption. If all the maps have such legends, there is no need to add captions. Note this on the design brief and be sure to include the maps in the list of illustrations.

Graphs and diagrams

Graphs and diagrams may have been prepared for another purpose and shoved into the manuscript unaltered, or they may be derived from originals that used different conventions. This tends to result in meaningless variation. Comparable items must be easy to compare. I once worked on a series of bar graphs showing gender differences in school achievement in various subjects; some of them had 'Boys' to the left and 'Girls' to the right, whereas others had 'Females' to the right and 'Males' to the left. Moreover, in some graphs the bars overlapped while in others they stood separate, and the fill pattern and fonts varied wildly. To ensure consistency, I chose one graph as a paradigm, and then exhaustively compared every aspect of the other graphs with it and marked those that did not conform.

Typical graphs are line graphs, bar graphs, pictorial graphs and pie charts. Each has a different emphasis: ensure that the appropriate type is used. On line and bar graphs, check that both axes are labelled and eliminate repetition. For instance, if the vertical axis is laboriously labelled *0%*, *10%*, *20%* and so on, delete the percentage signs and add *(%)* to the caption or the axis label. A horizontal axis labelled *June 2000*, *June 2001*, *June 2002* can be streamlined by adding *year ended June* to the caption.

Diagrams are known in the book trade as figures. They can take many forms: graphic representations of concepts or processes, working diagrams, mind maps, screen dumps, floor plans, flow charts or genealogical trees. There are conventions for the last three of these; study similar publications to get them right.

Nick Hudson makes some helpful suggestions for creating graphic models in his essay on 'Obscurantism':

> Words and short sentences are placed randomly in boxes distributed over the page, and joined with dotted lines and arrows. Some of the boxes should be shaded, and the arrows should be double-headed, to avoid any risk of there being a path through the system. Boxes of different shapes can add greatly to the mystery and the aesthetic effect.[1]

For most publications, a format that is longer than it is wide fits best on the printed page. If the author's sketch is not absolutely clear, annotate it, or draw a better sketch, or provide a photocopy of a similar pic so that the illustrator can understand the author's intention. Edit the labels as described above, and ensure that the caption provides sufficient information for a casual reader to understand the import of the pic without consulting the text.

Figure 6.1 shows the editing on hard copy of a diagram that the author has supplied. Substantive editing (which must be cleared with the author) is needed because the top row of boxes presents several problems:

- The content distracts the reader's focus from the purpose of the diagram, as defined by the caption: to show the factors that make up soil.
- The arrows imply that insects do not interact with people.
- Logically, a box should be added for birds, but this creates further problems for the arrows that show interactions.

Copyediting changes include:

- clarifying that trees are one kind of plant
- changing 'pH', a measurement, to 'acidity' to match 'salinity'
- making the capitalisation consistent
- marking the pic number and the location of the figure in the manuscript
- circling the caption to show it is not to be set (the design brief states where the edited caption copy is to be found).

In editing the caption copy, of course, you will delete the word 'all'; the author, preoccupied with soil, has forgotten about life in the oceans.

Drawings and cartoons

The editor's input into creative illustrations usually consists of briefing the illustrator or cartoonist. The brief may include sketches, photographs or relevant text from other books, along with a verbal description for each pic. Stipulate that pix are not to show unsafe activities or discrimination on grounds of gender, religion or ethnic origin. Cartoons, especially, should be reviewed for possible offensive implications.

Edit any labels and prepare caption copy and entries in the list of illustrations if required. If a pic such as a historical cartoon already includes a caption, you might decide to improve legibility by cropping the caption from the artwork and including it in the printed caption; mark this on the rough.

Boxed text

Boxes or panels are used to set off supplementary material from the main text. They are handy for such things as definitions, background information and extension activities.

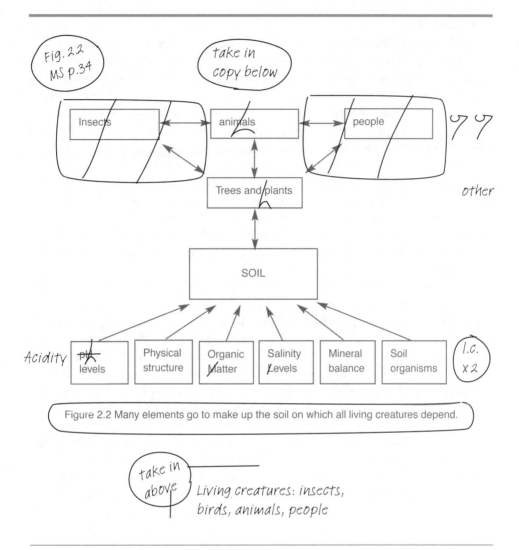

Figure 2.2 Many elements go to make up the soil on which all living creatures depend.

FIGURE 6.1   Editing a diagram: junior science textbook

It may be convenient to treat boxes as an extra category of illustration, especially if they require special typographical treatment for such items as newspaper headlines. A box usually has a heading (within the box) rather than a caption (outside the box). Boxes may be numbered, especially if they are referred to in the text, and in some books they are included in the table of contents or the list of illustrations.

Pix on screen

Graphic images are a vital part of screen publications. Besides line drawings and halftones, the screen can present information as animation, video and three-dimensional images. It also provides options unknown in print, such as zooming and direct feedback to the publisher or author. The technological requirements for graphics are evolving; an editor working in this medium must keep up to date or seek professional advice. It is essential to work closely with designers and technicians.

As explained in Chapter 4, design for the screen should not draw attention to itself. Excessive sophistication can be counter-productive. You may think it cute to animate a diagram, but the reader may find it simply irritating. Fine distinctions in colours beyond the 216 of the standard web palette may exceed the capacity of the reader's monitor. When converting a print publication for the screen, review the pictorial content for suitability to the medium and replace the pix or add new ones as appropriate.

You have probably had the experience of swearing at your computer while waiting for a huge graphics file to appear. For screen publications the editor assesses all graphics in terms of relevance and download time and removes those that are purely decorative. If a large graphics file is really needed, include a thumbnail of the pic and a hyperlink so that the file does not slow the main display. Compatibility with various browsers is also a consideration. Any screen publication needs to be rigorously tested to ensure that it will work on all popular platforms and configurations, and that it is accessible for people with a disability (see Chapter 4).

Artwork that is to appear on screen should be edited, either on screen or on hard copy, as described above. Assemble the artwork files in a separately labelled folder, so they can be readily linked to different locations in the publication. A publication on DVD or CD requires artwork for the label, the tray inlay and any accompanying booklet, in addition to the graphics that appear on screen.

Captions for pix on screen should be cogent. Readers scan the screen and seek the main information about the pic; wordiness will put them off. If necessary, extra information can be provided as a hyperlink or pop-up box.

For more information on screen graphics, see the *Style Manual*, Chapter 24.

Tables

Tabulation is a powerful means of organising information, both words and figures. Tables express relationships between different categories of information and expose the gaps where information is missing. Text tables (which contain words rather than numbers) are especially powerful; they may be elaborate, with subheadings and subdivisions. There is a lot to know about tables, as explained in the *Style Manual*, Chapter 19. Many authors do not understand how to exploit the possibilities of tabulation; the editor's specialist knowledge can be of great help, but extensive revision is time-consuming.

Appraisal

The editor appraises the tables, like all the other elements of the manuscript, in terms of their suitability. Consider whether their substance would be better presented as, say, a graph or a list.

Desktop publishing programs can make a good job of simple tables, but they cannot produce sophisticated effects such as minute variations in space. Tables prepared in a word processor often lose in the translation to page layout software, so it is usual to edit tables on paper.

Substantive editing

Once the tables have justified their existence as tables, consider them in relation to the text and decide their placement, as described above for pix. Tables that consist of only four or five lines are unlikely to be repositioned; if all the tables are of this type, they do not need to be numbered.

Review the structure of each table, and in consultation with the author and publisher decide whether it needs improvement. Perhaps you can combine several small, comparable tables into one to facilitate comparison, or split an unwieldy table that runs for several pages into two or three. Analyse the information in each table and ensure that its arrangement is logical: you may need to reword column headings or subdivide them with spanner rules (short rules that span only a few columns; see Figure 6.2). In a text table it might make sense to swap the position of the columns from left to right to achieve a logical flow. In number tables, a tint on alternate rows or a space after every fifth row may improve legibility.

Even if the budget does not permit a complete restructure, a table may be improved with some minor adjustments. Make sure that the table title describes the table fully, so that browsing readers who come upon it can understand what it's about. Eliminate repetition by removing repeated items from the body of the table to the column heads or table title. Authors often forget to provide a heading for the stub (left-hand) column, so you may have to invent something appropriate.

For most publications, tables should be long rather than wide. Sometimes you will need to restructure a table that has many columns and few rows so that it has few columns and many rows. There is no need to retype the whole table; just copy out the new column heads, the new stub column and a couple of columns of numerals or text to show the pattern for the typesetter to follow.

Notes to tables

A table may have several types of notes—general notes that apply to the whole table, notes that are keyed to specific parts of the table, notes on probability levels, and source notes. See that the various categories appear in the same order under each table, and mark them to distinguish them from the text (colour code on paper, styles in e-copy). Authors often key a general note to the table title, but general notes obviously apply to the whole table and do not need a note reference mark. Where there are several kinds of notes, you may add headings such as 'Notes' and

'Source' to distinguish them. In number tables, the note reference marks should be superscript letters or symbols (asterisk, dagger) to prevent confusion.

Do not attach endnotes or footnotes to tables. The placement of the table is determined by the pagination; if the table is moved from its original position during the layout stage, the note numbering may be disrupted. Convert such endnotes or footnotes to table notes, which appear below the table wherever it is positioned. The editor foresees such potential problems and prevents them by making minor adjustments, thus saving costs for the publisher.

Copyediting

The next step is to edit the tables for clarity and consistency. If a manuscript contains more than two or three tables, print them or remove them from the manuscript (having first numbered all the pages) and work on them together. The table in Figure 6.2 is fairly complicated, but it is well constructed. The only editorial interventions are an addition to the table title, a heading in the stub column, and the clarification of the layout for the designer.

Edit the column headings and other wording for language and for style (capitals, punctuation, italics). Make sure all the units of measurement are identified. Spot-check the totals in number tables, and if something doesn't add up refer it

Table 9.1 Household production of foodstuffs as a percentage of total production

Australia, 1951/52 – 1991/92 [en]

	% total production		
^Food production [bold]	1951/52	1971/72	1991/92
Raising [bold]			
Total vegetables	5.5	5.3	4.8
Potatoes	4.9	3.1	2.0
Total fruit	2.8	1.4	1.2
Citrus	4.8	4.5	5.0
Poultry: meat	n.a.	1.8	0.9
Poultry: eggs	44.9	29.4	n.a.
Gathering [bold]			
Fish	9.1	9.1	9.1
Manufacturing [bold]			
Jam	1.6	2.6	n.a.
Processed fruit*	0.5	0.3	0.4
Butter	3.2	0.0	0.0

[spanner rule] [align] [replace rules with 1 line #]

n.a. = not available

*Canned apricots, peaches, pears and pineapples only.

[ital] Sources: 1951/52, Commonwealth Bureau of Census and Statistics, *Report on Food Production and the Consumption of Foodstuffs*; 1971/72, Commonwealth Bureau of Census and Statistics, *Apparent Consumption of Foodstuffs and Nutrients*, No. 10.10; 1991/92, Australian Bureau of Statistics, *Apparent Consumption of Foodstuffs and Nutrients*, Cat. No. 4306.0.

FIGURE 6.2 Editing a table: academic social history

to the author. If percentages do not add to 100 because of rounding, consider whether the reader is sophisticated enough to assume this or needs a general note.

Tables, like graphs and diagrams, are particularly liable to meaningless variation, which can puzzle the reader. To ensure consistency between tables, go through them all looking only at the table titles. Then go through again to compare the column headings, and again for the stub columns, and again for the source notes, and so on. Tedious as it is, this is the only way to ensure that comparable tables are identically worded (where appropriate) and laid out.

After you've edited the tables, put them back in their correct places in the manuscript. If the tables are presented separately from the text, key them to their places in the manuscript as described above for pix. The pages of the table copy are numbered T1, T2, etc. If you have worked on a printout, add a note to the design brief to make sure that the edited version is the one that is typeset.

Copy and paste the table titles, shortening them if necessary, to the list of illustrations, as described above.

Mark-up

It is preferable to minimise the number of rules in a table and deploy white space to set off the various elements, but sometimes rules are required for legibility. The effect should be an uncluttered layout that aids comprehension.

In bookwork, the editor's job is to decide how best to present the information, and to mark up styles and layout for the designer. Thus you write instructions such as 'hanging indent' or 'more space' or 'centre column on decimal point'. Implementing these instructions requires specialist knowledge of typesetting software and is best left to the typesetter.

Careful mark-up of the manuscript copy of tables can prevent expensive corrections in proof. Take care to distinguish horizontal rules from the underlining that indicates italic. Where a table extends over more than one page of copy, mark arrows and the word 'continues' to show whether the continuation is to be placed at the bottom or at the side. For a large table, indicate on the manuscript copy where it may be split in page make-up, and instruct the typesetter what is to be repeated at the top of each new page: normally the table number — 'Table 4.1 contd' — and the column headings. Typesetters sometimes spread a narrow table by spacing out the columns to match the measure (line length) of the text, but the extra space can hinder comprehension if the reader's eye has to travel too far from one cell to the next. The editor prevents this discomfort by marking the manuscript copy 'set to natural measure and centre on text'.

Column headings are either aligned left or centred, but should be consistent throughout the publication. In text tables the wording is set flush left and unjustified; a hanging indent may improve legibility.

For screen publications, tables that have been prepared on a word processor or desktop publishing program may not convert well to the mark-up language. Carefully check the alignment of rows and cells, and examine such features as borders and shading.

Completeness and consistency

COMPLETENESS AND CONSISTENCY make a publication fit for purpose, to use the terminology of the Trade Practices Act. Readers feel cheated when they are referred to a non-existent illustration or are unable to follow information to its source. The editor is responsible for overseeing the integrity of a publication, as Chapters 13 and 14 of the *Style Manual* explain. Of course completeness and consistency apply to all parts of the publication, but here we survey the non-text items; proofs and quality control are discussed in the next chapter.

Eliminate meaningless variation

A large part of copyediting consists of imposing consistency on the linguistic and visual elements of a publication. The rationale for this is that meaningless variation distracts the reader. He may not consciously notice, for instance, that *enquiry* is sometimes spelt *inquiry*, but too many such variations will disturb him at a subliminal level and impede his absorption of the meaning.

The editor establishes an appropriate style, or follows house style, and ensures it is applied consistently throughout. As you gain experience you will do this routinely, knowing which expressions are likely to give trouble. You must ensure consistency not only in spelling but in all the matters listed in Standard E—the expression of numbers, the style and wording of the headings and captions, the layout of lists, quotations and tables, and so on (see Appendix).

Variations in terminology will confuse the reader more than inconsistent capitals and hyphens. Why does the author say *England* in one place and *Britain* in another? Is a distinction intended? Or maybe it should actually be *the United Kingdom*? The reader can waste time over puzzles like this. I worked on a book by three authors, about economic policy or some such abstruse topic, which frequently mentioned the government in Canberra. One author had referred throughout his section to the *Australian government*, one to the *federal government*, and one to the *Commonwealth government*. All three terms are correct but the variation was confusing, especially as the book was to be sold overseas, where readers are not familiar with Australia's constitutional arrangements.

Although you eliminate meaningless variation, you should not be mindlessly consistent for the sake of it. For instance, most Australian book publishers require that dates be expressed as day, month, year—*1 May 2004*. Yet the term *September 11*, which follows US usage, has entered the language as a convenient descriptor for the terrorist attacks on New York and Washington in 2001. As a meaningful variation this should be encouraged, even if you think it looks odd next to dates in the conventional form.

Prelims

The preliminary pages (prelims) are the reader's entry to the book; when you are preparing them, consider how the reader will use them. He skips the title page, because he's already seen that information on the cover, and looks for the table of contents, the key to the book. He doesn't want to have to turn a lot of pages to find it, so place it as near the front of the book as you can.

You look through the prelims when you appraise the manuscript, but it's best not to make any major changes to them until you have read through the entire text and all other material—appendixes, references, captions. You need to have a thorough understanding of the contents of the book before tackling the prelims.

Prelims are usually numbered with lower-case roman numerals in a separate sequence from the text, so that extra material can be added in proofs or for a new edition. If your client has a house style for the prelims, follow it. The usual sequence for non-fiction is:

- half title: may include a biographical note on the author
- list of other books in the series or by the same author
- frontispiece
- title page
- imprint page (containing legally required information, CIP data, disclaimers)
- dedication or epigraph
- table of contents
- lists of illustrations, usually in the order maps, plates, figures, tables (see Chapter 6)
- list of contributors
- foreword (by someone other than the author)
- preface (by the author)
- acknowledgements
- note on the text, transliteration or terminology

- conversions for measurements and currency
- list of abbreviations
- other lists: legal cases or statutes, biological species, *dramatis personae*, chronology
- glossary
- general map
- genealogical charts.

Obviously, few books contain all of these items, and the sequence may vary: a dedication or epigraph, for instance, can be placed on a verso (left-hand) page facing the first page of text; novels often have an extra title page on a recto (right-hand) page immediately preceding the text. If possible, begin the table of contents, foreword and preface on recto pages. To speed the reader's entry into the book, some publishers slim down the prelims by placing bulky or peripheral items in the endmatter. Such items may include conversions, abbreviations, other lists, glossary, genealogical charts.

The prelims may need streamlining or structural editing; consider their suitability in conjunction with the order of book (Chapter 3). Take care with items headed Foreword, Preface and Introduction. A foreword is by someone other than the author; the preface is by the author. It may be appropriate to include personal and copyright acknowledgements in the preface, with or without a subheading. If the Introduction is a purely personal note by the author it can be renamed Preface; if it's an essential part of the main text it may be numbered as Chapter 1. Similarly, the Conclusion may be given a chapter number.

Other publications follow slightly different rules. In government and corporate circles, the prelims of a report or submission may contain a letter of transmittal to the responsible minister or the client. A lengthy report benefits from the inclusion of a summary of findings, which may be headed Conclusions and Recommendations or Executive Summary. A paper for a conference or learned journal begins with a synopsis of the contents, usually headed Abstract. An instruction manual or reference work might include an explanation headed How to Use This Book.

Although the prelim pages have roman numerals in the finished publication, page numbers on the copy for setting are P1, P2, etc.

Table of contents

It is the editor's responsibility to prepare copy for the table of contents to accompany the edited manuscript. Although I refer to it here as 'table of contents', the list should be headed simply Contents. The page numbers are represented by double zeroes in the copy, and the editor adds or verifies them in page proofs.

The table of contents lays out the book's scope and purpose, so that the reader can decide at a glance whether the book has anything of interest to him. It is set out so that the structure and proportions of the material are apparent, providing sufficient detail for the reader to grasp the nature of the book, but not so much that the framework is obscured. Avoid clutter both in wording and in typography. In non-fiction books the reader's purpose may be different from the author's; he may have a particular query in mind. For instance in a book titled *Restoring the Land: A practical approach*, the reader may be seeking information on LandCare groups or on suitable species to plant in his area. The contents page should have sufficient detail to show whether the book is likely to be of use for such tangential enquiry.

In a non-fiction book the table of contents derives from the guide to headings (Figure 9.4). The editor decides how much detail from the guide is useful to the reader. The prelims, chapter headings and endmatter are always listed, but you may include one or more grades of subheadings. A novel has a table of contents if the chapters have names, or if it's divided into named parts.

The left-hand column of Figure 7.1 shows a table of contents for a book on traditional Chinese medicine as received from the author. This undifferentiated list is intimidating: it gives the reader no idea of the scope or plan of the book, and if he is seeking, say, information about treating haemorrhoids, he must read every line in order to find out that the topic is not covered. My solution, which is not the only possible solution, was this:

- I grouped the given headings into chapters, and asked the designer to emphasise the chapter titles on the contents page by their typographical treatment.
- Because it was a small book, 120 manuscript pages, I decided not to number the chapters.
- I removed the subheadings from the table of contents (but not from the text).
- I changed the wording of the first chapter title because the terminology was inconsistent and because it was expressed as a question. As a general rule, 'What is' questions do not make good headings.

There are some points of substantive editing to note on this book.

- I streamlined the prelims by incorporating How to Use This Book as subheading in the Introduction.
- Because all non-fiction books should have an index, I added Index to the table of contents and to the documentation, and made a note to consult the publisher and author about it.
- In the chapter entitled Maintaining Good Health I changed the order of the subheadings (and made the corresponding change in the text), in keeping with the book's emphasis on lifestyle and diet rather than medication.

I also made a note on my task list to look at the text under the heading Five Evils. The original table of contents lists only four, and no evil should be allowed to wander unchecked.

Original table of contents

Introduction
How to use this book
What is herbal medicine?
Yin and yang
Qi
Meridians
  Spleen/Stomach
  Lung/Large intestine
  Heart/Small inestine
  Liver/Gall bladder
  Kidney/Bladder
Blood
Fluids, shen, jing
Five phases
  Five phases of correspondences
Five evils
  Wind
  Damp
  Dryness
  Cold
Emotions
Traditional Chinese medicine consultation
Menstruation
Infertility
Pregnancy
Menopause
Migraine
Herpes
Common cold
Depression
Obesity
UTI (urinary tract infection)
Self-medication
Lifestyle
Diet
Final note
Appendix 1—Moxabustion
Appendix 2—Soup recipes
Appendix 3—Medicated liqueurs
Shopping list
Suggested reading

Revised table of contents

Introduction 00

An outline of traditional Chinese medicine 00

Yin and yang 00
Qi 00
Meridians 00
Blood 00
Some other concepts 00
Five phases 00
Five evils 00
Emotions 00
The consultation 00

Particular conditions 00

Menstruation 00
Infertility 00
Pregnancy 00
Menopause 00
Migraine 00
Herpes 00
Common cold 00
Depression 00
Obesity 00
Urinary tract infection 00

Maintaining good health 00

Lifestyle 00
Diet 00
Self-medication 00
Final note 00

Appendixes 00

1 Moxabustion 00
2 Soup recipes 00
3 Medicated liqueurs 00
4 Shopping list 00

Suggested reading 00

Index 00

FIGURE 7.1 Setting out a table of contents: self-help book on health

Endmatter

A conclusion or epilogue is part of the main text of the book and precedes the endmatter. An afterword may be placed before the endmatter, or after everything else but before the index.

The usual sequence for endmatter in non-fiction books is:

- appendixes (including various types of lists)
- endnotes
- references or bibliography
- glossary
- list of contributors
- acknowledgements
- particular indexes (of places, of scientific names, of first lines)
- general index.

In addition, a textbook may have a lengthy section of answers to questions, which precedes the index.

Appendixes often consist of supplementary documents or statistics, but almost anything can fit under this rubric. The book on traditional Chinese medicine has a shopping list and recipes as appendixes; a book on public speaking might have sample speeches. Appendixes offer flexibility and can be a means of pacifying an author who simply must include information that doesn't fit anywhere else. In some cases, though, a brief appendix might be better incorporated in the main text. Naturally, you will check whether copyright permission is needed for material used in appendixes.

Most non-fiction books, and all textbooks, should have a bibliography, even if it's just a list of half a dozen titles headed Further Reading. If there isn't one, ask the author to compile it. All non-fiction books (except those arranged in dictionary format) need an index. The editing of references and indexes is discussed below.

Jacket and cover

The editor rarely gets much say in the design of the dust jacket or cover, but it is usually your responsibility to compile copy for typesetting. Type it up according to the publisher's house style and mark on it the placement of any material that you don't have, like the cover design credit, ISBN, barcode and colophon. A hardcover book needs six pieces of copy: jacket front, jacket front flap, jacket spine, case spine, jacket back, and jacket back flap. A paperback needs three pieces: the front cover, the spine, and the back cover.

Blurb

The blurb appears on the front flap of the jacket or the back cover of the paperback. The editor supplies a draft blurb when the editorial brief requires it.

Drafting the blurb can be fun, especially if the book has sparked your interest. The aim is to convince readers that the book is terrific—in fact, to sell it. Before you begin, ascertain the marketing strategy for the book. Then skim through the publishing proposal if you have it, and also the book's preface, introduction and conclusion, and steal any notable ideas and phrases. Explain what is remarkable about the book—for non-fiction, it puts forward a controversial argument or illuminates a neglected topic; for a novel, it is imaginative and absorbing; for a textbook, it is written expressly for the syllabus and contains pedagogical aids. Mention the author's previous successes or particular expertise in the field. Be creative and communicate your enthusiasm: include striking quotations from the text, list the book's themes as dot points or questions.

Blurbs seem to attract clichés; avoid *groundbreaking, compelling, savage indictment of, sheds new light on, this book will be of interest to all who* ... and *this book will change your life.*

References

Sources of quotations, grounds for controversial statements, acknowledgement of other people's work, further reading—references are part of most non-fiction books. Every job description includes a few boring chores, and for editors checking references is one of them. Editorial work on the referencing should be in keeping with the scale of the project. Maintain a sense of proportion. Most readers skip the references, and editorial time spent fiddling with the commas won't make any extra sales.

Figure 7.2 outlines the two most common referencing systems; Chapter 12 of the *Style Manual* gives full details of them and a couple more besides.

Accurate citations

Although the dollar value of footnotes is low, two recent historical controversies have drawn attention to their importance. In England a defamation case brought by the historian David Irving resulted in exhaustive examination of the sources cited in his books. He was found to have distorted and denied evidence of the Holocaust; as a result he lost both the case and his scholarly reputation. In Australia allegations that Aboriginal history has been fabricated, particularly with regard to massacres by whites, have hinged on the accuracy of citations. The author is responsible for accuracy, but the editor is alert for improbabilities and inconsistencies.

Authors frequently make mistakes in references. You will find discrepancies in every kind of information: the spelling of authors' names, the order of joint authors' names, the wording of titles, the publication dates, the volume and page numbers. Take special care where authors cite their own works: they often get some details wrong because they cite from memory.

Characteristics	Documentary-note system (notes and bibliography)	Author–date system (Harvard system)
In-text citation	superscript figures (or reference marks: asterisk, dagger, etc.)	name and year of publication, in brackets
Refers to:	footnotes or endnotes, which refer to the bibliography	list of references
What information does it provide?	citation of sources and comment on text	citation of sources
Position of indicator	at end of sentence or paragraph if possible	immediately after name or at end of sentence
Disadvantages	means nothing unless reader leaves text and goes to the notes	does not permit comment not good with long names
Advantages	text indicator does not distract the reader notes can supplement and qualify the text	brief and neat
Main subject areas	history, biography, literary criticism	physical sciences, social sciences

FIGURE 7.2 Two systems of referencing compared

If the referencing is seriously deficient, it will have to go back to the author with tactful, detailed instructions explaining what is required. If there are only a few discrepancies, ask the author to supply the information you require to fix them. But where the author is unreliable or slow and there are only half-a-dozen or so bibliographic queries outstanding, it's quicker to chase them up yourself in an online library catalogue. The national libraries of Australia and New Zealand, as legal deposit libraries, theoretically have a copy of every book published in their respective countries, and their catalogues are searchable. The Electric Editors website has links to the catalogues of the British Museum and the US Library of Congress.[1]

Take care in citing conference papers. These are the cutting edge of scholarship, the formative stages of ideas that have not yet been worked up into articles or books; scholars may want to follow them up. Give all possible details, including the date of the conference, the location, and the name of the sponsoring organisation.

Substantive editing

Exhaustive documentation of sources may be a bid for academic credibility or a hangover from a previous incarnation of the book as a doctoral thesis. Before you begin work on the references, ask the basic questions that apply to all elements of the book: are they really necessary, and do they suit the purpose and intended readership?

Even though you can see that the references would benefit from substantive editing, don't embark on major changes unless you have agreement from the publisher and the author and have made full allowance for the cost. Some techniques for streamlining notes are described below.

Task	Documentary-note system	Author–date system
In-text citations	Highlight all superscript figures or note them in the margin. Check their placement: move them to the end of the sentence or paragraph if possible. Check for excessive frequency; combine if possible.	Highlight all in-text citations or note them in the margin. Check their placement; move them to the end of the sentence or paragraph if possible. Check for excessive frequency; combine if possible. Edit in-text citations for spelling of authors' names and consistent punctuation: commas, colons, ampersands.
Bibliography or References	Edit for completeness and consistency.	Edit for completeness and consistency.
Sense	Compare the sense of the text with the notes; if they don't correspond, the note numbering may need revision; consult the author.	Compare the sense of the text with the citations; if they don't correspond, consult the author.
Meaningless variation	Check the notes against the bibliography for discrepancies in the spelling and order of authors' names, wording of titles, place and year of publication.	Check the in-text citations against the list of references for discrepancies in the spelling and order of authors' names, year of publication.
Repetition	Compare text and notes; if the author's name is given in the text, it need not be repeated in the note. Compare notes and bibliography; the citations in the notes can be cut to authors' family names and short titles because the bibliography provides full publication details.	
Sequence	Check alphabetical and chronological sequence of bibliography. Check numerical sequence of text indicators and notes.	Check alphabetical and chronological sequence of the list of references.

FIGURE 7.3 Procedures for copyediting references

Copyediting

There are two main requirements in copyediting references: that the citations are sufficient to enable the reader to locate the works, and that the chosen style is applied consistently. As usual, you are trying to eliminate meaningless variation without making too much work for yourself.

Figure 7.3 shows how to copyedit references for the two most common systems on paper; the same principles apply on screen. Be sure to check the references against the text for sense: sometimes a discussion about a book by Author A is accompanied by citations of works by Author B. Do not edit spelling in the titles of books and articles. Book publishers prefer not to duplicate information in the notes and the bibliography (to save space), but students and researchers prefer to have the information in full in both places (to save photocopying).

Style

For the editor at the typeface, the *Style Manual*'s rules on matters of citation are a counsel of perfection. Publishers tend to lose enthusiasm for their preferred style when you tell them how much it will cost to apply it. Unless the editorial brief requires you to impose a strict house style, go with the flow. Where the author has a system that is reasonable and consistent, or even fairly consistent, stick with it.

For detailed citation of archival sources, you must rely on the author. It is usual to supply:

- the name of the writer; for correspondence, the name of the recipient
- the title of the document, if it has one
- the date the document was composed; if unknown, give an approximate date in square brackets
- the name of the repository
- the title of the series, and sub-series where required
- the number of the volume, file, box or bundle.

In a book for the general reader, a brief note about the archives the author has consulted is usually preferable to detailed citations.

An infinite variety of styles can be devised for citations of printed sources, with minor differences in punctuation, capitals and sequence. For instance, here are three possible styles for author–date citation of a chapter in a book, any one of which is acceptable:

- O'Nym, Pseud, 2000, 'Waltzing the wafer: Gender and class in the sociology of ice-cream' in F. Likiardopolous and and P. G. Ng, eds, *Wafer, Cone or Dixie Cup: A history of Australian ice-cream preferences*, Camford University Press, Melbourne, pp. 148–80.

- O'Nym, Pseud (2000). 'Waltzing the Wafer: Gender and class in the sociology of ice-cream', chapter 6 in *Wafer, Cone or Dixie Cup: A history of Australian ice-cream preferences*, F. Likiardopolous and and P. G. Ng (eds). Camford University Press: Melbourne.
- O'Nym, P. (2000) 'Waltzing the Wafer: Gender and Class in the Sociology of Ice-cream'. In *Wafer, Cone or Dixie Cup: A History of Australian Ice-cream Preferences*, pp. 148–80. Ed. F. Likiardopolous and and P. G. Ng. Melbourne: Camford University Press.

Similarly, there are many acceptable variations of arrangement, capitalisation and punctuation for citing books; it doesn't matter which is followed as long as it's consistent. For instance, the publication details may be given as:

- Sydney: Linen Press, 2002.
- Linen Press (Sydney, 2002).
- Linen, Sydney, 2002.
- Sydney, 2002.

Some authors state the place of publication as a suburb rather than a metropolis: *Allen & Unwin, St Leonards, NSW*, rather than *Allen & Unwin, Sydney*. The latter is preferable, especially if the book is likely to be sold overseas. When citing university presses, there is no need to state the place name if it is also the name of the press: *University of New South Wales Press, Sydney*, and *Oxford University Press, Melbourne*, but *Melbourne University Publishing*. When the place of publication is little known, add the name of the state (Australia and United States) or county (Britain) in its standard shortened form, and do this also if the place has a common name like Newport or Richmond.

In general, as long as the author has been logical and consistent, don't fuss: altering caps and commas is busywork. Spend the necessary time, though, to make sure all the required information is there and in the right order. Conceptualise it as a table and make sure all the appropriate cells are filled in, as shown in Figure 7.4.

Endnotes and footnotes

Even with sophisticated typesetting software, footnotes are tricky to deal with and at page proof stage they require copyfitting (Chapter 8). Because this raises costs, publishers generally prefer endnotes.

Before you undertake any substantive editing of the notes, consider whether extensive renumbering is worthwhile. Correlating the two sequences—the superscript numbers in the text and the numbers on the notes themselves—can be tedious and confusing, even on screen. Do not attempt changes that will result in renumbering without agreement from the author and the publisher.

Except in the most formal academic contexts, it is not necessary to provide a citation for every statement and quotation. Sometimes an author mentions the same source half a dozen times in one paragraph and supplies a separate note for

Author	Extra 1	Title	Extra 2	Publication details
Marr, David,		*Patrick White: A Life,*		Sydney: Random House, 1991.
Axelrod, R.	1984.	*The Evolution of Cooperation.*		Basic Books, New York.
Grieve, Norma, and Burns, Ailsa.	eds.	*Australian Women: contemporary feminist thought*		Oxford University Press. Melbourne, 1994.
Burns, Robert	(ed. John Hill),	*Collected Poems.*		A. and C. Black, Edinburgh, 1923.
Roughsey, Elsie,		*An Aboriginal Mother Tells of the Old and the New,*	ed. Paul Memmott and Robyn Horsman,	Fitzroy: McPhee Gribble, 1984.
Gowers, Sir Ernest,		*The Complete Plain Words,*	2nd edn, rev. Sir Bruce Fraser,	HMSO (London, 1973).
National Inquiry into the Separation of Aboriginal and Torres Strait Islander Children from their Families,	1997.	*Bringing them Home*	(Sir Ronald Wilson, president).	Human Rights and Equal Opportunity Commission, Sydney.
Australian Academy of Science Committee of National Parks,		*National Parks and Reserves in Western Australia,*	Occasional Paper No. 3,	Australian Academy of Science, Perth, n.d.
Andrews, A.,		*The First Settlement on the Upper Murray, 1835–45,*		Sydney: D. S. Ford, 1920 (Library of Australian History, Sydney, facs. edn, 1974). Library of Australian History, Sydney, [1920] 1974.

FIGURE 7.4 Typical styles for citing books

each reference. If the publisher has agreed to pay for substantive editing and renumbering of the notes, condense these repetitive notes into one, beginning it with some remark like 'This section draws on' or 'The following account is taken from', and giving a span of page numbers. Similarly, in the author–date system you can combine identical in-text citations into one, and place it either near the beginning or at the end of the paragraph.

The author–date system can be obscure if slavishly applied. For the reader, a passage that discusses 'Adam-Smith (1978, 1982)' is meaningless unless he turns to the list of references, whereas 'Adam-Smith in her books *The ANZACs* and *The Shearers*' gives all the necessary information right there on the page.

Abbreviations that are used only in the endnotes may be listed at the beginning of the endnotes rather than in the prelims. Authors may introduce an abbreviation at the first mention in the form 'National Library of Australia, hereafter NLA'. This is not helpful for the reader; if he forgets, he has to search back through the notes for that first mention. Compile a list of abbreviations if there are more than two or three.

Persuade the author not to use Latin abbreviations such as *op. cit.* and *et seq.* (unless replacing them would require a lot of work). *Op. cit.*, meaning 'in the work cited', can be replaced by the title of the work (shortened if necessary), and *et seq.*, meaning 'and following', can be replaced by actual page numbers or 'ff.'. Two useful Latin abbreviations are *et al.*, meaning 'and others', referring to multiple authors, and *ibid.*, meaning 'in the same place'. These two are space-savers and fairly widely known. Remember that *ibid.* cannot be used if the preceding note cites more than one work, and it may become incorrect if the preceding note is altered.

Endnotes have the chapter headings as subheadings. Verify them against the table of contents for wording and style. If the chapter headings are lengthy, the endnote subheadings can be the brief versions that are used in the running headings (Chapter 4).

Bibliography

Give the bibliography an appropriate title. For the author–date system it is always called References, but in other cases it may be Select Bibliography or Bibliography of Works Cited or Further Reading or simply Bibliography.

An author sometimes subdivides the bibliography into several sections and subsections, such as archival sources, primary sources, official sources, articles, books, and theses. This approach is required for a thesis but should be simplified in a book derived from it; scholars who require detailed information will consult the thesis. The general reader prefers an explanatory Note on Sources to exhaustive lists of archival material that he will never consult; he does not want to plough through half a dozen alphabetical sequences to find a particular work. Again, substantive editing must be fully costed and cleared with the author and publisher.

Verify bibliographies and reference lists for alphabetical order, and for chronological order where more than one work by the same author is cited. Legibility is improved by substituting a 2-em rule for repeats of an author's name, but don't mark this until *after* you have arranged the citations in the correct order.

Here are a couple of handy tips for working with bibliographies.

- To compare the bibliography with endnotes or in-text citations, place them side by side on your desk or use a split screen (Chapter 10 under Comparing Two Documents).
- When you're checking citations in the text or notes against a hard-copy bibliography, secure the bibliography with a spring paperclip on the top right-hand corner; this holds the pages in place while you flick through, focusing on the left side of the page, to find particular citations.

Indexes

The preparation of an index is an exercise in imagination in which the indexer tries to think of every way in which a reader might want to access the content of the book. A history of Australian Rules football, for example, might be consulted by readers who want to know about the effects of World War II on the game; particular players, clubs or grounds; the development of the role of coaches; or the preparation of playing surfaces. The indexer tries to accommodate all such needs with careful choice of entries and cross-references. There is more about this in Chapter 15 of the *Style Manual*.

Indexes are usually edited on screen. If the index is professionally prepared, the editor need only make a quick check to ensure that the indexer is competent and to correct typos and consistency with the text. Usually, though, the index is prepared by an amateur—the author. In most cases this is a false economy. An amateur index usually needs both substantive editing and copyediting.

The index cannot be finalised until the book is in page proofs. By the time the editor receives it, the production process is well advanced and the budget and schedule have little room for movement. If the index is not up to standard, there is no time to return it to the author—and anyway, this is probably the best she can do. In extreme cases you might ask the publisher for more time and money, but usually you have to make the best of what you have.

Substantive editing

The organisation of the index should be self-evident; no specialised knowledge of the book's content should be required to locate entries quickly. In most books a single level of subentries is sufficient, and few need more than two levels. Professional indexers recommend allowing space for the index equal to 12–15 per cent of the text in a specialist work; 8–10 per cent in an academic book or textbook; and 3–5 per cent in a general or popular book.[2]

To edit the substance of an index, tackle it from two different angles:

- First, concentrate on the words and ignore the page numbers. Is the index conceptually sound? Are major topics omitted? Are sufficient synonyms provided? Test the cross-references: if an entry reads 'education: *see* schools', check that there is in fact an entry for 'schools'.

- Now look at the page numbers. Butcher in *Copy-editing* recommends that an entry that has more than six page numbers should be divided into subentries, but this is rarely attainable. Conversely, where several subentries all refer to the same two or three page numbers, they can be collapsed into one.

Continue this phase until you run out of time or you are satisfied with the conceptual integrity of the index.

Copyediting

Here is a systematic procedure for copyediting an index on screen:

1 Make any global changes that are needed: apply correct spellings, italicise *see* and *see also*, convert hyphens to en rules in spans of numbers.
2 Sort the entries into alphabetical order; in Microsoft Word this is done with Table > Sort. Check that the result accords with house style on such points as treatment of numbers and *Mac, Mc.*
3 Insert a one-line space before each alphabetical block.
4 Read the words (ignoring the page numbers), checking for typos and punctuation and for errors introduced by global changes. Correct inconsistencies of style—spelling, capitals, italics—by checking doubtful words against the word list or the page proofs.
5 Read the page numbers, checking for consistent style and punctuation and for correct order. Look for digits that are omitted or repeated and for nonsense numbers like *155–4*. Turn to the page proofs and find the correct page numbers; as a last resort, delete doubtful numbers.
6 Save the edited index as a new file and name it appropriately (Chapter 10 under Electronic Files).

8

Proofs

ANGUS & ROBERTSON, in the glory days when Beatrice Davis was their senior editor, used to consider three typos per book was a reasonable amount,[1] and that's still a target to aim at. Of course, there is huge potential for mistakes in any publication—all those letters, words, names, dates, facts, numbers and typography—and the closer you are to it the harder it is to see them. It's common for experienced editors to glance at a proofread page and immediately spot an error that the proofreader has missed. This is not a sneer at proofreaders; it just demonstrates how hard it is to detect errors in print. It's fatally easy to miss typos in the displayed type of titles and headings.

Some editors claim that the process of reading actually creates typos. The action of passing one's eyes over the text, they say, disarranges or moves the letters; consequently, the more often a page is read, the more errors there are. Despite considerable anecdotal evidence about this effect, rigorous scientific investigation has proved that it is illusory. Editors should, however, understand the operation of Muphry's Law of Proofreading, as stated by John Bangsund:

> Muphry's Law is the editorial application of the better-known Murphy's Law. Muphry's Law dictates that (a) if you write anything criticizing editing or proofreading, there will be a fault of some kind in what you have written; (b) if an author thanks you in a book for your editing or proofreading, there will be mistakes in the book; (c) the stronger the sentiment expressed in (a) and (b), the greater the fault; (d) any book devoted to editing or style will be internally inconsistent.[2]

In the olden days, the first proof was of the text only, without tables or illustrations. The metal type was set up in shallow trays called galleys and the proof was printed—or 'pulled'—on long slips of paper called galley proofs, each holding the equivalent of about three printed pages. Thus the text was finalised before the pages were made up.

Modern production methods have dispensed with galley proofs: the first round of proofs is usually laid out as pages. Sometimes, though, there is a preliminary stage called galley-on-page, in which the typesetter drops the text into the page format but does not paginate it, letting the breaks and headings fall where they may. Clarify what stage you are working on so you know what to mark; you will not bother adjusting widow lines if you are working with galley-on-page, or correcting details of illustrations that are 'positional only'.

A straightforward book that is mostly text usually has only one or two rounds of proofs. Later stages are described below. For proofreading fees, see Chapter 11 under Hourly Rates.

The proofreader's role

The proofreader verifies the typesetting against the type specification, and therefore needs to understand matters such as point sizes and the characteristics of type families and fonts. These topics are explained fully in the *Style Manual*, Chapter 18.

Some editors like to proofread the books they have edited, but it is valuable to have someone else do it: another eye will find errors that you have missed. Pay close attention to the corrections on the proofs of your jobs. The work of skilled proofreaders can provide a thorough education in spelling, typography and mark-up.

Proofreading is vital for quality control, but the proofreader's responsibility is narrower than the editor's: it is to verify that the edited manuscript has been faithfully rendered in type according to the specifications. The proofreader does not interrogate substance and structure as the editor does, but concentrates on seeing that the editor's and designer's instructions have been carried out. Proofreaders do draw attention to what appear to be major substantive errors, such as omission of a whole area of the topic, because it's always possible that there's been some awful mistake. They also query obvious errors of fact, sense, grammar and consistency. But in general, proofreaders have confidence that the publishing team has thought things through and concentrate on checking what the typesetter has done. The tasks of proofreading are covered in Standard E, paras 3–5 (see Appendix), although the proofreader does not prepare any copy or edit the index.

A client may ask a freelance editor to do 'blind proofreading', in which the proofs are read without any previous version—manuscript or proof—to refer to. In this situation you cannot verify numbers or the spelling of names, and if no word list is supplied you have to compile one as you go. In many cases, so-called blind proofreading amounts to copyediting, and should be charged as such. A detailed editorial brief can prevent this sort of confusion.

Proofreading marks

The conventional proof correction marks are logical and easy to learn. Make use of the feedback that proofs provide: if a typesetter has misunderstood your handwriting or a mark you have made, think how you can mark it more clearly on future jobs. Remember that authors and desktop publishers may not know the standard marks; when sending marked manuscript or proofs, supply a list of the ones you have used.

Corrections on proofs are colour coded, with author's and editor's changes in blue and typesetting errors in red, unless the publisher has some other preference. On proofs marginal marks are always required, but on a hand-marked manuscript some marginal marks that are used frequently, such as *delete*, *hyphen* and *sp. out*, may be omitted if the text mark is prominent and unambiguous.

Some points to note:

- Instructions should be circled to distinguish them from copy to be typeset.
- Where several marginal marks occur on the same line, follow each one with an oblique stroke.
- If you have trouble making a recognisable 'delete' sign, practise! It may help to visualise it as a lower-case d followed by an oblique stroke.
- If a correction includes ambiguous characters—figure one, capital I and lower-case ell; capital O and zero; apostrophe and comma; hyphen, en rule and em rule —you may need to annotate them for clarity.
- To add a diacritic, cross out the unaccented letter and write the accented letter in the margin. If you suspect the typesetter is inexperienced, write the name of the accent: *Spanish tilde*, *Maori macron*.

The common proofreading marks are set out in Figure 8.1. For more information and examples, see Appendix C of the *Style Manual*.

Mark-up

The proofreading marks in Figure 8.1 are used for both manuscripts and proofs, but the exact application of them varies. It used to be the practice to mark alterations within the text on manuscripts because the typesetter read every line when keyboarding; on proofs, they were marked in the margins because the typesetter took the text for granted and looked only at the margins. Modern production methods have turned the manuscript into a quasi-proof, and mark-up has changed accordingly.

Mark-up has two purposes: to make corrections to the content, and to interpret the material for the designer and typesetter. Figures 8.2–8.4 show that identical copy may be marked up differently, depending on two things: the production process (see Figure 10.1), and the stage it has reached.

Instruction	Textual mark	Marginal mark
insert copy in the text	caret ⋏	*write the copy to be inserted*
take in copy from another page or document	caret ⋏	(take in copy) *and identify source*
delete copy	cross out the characters to be deleted	℘
delete and close up	cross out the characters to be deleted and add linking marks	℘
leave as printed	mark dotted line under the characters to be retained	(stet)
add space	caret ⋏	# *amount of space may be shown, e.g. 6 pt, 1 line*
close up (remove space)	linking marks	(close up)
transpose characters or words	∪∩ between characters or words	(trs)
transpose sentences or paras	circle the copy and connect it to the correct location with an arrow	(trs)
take words or characters over to next line	[around words or characters to be moved	(t.o.)
take words or characters back to previous line	] around words or characters to be moved	(t.b.)
move right	[around copy to be moved	
move left	] around copy to be moved	
raise lines	⌐_⌐ under lines to be moved	raise
lower lines	⌐⌐ above lines to be moved	lower
correct the vertical alignment	‖ beside lines to be adjusted	(align)
unjustify or set ragged right	vertical line at right of text to be changed	(r.r.)
wrong font	circle the characters to be changed	(w.f.)
indent 1 em	☐ at beginning of line to be indented	
indent 2 ems	☐☐ at beginning of line to be indented	
begin a new para	[before first word of new para	(n.p.)
do not begin a new para (make first line full out or flush left)	] at beginning of unwanted para	(f.o.) (f.l.)
join two paras	⌐⌐ between paras to be joined	(run on)

Instruction	Textual mark	Marginal mark
change to lower case	circle the characters to be altered; or strike through each character from the top righthand corner	(l.c.)
change to capitals	triple line under the characters to be altered	(caps)
change to small capitals	double line under the characters to be altered	(s.c.)
change to italic	single line under the characters to be altered	(ital.)
change to bold	wavy line under the characters to be altered	(bold)
change to roman	circle the characters to be altered	(rom.)
underline	single line under the characters to be altered	(underline)
change double quotation marks to single	circle the double quotation marks	(single quotes)
replace with superscript character	$\mathcal{Y}$	(super.)
replace with subscript character	$\wedge$	(sub.)
spell out number or abbreviation	circle the characters to be altered	(sp. out) add the full spelling if required
insert hyphen	caret and hyphen	(hyphen)
insert en or em rule	caret and en or em rule	(en) (em)
change to en or em rule	circle character to be changed	(en) (em)

FIGURE 8.1 Symbols for text mark-up and proof correction

Hard-copy manuscript

Figure 8.2 shows the traditional method, where the manuscript is edited by hand on hard copy.

- The mark-up shows both editorial alterations and instructions for the designer and typesetter.
- The marginal lines that identify special setting—lists, set-down quotations, boxed text, questions, exercises— are usually in colour, and the colour code is explained in the design brief.
- Where general instructions in the type specification cover such items as the style for the chapter heading, there is no need to mark up each instance: just write 'to style'.
- Note that copy that is to be edited by hand must be printed double-spaced.

~~CHAPTER~~ 4

SMALL BUSINESS AND THE LAW

A small business can be defined in various ways, according to factors such as the number of people it employs or the value of its sales ~~each year~~. Generally the defintion includes businesses that have less than twenty employees. Most small businesses share two characteristics the owner manages the business and ~~he or she~~ provides most of the capital.

Types of Business Organisation

Sole trader

For a sole trader, the business has no legal identity separate form the owner. The main advantage of sole trading is that the owner has total control. The disadvantages are:

- the owner's private assets may be required to meet business debts;
- it can be hard to obtain finance or external equity;
- the owner incurs captial gains tax if the business is sold; ~~and~~
- the owner's illness or death may damage the business.

 A sole trader pays personal income tax on the profit (income minus expenses) of the business.

Partnership

The law deems that a partnership can exist where people act like partners, even though they have never explicitly agreed to form a partnership. A partnership exists when ~~certain~~ three factors apply:

- a business is being carried on; ~~and~~
- the business is being carried on in common (either by the partners or by an agent acting for them) ~~and~~
- the aim of the business is profit.

Although you do not have to comply with any formalities to set up a partnership, it is wise to draw up a written agreement. It should specify the obligations, rights and liabilities of the partners in case of disputes, and such matters as capital contributions, entitlements to salaries, and rights when the partnership is terminated.

FIGURE 8.2 Mark-up on a manuscript edited by hand on hard copy: junior commerce textbook

Printout of edited manuscript

Figure 8.3 shows the same copy as in the previous figure, but the production method differs. The editing has been done on screen, and the edited manuscript is presented as a marked-up printout.

- Because the editorial alterations have been made on screen, the mark-up consists of instructions for the designer—namely, the styles used.
- For most manuscripts the editor needs to mark up only a few pages or one chapter.
- The styles correspond to the list in the design brief, and the letter *x* in their names indicates custom styles created by the editor.
- Track Changes would normally be removed before the edited manuscript is printed, but the changes are shown here for comparison with Figure 8.2.

---

xch no   ~~CHAPTER~~ 4

xch head   **Small Business and the Law**

A small business can be defined in various ways, according to factors such as the number
xpara f/o   of people it employs or the value of its <u>annual</u> sales ~~each year~~. Generally the defintion includes businesses that have ~~less~~ <u>fewer</u> than twenty employees. Most small businesses share two characteristics~~,~~: the owner manages the business and ~~he or she~~ provides most of the capital.

xAhead   **Types of Business Organisation**

xBhead   **Sole trader**

For a sole trader, the business has no legal identity separate f~~ro~~om the owner. The main advantage of sole trading is that the owner has total control. The disadvantages are:
- T~~t~~he owner's private assets may be required to meet business debts~~,~~.
xbullet list •   ~~it can be hard to obtain~~ f~~F~~inance or external equity <u>can be hard to obtain</u>~~,~~.
- T~~t~~he owner incurs captial gains tax if the business is sold~~; and~~.
- T~~t~~he owner's illness or death may damage the business.

xpara7   A sole trader pays personal income tax on the profit (income minus expenses) ~~i~~of the business.

Partnership

The law deems that a partnership can exist where people act like partners, even though they have never explicitly agreed to form a partnership. A partnership exists when ~~certain~~ <u>three</u> factors apply:
- a business is being carried on~~; and~~
- the business is being carried on in common (either by the partners or by an agent acting for them)~~; and~~
- the aim of the business is profit.

Although you do~~n't~~ <u>not</u> have to comply with any formalities to set up a partnership, it is wise to draw up a written agreement. It should specify the obligations, rights and liabilities of the partners in case of disputes, and such matters as capital contributions, entitlements to salaries, and rights when the partnership is terminated.

FIGURE 8.3   Mark-up on the printout of a manuscript that has been edited on screen: junior commerce textbook

Proofs

Figure 8.4 shows that a different approach is required if the same copy as in the previous figures arrives on your desk as proofs. As explained above, the proofreader has a much more limited task than the editor. It is not possible to make improvements to the wording at this late stage in the production process, unless the cost of such alterations has been cleared with the publisher.

- The distinction between *less* and *fewer* is on the way out. It is appropriate to correct it in this case because textbooks are written in formal English, but in a popular or colloquial publication this correction could be regarded as pedantry.
- The changes to the chapter heading would be made only if they were required for consistency with the rest of the book.
- As already mentioned, it is customary to mark author's and editor's corrections in blue and typesetting errors in red.

Proofreading methods

The traditional method of reading proofs was for a 'copyholder' to read the text aloud to the proofreader, indicating capitals, italics and so on with a code of taps. It's hard to get that sort of help nowadays, so you have to verify everything by eye.

Reading first proofs

Begin by placing the proofs in front of you and the edited manuscript to one side. Have the documentation within reach—type specification, word list, sample setting. Mark the proofs as explained above. You may choose to read the text once very thoroughly, or go through it twice at a faster pace. The major difficulty in proofreading is that you see what you expect to see. As we saw in Chapter 2 under Reading, it's hard to spot *conservation* when the sense leads you to expect *conversation*.

When you are proofreading, whether text or displayed type, slow down your eye-movement by placing a piece of card under the line of type and holding it there until you are satisfied that all the letters and words are in the right places and correctly spaced. After you have marked an error, reread every word in the line in case there's another error lurking. You can do a better job if you know what kind of errors to look for (Chapter 10 under Typical Errors).

As you proofread the text, compare every paragraph of the proofs against the edited manuscript in case something has been omitted. Verify optional spellings and all numbers in the proofs, character by character, against the manuscript. Where complicated matter with a lot of numbers, such as statistical tables, has been rekeyed, the old-fashioned method of having it read aloud while you look at the proof is the only sure way to get it right.

After reading every word, make several more passes through the proofs, page by page, to check all the elements listed in Standard E (see Appendix). For instance:

⁊ **CHAPTER 4**

SMALL BUSINESS AND THE LAW

u. & l.c.

A small business can be defined in various ways, according to factors such as the number of people it employs or the value of its sales each year. Generally the defintion includes businesses that have less than twenty employees. Most small businesses share two characteristics; the owner manages the business and he or she provides most of the capital.

fewer /

6pt #

Types of Business Organisation

Sole trader

For a sole trader, the business has no legal identity separate from the owner. The main advantage of sole trading is that the owner has total control. The disadvantages are:

trs

equal #

* the owner's private assets may be required to meet business debts;
* finance or external equity can be hard to obtain;
* the owner incurs captial gains tax if the business is sold; and
* the owner's illness or death may damage the business.

A sole trader pays personal income tax on the profit (income minus expenses) if the business.

o/

Partnership

The law deems that a partnership can exist where people act like partners, even though they have never explicitly agreed to form a partnership. A partnership exists when certain factors apply:

* a business is being carried on; and
* the business is being carried on in common (either by the partners or by an agent acting for them); and
* the aim of the business is profit.

Although you don't have to comply with any formalities to set up a partnership, it is wise to draw up a written agreement. It should specify the obligations, rights and liabilities of the partners in case of disputes, and such matters as capital contributions, entitlements to salaries, and rights when the partnership is terminated.

t.b.

FIGURE 8.4 A corrected proof: junior commerce textbook

* *Headings, tables, pix, captions:* If the book has a complicated scheme of headings, go through the proofs looking at nothing but the headings in order to check that every aspect—grading, wording, capitalisation, font, surrounding space—accords with the edited manuscript and the type spec. Depending on the book, you may have to make separate passes to check the tables, pix and captions.

- *Numbering of endnotes:* Verify the sequence of superscript numbers in the text and in the notes, and ensure that the last number in each chapter matches the last number in the endnotes.
- *Running heads:* Proofread the running heads and verify them for wording and style against the table of contents and the chapter openings. If an alteration is needed in the running heads, there is no need to mark each one; just mark the first occurrence and add a note such as 'change recto running head to end of chapter, p. 43'.
- *Typography:* Go through page by page once more, looking only at the typography: the spacing above and below headings, illustrations, lists and so on; the word spacing; widow lines and orphan headings; the placement of illustrations; breaks in tables and lists. Check the line breaks and word breaks. No more than two consecutive lines should end with a hyphen or begin or end with the same word; adjust the setting by taking over or taking back syllables and words or, as a last resort, rephrase. Do not end a recto page with a hyphen.

Word division (where a word is broken at the end of a line) is an area with complicated rules and many exceptions. Word-processing programs are not capable of subtleties and may produce conundrums like *co-athanger*. Rather than making a decision according to the rules in each instance, save time by following a dictionary that shows word breaks, such as *Collins Gem Dictionary of English Spelling*.

The final task is proofreading the prelims, and it's quite complex. The larger the type, the easier it is to miss a typo; carefully proofread every word and double-check displayed type. Verify the wording and page numbers given in the table of contents and the list of illustrations by turning to the relevant pages. A lot of things can go wrong in the prelims—spelling of the author's name, changed title of book, order of pages, page numbers, running heads, missing CIP data or sponsorship credit—so check and double-check.

Collating first proofs

Editors may or may not do the proofreading, but their duties usually include collating first proofs. In this procedure you review the corrections that the author and proofreader have made, and clarify and co-ordinate them for the typesetter.

Don't be afraid to disallow the author's corrections if they are excessive. Proofs are a chance to correct the typesetting, not to improve the prose, and you should make this clear to the author before she receives them. In extreme cases where an author insists on extensive changes in proof, the cost may be charged against her royalty.

The editor also reviews the proofreader's corrections in relation to the quality required. For instance, on a cheap job you might leave inconsistent capitals or hyphens if the word is seldom used, the meaning is clear, and the two forms do not occur within a page or two of each other.

Collating proofs for a book of average size typically takes a couple of days. Generally you receive the edited manuscript and two sets of corrected first proofs, the author's and the proofreader's, together with the type spec and the word list. You might get extra sets of proofs if there are joint authors or a publication committee or an outside expert; in this case, clarify which corrections have priority.

Here is a systematic procedure for collating proofs.

1 *Label what you've got:* You begin by labelling all these piles of paper as 'edited MS', '1st proofs, author's set' and so on; add the date.

2 *Transfer all the corrections to one set of proofs:* Choose the set that is most legibly marked, usually the proofreader's, to be the marked set. Place it in front of you and the author's set to one side; go through them both page by page. Assess the author's corrections and transfer the essential ones to the marked set, using the required colour code. If any essential corrections cause pagination or other problems, mark them in pencil on the marked set for later attention. Repeat this process with any other sets of proofs until you have all the approved corrections on the marked set.

3 *Check all corrections, solve problems:* Go through the marked set again page by page, ensuring that all the marks, including the proofreader's, are necessary, correct, legible and unambiguous. As you go, deal with the proofreader's queries and solve any problems created by the corrections. Do any copyfitting that is needed, as described below. On this pass you aim to fix every problem except the half-dozen or so that are really too hard.

4 *Check the headings, tables, pix, captions, running heads:* Ensure that the proofreader has done a thorough job. If not, verify them as described above.

5 *Check the typography:* Go through the marked set page by page once more to assess the typography in case the proofreader has overlooked something. On this pass, solve all outstanding queries; if any remain, tag them for the attention of the designer or the publisher, as appropriate.

6 *Check the prelims:* There is a lot of work in these few pages, as described above. The proofreader may not know the house style or may neglect to check some detail like the running heads. Take your time and get them absolutely right.

7 *Label the corrected proofs:* Label the marked set clearly as 'marked 1st proofs: use these for corrections'.

Collation sounds orderly enough as described here, but if the proofs come through in batches on a book that's running late, the degree of difficulty rises steeply. I remember the proofs of a thousand-page economic textbook with two authors and a tight schedule. For about a fortnight I received daily batches from the authors in Adelaide and Sydney and the proofreader in Byron Bay, which I had to collate and forward within twenty-four hours to the typesetter in Melbourne. Where the authors' corrections contradicted each other I had to judge which was preferable, and I had to keep careful records of style decisions so that the later batches could be made consistent with the earlier ones. Amazingly, it all got done without a hitch and we made the publication date.

Sometimes you hand over the collated proofs to the publisher as soon as they are completed, but normally you hold them until the index arrives. Authors are often flagging by this stage and need encouragement.

Long alterations

If the author requires alterations in proofs of more than a line or two (and the publisher agrees), prepare e-copy for the typesetter and attach a printout to the proofs. If there are several insertions, key them to the proofs as *Copy A*, *Copy B*, etc., thus:

1 Prepare the e-copy. With any luck, the author has sent the additions in electronic form; if not, you will have to type them. In either case, they need to be copyedited to conform with the text.
2 In the e-copy, arrange the new material under subheadings like 'Copy A, take in on proof page 179'.
3 Give the electronic file a descriptive name, such as *1st proofs Additions*.
4 On the relevant proof page, mark the appropriate place and write 'take in Copy A from 1st proofs Additions'.

Be sure to send the file and an identical printout of it with the proofs.

Copyfitting

The task of copyfitting in page proofs is the responsibility of the editor, not the proofreader. It is a challenge to your ingenuity. Authors seem to think that pages are elastic, but each one can hold only a specific number of lines. Copyfitting is required when some correction—the addition or deletion of a few words or a change to a heading—creates an extra line or removes one. Unless compensating changes are made, this small change may mean that the whole chapter, possibly the whole book, has to be repaged. A late decision to add or remove a paragraph or an illustration can create havoc.

Provided the change is essential, the editor has to make or lose lines to minimise disruption to the pagination. Copyfitting may also be required in order to place a footnote on the same page as its text indicator.

If you are absolutely sure that copyfitting is needed, it's wise to rough it out in pencil and test all the ramifications before you mark it in ink. Tackle it like this:

• Look at the problem page and one or two before and after it. Determine whether they are recto (odd-numbered) or verso (even-numbered) pages and whether moving the lines of text back or forth is likely to cause an awkward break, or detach an illustration from the related text, or create a widow line or an orphan heading.

- If the problem page is within a page or two of the end of the chapter, your task is easy. Just mark 'take back' or 'take over' on the appropriate amount of text from page to page until you reach the end of the chapter, checking that you don't create any widows or orphans on the way.
- If the problem page is not near the end of the chapter, or if the last page of the chapter is already a full page, you will have to make some adjustments. First, see whether you can accommodate the change by some simple rearrangement of space around headings and illustrations, either on the problem page or on adjacent pages.
- If not, you will have to edit the text. To lose a line, look for a paragraph with a short turnover (final line) and see if you can delete enough words to bring the turnover back to the previous line. If the writing is good, this can be really difficult to do. Adding a line is usually easier: look for a paragraph with a long turnover and add a word or two; or see if you can break a long paragraph into two; or, if the word spacing is tight, instruct the typesetter to rerun the paragraph with extra word space to make a line.
- As a last resort, facing pages can both be one line long or one line short.

When making changes for copyfitting, explain to the typesetter what you're up to by writing notes on the proofs, such as 'these alts are to make room for change on next page' or 'run facing pages evenly one line long'. If the typesetter knows what you're trying to do, she might think of a better way to do it. Also, she will know to ignore these alterations if a later change, such as the removal of an illustration, renders them unnecessary.

Ideally, the index is not prepared until the book is in final page proofs, but often you are copyfitting while the author is indexing. When you receive the index copy, you will have to check all the index entries that relate to the altered pages and correct the page numbers in the index. If subheadings or pix have been moved from one page to another, correct the page numbers in the table of contents or the list of illustrations.

Fixing layout problems

The appearance of the page should be inviting; the arrangement of text, illustrations and space helps to convey the meaning. Where two pix are separated by only a couple of lines of discussion, for instance, place the pix together at the top or bottom of a page and join the discussion of them to the previous or following text. A typesetter accustomed to bookwork will do this; desktop publishers may need instruction.

In justified text, the space between words varies. In tight setting the word space is equivalent to one-quarter of an em, or about the width of a comma. Loose or 'windy' setting may create vertical rivers of space, which draw the reader's eye down the page and hinder the lateral movement that is essential for reading. If you trust the typesetter, mark the lines or paragraphs that need adjustment and write 'spacey' in the margin. If detailed instructions are needed, indicate word-breaks and mark 'take back' for specific words and characters.

Layout problems may have to be solved by altering the text, as described under Copyfitting, above.

Checking second proofs

A second round of proofs may be needed if the first round is heavily corrected. Do not proofread second proofs word by word; just verify that all the alterations have been made correctly and no new errors have been introduced. Look at the line above and below the alteration to ensure it isn't misplaced. If any text or pic has been moved, compare the beginning of each text line against the first proofs to ensure that nothing has been left out or put in the wrong place.

Recheck the prelims. If the pagination has changed, correct the page numbers in the table of contents, the list of illustrations and the index. Check also that the extent hasn't changed. I once worked on a textbook that had a few problems and went through half a dozen rounds of proofs; somehow during the process it acquired two extra pages, creating a last-minute panic.

Adjusting for an even working

Because books are usually printed in large sheets that hold sixteen pages, it's best to aim for a total number of pages that is a multiple of sixteen, known as an even working. If there are one or two pages over, the printer will have to add at least a half-signature, which will be mostly blank. Small adjustments can often avoid such unnecessary costs. The best way to explain this is with an example.

Suppose you have a book in page proofs, and when you receive the index you realise that it's bigger than expected. Your calculations show that it is one page too long to permit an even working. No changes can be made to the pagination of the text now that it has been indexed, so the alternatives are:

- delete 55 lines from the index
- add an eight-page half-signature to the book, seven pages of which will be blank
- adjust the prelims.

Obviously the third option is the simplest and cheapest. The order of the prelims is shown in Figure 8.5, which also shows two possible solutions. In the first, the dedication is moved to the verso facing the first page of the text, thus saving two pages of the existing prelims (v and vi). In the second, the list of abbreviations is moved to the verso of the illustrations list, again saving two pages (xiii and xiv). As a last resort, you could place the dedication at the top of the imprint page, set off by large type and white space from the publication details (saving pages v and vi), but the result looks awkward and the author may object.

If there is no way to save pages in the prelims, an alternative is to set some or all of the endmatter in smaller type or double columns in order to gain the necessary space.

Existing prelims		Solution 1		Solution 2	
i	half title	i	half title	i	half title
ii	series note	ii	series note	ii	series note
iii	title	iii	title	iii	title
iv	imprint	iv	imprint	iv	imprint
v	dedication	v	contents	v	dedication
vi	(blank)	vi	contents *contd*	vi	(blank)
vii	contents	vii	list of illustrations	vii	contents
viii	contents *contd*	viii	(blank)	viii	contents *contd*
ix	list of illustrations	ix	preface	ix	list of illustrations
x	(blank)	x	preface *contd*	x	list of abbreviations
xi	preface	xi	list of abbreviations	xi	preface
xii	preface *contd*	xii	dedication	xii	preface *contd*
xiii	list of abbreviations				
xiv	(blank)				

FIGURE 8.5   Adjusting for an even working

Later proof stages

The freelance editor's responsibility generally ends with the second proofs; later stages like dyelines and machine or press proofs are checked in house. They are particularly important for heavily illustrated and colour publications. The in-house editor checks that all corrections marked on the previous stage have been made and no new errors introduced, and also verifies the accuracy of the colour and the positions and sizes of the pix. The *Style Manual*, Chapter 25, has more detail about proof and prepress stages for books.

By the time advance copies are delivered, it is too late to correct mistakes unless they are significant enough to stop the presses—such as pix that appear upside down or the omission of a signature of pages. In desperate cases significant errors of fact or attribution discovered at this stage are corrected in an errata slip attached (tipped in) to the prelims, but this is very expensive and looks amateurish.

9

Editing methods

THE REQUIREMENTS FOR substance and structure are discussed in Chapter 4 and language is covered in Chapter 5. This chapter explains in detail the tasks that make up the process of editing. They are divided, somewhat arbitrarily, into copyediting, language editing and substantive editing, but there is always considerable overlap and the editor may perform elements of all three on each pass through the manuscript.

Copyediting: a twelve-step program

Copyediting is the heart of the editorial process, comprising the essential tasks that must be done to prepare any document for publication—correcting spelling and grammar and checking for inaccuracies and inconsistencies. Copyediting can take place at various levels, depending on the quality of the original document and the time and money available. It includes language editing and it blurs into substantive editing. The advice given here is for the sort of manuscript that comes with the optimistic instruction, 'It's just a straight copyedit—shouldn't need much at all.'

I present here the systematic procedure for copyediting that I apply to each job, which I vary at times, adding more steps when I need them. It's not a franchise, just a model that you can adapt to your own working methods to increase efficiency. Because every publication is different, emphasis on their similarities enables you to concentrate on the differences that are significant. By channelling your energy you increase its strength. Applying the same framework to every job frees you, in the same way that routine does, to concentrate on the important things—but, like routine, it should not become an end in itself.

The Rough and Smooth Edits described below are notional: they could be called First and Second. They describe not an absolute state but a level of editorial achievement that depends on where you start: good writing even before the Rough Edit may be more polished than poor writing after both Rough and Smooth Edits. The aim of the Rough Edit is to identify the problems and solve all the easy ones. Having dealt with the obvious, you can read more fluently in the Smooth Edit to detect more subtle defects and determine what has to be referred to the author.

1 Appraisal

The method of appraising a document is explained in detail in Chapter 4. Don't begin editing until you have a project plan and a detailed editorial brief (Chapter 3) and have discussed your proposed changes with the author. At this time also, ask about any missing copy—acknowledgements, permissions, bibliography. Who is responsible for producing the copy, and is it your job to chase them?

2 Mark-up or apply styles

Mark-up is the means by which the editor and the designer explain the author's intentions to the typesetter, as explained in Chapter 8.

Make a complete pass through the manuscript to distinguish text from non-text. The traditional method of distinguishing non-text items—quotations, tables, exercises, captions—is colour coding, ruling coloured lines in the left margin. Instead, the publisher may require you to write design codes next to each component; thus a table might be coded *TN* for the table number, *TT* for the table title, *T1* for the column heads, *Tab* for the body of the table, and so on. I perform mark-up as a separate operation, reading just enough on each page to identify the various elements. At this stage I'm concentrating on the typography rather than the words. I also highlight the in-text citations—superscript figures or author and date—so I can verify them later against the notes and list of references.

As part of the mark-up I identify headings, but I don't grade them at this stage unless the author's scheme is really simple and consistently applied. Instead, I mark a circle next to each heading and subheading. Later, in a separate operation, I go through and write a letter in the circle to show the heading grade.

You don't expect to find everything that has to be marked on this pass, but you do all the obvious stuff. As you go, add to your editorial task list and make notes of points that the designer and typesetter need to know. Colour coding and mark-up are good jobs to do when not you're not feeling very bright—on Friday afternoon, if you can manage it. Depending on the manuscript, the time of day and my mood, I alternate mark-up with the next step, the Rough Edit of the text, chapter by chapter.

On screen, the equivalent to mark-up is applying styles. For headings, I use the defaults in Microsoft Word—Heading 1, etc. As with hard copy, on the first pass I concentrate on identifying the headings as such and don't fuss about the heading grade; later I come back and refine the hierarchy, using Outline View to promote or demote the headings from one grade to another. If the publisher requires custom styles, I then convert the default headings with global changes.

3 Rough Edit of text

Don't dither during the Rough Edit of the text; keep moving through it fairly fast. Your aim is to find all the problems, solve everything uncontroversial, and query or note everything else. Edit in ink, blue or red according to the publisher's preference, and compile a word list and a task list as you go.

In the Rough Edit you can do obvious things—correcting the style of dates, spelling out % as *per cent*, fixing the end punctuation in relation to closing quote marks. Do any bits of mark-up that were missed, along with the easy and obvious language editing, such as correcting grammatical mistakes, wrongly used words and punctuation. As you get into the later chapters, you can make some decisions about capitals and variant spellings and apply them. If heavy language editing is required, it is best to add an extra step to the process, concentrating solely on grammar and vocabulary.

Mark everything that can't be solved quickly, such as passages that seem to repeat something said earlier and names that might be misspelt, for later attention. When I encounter a paragraph of knotty prose that I can't disentangle, I pencil a wavy vertical line in the margin. I use a soft lead (2B) for queries; it's dark enough to photocopy or fax if necessary, and it's easy to rub out.

I position my queries and instructions methodically: any query that has to be referred to the author, I mark in the left margin of the manuscript; anything I think I can solve, I mark in the right margin. Similarly, I always mark the location of pix and tables in the left margin. When you're looking for these marks—to check that the table numbers are in sequence, say, or to locate a particular query—it's easy to thumb through one side of the manuscript, instead of having to study every page and read and dismiss all the irrelevant marks.

On screen, I use the Comment function for queries for the author, and I type *xxx* in the text for queries that I must attend to. Unedited passages and other problems that need attention later can be displayed in colour. Queries and instructions for the designer can be enclosed in double square brackets; be sure to mention this on the design brief. If they are numerous you can create a style for them with a name such as Design Note.

At this stage, also, it's important to make global changes. As we all know, enthusiastic global changes can have unintended consequences. A textbook in which *TOR* was spelt out as *terms of reference* with a late, hurried global change was rescued by the proofreader, who queried *unsatisfacterms of referencey*. Make global changes early, so you can detect any surprises in a later reading.

4 Rough Edit of everything else

You now do a Rough Edit of all the other parts of the manuscript besides the text. As you go, make notes of further tasks to be done and queries and instructions for the designer and typesetter.

Read the references, identifying all the problems and solving the easy ones.

The Rough Edit of the bibliography, for instance, may require three or four passes in which you concentrate on different points of style and verify alphabetical order. Then check the notes against the bibliography and against the text, and query any discrepancies; verify the sequence of the note numbers both in the text and in the notes and correlate them. For the author–date system, check the text citations against the list of references (Figure 7.3).

Similarly, work through the tables and illustrations (Chapter 6). If there are more than two or three tables, remove them all from the manuscript and work on them together to ensure consistency. For illustrations, examine the artwork and the captions and check their sequence. Edit the pix and the captions. Go through the manuscript to mark the location of the pix in the margin. Compile the artwork brief and the list of illustrations for the prelims (Chapters 3, 7), and check that permissions have been obtained (Chapter 2).

As a separate operation, go through all the headings and subheadings. Ensure they relate to the following text; correct them for sense and style; grade them according to the guide to headings (Figure 9.4); and verify them against the table of contents (Chapter 7).

Last, do a Rough Edit of the prelims (Chapter 7).

5 Smooth Edit of everything

You've knocked the manuscript into shape. Now you go through each part of it once more, but this time your aim is to solve everything you possibly can. Because you've removed most of the distractions—misspellings, grammatical mistakes, stray capitals—you can put yourself in the position of the reader, concentrating on the sense and taking a broad view of the book as a whole. At this stage you do any remaining language editing, and pick up inconsistencies and contradictions in the story or argument. This stage also reunites the text with the non-text material, so you can consider the relations between them.

Try to solve all the outstanding queries as you go, though you will usually find a half-dozen or so that are too hard. If a query or a passage of text is really holding you up, mark it and leave it until Step 6; you can then either decide that it's bearable or refer it to the author or designer.

On screen, don't make any global changes at this stage because this is your last read. You can still do a search and replace, where you change each instance individually, but any errors introduced at this stage will not be detected.

6 Compile queries for the author

All communications with the author must be tactfully phrased, and your queries should be precise and clear. The presentation of the queries depends on the production method and the author's expertise (Chapter 10). Explain to the author how she is to respond; if she is to make her changes directly in the e-copy of the edited manuscript, she may need a detailed brief.

7 Documentation, extra copy

Documentation includes the order of book, the word list, the design brief, the artwork list, and any forms that the publisher requires. The design brief explains the colour coding or styles you have used and includes the order of book, word list and style sheet. It may also include a note to the typesetter concerning global changes to be made, or you may fill in a detailed type specification (Chapter 3).

Extra copy that you prepare at this stage includes copy for running heads, jacket and cover. You may also have to prepare a list of illustrations for the prelims, a list of abbreviations, captions or a draft blurb (Chapter 7).

This stage can be delayed, or you may combine part of it with the previous one—the word list and some of the extra copy should be prepared early so they can go to the author with your queries. If you're pushed for time, you can leave most of the documentation until you finalise the job at Step 9, but it's better to complete it as far as possible while everything is fresh in your mind. At this stage also it's wise to reread the editorial brief and all correspondence and emails, just to make sure you have done everything that's asked.

Now you put the job aside (Chapter 10) until you hear from the author.

8 Incorporate author corrections

The method of incorporating the author's corrections depends on the production process (Figure 10.1). On paper, you copy them legibly by hand; on screen you make the changes on the e-copy. In either case, read the result carefully to ensure that you have not introduced any errors. When incorporating author corrections requires you to compare two documents, use the techniques described in Chapter 10.

9 Final check all

After you've made all the changes that the author wants, you're within sight of the end. You probably have half a dozen outstanding queries about meaning, style or design. Being nearly at the end of the job, you can tackle them in a determined frame of mind and either solve them or refer them to the author or designer. (Of course, we hope that there won't be any queries for the author at this stage, but occasionally, rather than delaying the whole job for a couple of minor points, you can leave them to be fixed in proof.)

On paper go through every page of the manuscript and all its bits and pieces to make sure that any instructions and remaining queries are legible and unambiguous, that they're circled (meaning 'do not set'), and that they're labelled appropriately for the author or the designer or the typesetter. Make sure that no unwanted marks remain.

On screen, similarly, search for *xxx* or whatever you have used to mark queries for yourself, make sure they have been resolved, and erase the query marker. If you have used Track Changes, ensure that all changes have been accepted or rejected. At this stage, run a spell check and a grammar check (to detect missing and misplaced words) and remove double word spaces. It's important to do these operations last, so they will catch any errors caused by inserting the author's corrections.

Ensure that you have prepared all the extra copy that is required. Complete the documentation. When you have edited on paper, you can now go straight to Step 12.

10 The printout

For screen editing there is an extra step, vital for quality control. Having printed the edited manuscript, skim it for sense and mark it up (Chapter 8). You will probably notice errors: in some cases you can simply mark them and leave them for the typesetter to correct, depending on the expectations agreed in the editorial brief. Note on the front page of the printout 'corrections marked on hard copy have not been made in e-copy'.

11 Proofing

With modern production methods, publishers are expecting editors to take on the responsibilities once assumed by compositors, proofreaders and typesetters. Step 11 goes beyond the traditional definition of copyediting a manuscript and results in a first or even a second proof, taking the job to a later stage in the production process.

- *First proof:* The editorial brief may require you to proofread the printout of the edited manuscript and key in the corrections. Methods for proofreading are described in Chapter 8. You do not need to reprint unless the alterations are extensive. Note on the front page of the printout 'all corrections marked on hard copy have been made in e-copy', and make sure it's true.
- *Second proof:* In addition, you may be required to print and proofread the corrected pages.

12 Despatch or handover

Now you've reached the last step. Fill in the handover form or write a covering letter listing any remaining problems, such as copy still to come or outstanding queries (Chapter 3 under Covering Letter). Record any decisions agreed to during the editorial process that will alter costs, such as an increase in the number of pix. Freelances prepare the invoice at this stage.

When sending e-copy as an email attachment or on a disk, make sure you send the final version and include all the necessary files. The printout should agree exactly with the e-copy. For post or courier, stack up the edited manuscript, artwork, documentation, invoice and disks, and make sure it's all present and correct. Package it (Chapter 10), and despatch.

Language editing

People talk about the mystique of editing, the attitude of mind, the innate intuition that makes a good editor. Some claim that editing is a vocation or an art. It is not a creative art like painting or composing, but it could be considered a reactive art like acting or surgery. Personally, I see it as a craft.

When I am editing, I ask myself a series of questions about every sentence. And this applies whether it's an accounting textbook, a verse novel or a scholarly biography.

- Is this sentence needed?
- Does it belong in this paragraph, under this heading, in this chapter?
- Does it follow logically from the one before?
- Is it precise and succinct? Is it well-written and grammatically correct? Apply the principles of good writing.
- Is its content probably accurate?
- Does its content need to be supported by referencing? (Well, maybe I don't ask that for the verse novel.)
- Does the sentence contain any specialist terms that need to be explained, either in the text or in a footnote or a glossary?
- Does it contradict statements made elsewhere in the book?
- Is it consistent in terminology and style (spelling, capitals, hyphens) with the rest of the book?
- Does it contain any cross-references (to another chapter, a table, an illustration) that need to be checked? Or should a cross-reference be added?

The process of answering these questions is called language editing or line editing, and it is one component of copyediting.

Language editing requires the most detailed concentration and is mentally exhausting. If I do it for more than six or seven hours a day, I begin to make stupid mistakes. Vary it with less demanding tasks like correspondence, mark-up and sorting pix.

Language editing can be performed at various levels; some jobs call for intervention, some for a delicate touch. The level of language editing is dictated partly by the quality of the writing and partly by the budget. If the publisher has asked for a quick-and-dirty or the budget is absurdly low, you can only correct the most egregious errors. It is easy to slip into editing language more closely than the budget allows. The running sheet (Figure 3.1) enables you to monitor your progress; if you are falling behind on the time allowed for language editing, you will have to be less fussy. If it's bearable, leave it. You might find it painful to pass up opportunities for improving the text, but you can only do what you're paid for.

We will look at three samples demonstrating different levels of language editing. In each case the edited version shown is only one of many possibilities. For clarity the sentences are shown on separate lines, but in reality they would be run on.

Medium

Normally there is time for a medium level of language editing, as shown in Figure 9.1. The breezy, colloquial tone of this example suits the intended readers, so it needed little attention. I only tweaked the language, straightening out the second and fourth sentences and making slight alterations to the next two. The edited version in Figure 9.1 is an example not of deathless prose but of what can be done in the time. With a larger budget, the writing could be further improved—the third sentence, with its lumbering gerund and anti-climactic ending, cries out for rephrasing—but on this sort of job there simply isn't time.

Extreme

In contrast, Figure 9.2 shows a manuscript that needs heroic editing and has an adequate budget for it. In the edited version, every sentence has been rewritten. The author's style is verbose: as well as improving the flow of the language, the editing has reduced the wordcount by almost 20 per cent. If this reduction can be maintained throughout, the book will be smaller and therefore cheaper to produce.

Original	Edited
[1] You are probably starting to realise that selling can be a complex business.	[1] You are probably starting to realise that selling can be a complex business.
[2] Not only do you have to understand the standard attributes of each product you are selling, you also have to be aware of the drivers that influence each customer.	[2] Not only do you have to understand the standard attributes of each product you are selling, but you also have to be aware of what drives each customer.
[3] Presenting benefits that meet the tangible needs of the customer is not difficult.	[3] Presenting benefits that meet the tangible needs of the customer is not difficult.
[4] You will find that, as you get more practice, once you have chosen the alternatives to suggest, you will be very familiar with the subject matter and you can relax and enjoy the process.	[4] As you get more practice, you will find that, once you have chosen the alternatives to suggest, you will be familiar with the subject matter and you can relax and enjoy the process.
[5] It is a little trickier to directly address the intangible needs that a customer might have.	[5] It is trickier to deal with the intangible needs that a customer might have.
[6] For starters, how do you recognise what these needs are?	[6] To start with, how do you recognise what these needs are?
[7] Once again, your active listening and questioning skills are the key.	[7] Once again, your active listening and questioning skills are the key.
[8] Train yourself to listen carefully to what each customer says and think about why he or she chose those particular words.	[8] Train yourself to listen carefully to what customers say and think about why they chose those particular words.

FIGURE 9.1 Medium-level language editing: TAFE textbook on customer service

Original	Edited
[1] Information at the level of the implementing agency is seen as more important than community may view it, but often less important than the Managing Agency.	[1] The implementing agency values information more highly than the community does, but less highly than the managing agency.
[2] Again, information is relatively rich, in that there is constant contact with the work itself, therefore words on a page relate to the direct experience of community realities as experienced by agency staff.	[2] At this level, information is relatively rich because of constant contact with the work itself; words on a page relate to the direct experience of community realities by agency staff.
[3] Because of their constant contact with the people and the work, there may well be assumptions made by implementing agency staff that leave reports to partners, nonsensical or at best incomplete.	[3] Because of their intimate knowledge of the situation, staff may make assumptions in their reports that render them hard to understand for those with no inside knowledge.
[4] Information needs would still be weighted in favour of needs for implementation, as opposed to needs for accountability or partner or donor education.	[4] At this level information is needed for implementation, rather than for accountability or for educating partners or donors.

FIGURE 9.2   Extreme language editing: manual for project officers

Light

Some material demands light language editing, and some publications cannot afford anything more. As Chapter 5 explained, the editing of transcriptions requires special care. Figure 9.3 shows how the editor can make reading easier with extra punctuation and judicious interpolations while faithfully representing the speaker's expression.

Specialist content

Normal reading focuses on the content words and passes over the function words. In language editing, especially of specialist non-fiction, a useful technique is to reverse this and read for syntax rather than sense. When reading in this way you ignore most of the nouns, verbs, adjectives and adverbs and pay attention to the function words and phrases, partially parsing each sentence to expose its framework. Your brain takes in something like this:

> It is important to recognise that the *rhubarb rhubarb* of the *rhubarb* was a product of the *rhubarb* which played a vital role in the *rhubarb rhubarb* due to the fact that the *rhubarb rhubarb* was accepted by the *rhubarb*.

Original	Edited
[1] Emu big story a lot of story, when we hunt emu, that is early job, get up way before sunrise; walk miles to get them, we go to their favourite watering hole, that's where they use to take their bath, morning shower and all that.	[1] Emu big story, a lot of story. When we hunt emu, that is early job. Get up way before sunrise. Walk miles to get them. We go to their favourite watering hole, that's where they used to take their bath, morning shower and all that.
[2] This was a real professional job, sharpshooters' job, real hunters that knew how to get those emu because emu rare, rare meat, you go a long way to get them.	[2] This was a real professional job, sharpshooters' job [with spears], real hunters that knew how to get those emu, because emu rare, rare meat; you go a long way to get them.
[3] Maybe 3/5 men in the tribe that were professionals, they go to dried out creek bed or watering hole and wait.	[3] Maybe three to five men in the tribe that were professionals, they go to dried-out creek bed or watering hole and wait.
[4] So what they would do, still early; climb up a tree near water hole, where the emu tracks were to the water hole before sunrise, climb up tree, they would see them come down to the watering hole, baby chicks, mother everything even kangaroos they used to come down, the hunters were waiting up tree, the emu have two guards standing either side while the other emus go for a drink or swim, emu guards looking this way, that way, looking up, they smart.	[4] So what they would do, still early, climb up a tree near water hole, where the emu tracks were to the water hole. Before sunrise, climb up tree. They would see them come down to the watering hole, baby chicks, mother, everything. Even kangaroos, they used to come down. The hunters were waiting up tree. The emu have two guards standing either side while the other emus go for a drink or swim; emu guards looking this way, that way, looking up; they smart.

FIGURE 9.3   Light language editing of nonstandard English: transcription of Aboriginal stories

This method of reading shows up the syntax and punctuation of the sentence so you can see whether they need correction. In the example:

- The introductory phrase, *It is important to recognise that*, could perhaps be deleted.
- The relative pronoun *which* alerts you to a relative clause that needs to be set off with commas (unless it is a defining clause).
- The circumlocutions *played a vital role in* and *due to the fact that* could perhaps be replaced by *shaped* or *influenced* and *because*.
- The word *by* signals the passive voice, which should be made active if possible.

Later, of course, you will read the text again in the normal manner to deal with the sense and terminology.

Substantive editing

Substantive editing can be defined as tailoring the structure, content, language and style of a publication so that the intended reader will find it attractive because it is clear, interesting, memorable, logical and easy to understand. It is, in fact, what the author should have done. The need for it is quite obvious, and it always requires close consultation between editor, author and publisher.

Substantive editing can take place at various levels. It is conceptual in nature and requires imaginative and exploratory thinking. It's not rarefied, though. The editing of structure can seem like woodwork—examining the grain, shaping pieces to fit, dovetailing the joints and sanding everything smooth.

At the simplest level, substantive editing may consist of changing the title of the book to reflect its contents: say, from *The Backyard Goat* to *Making Cheese at Home*. The other end of the spectrum is heroic editing, where the editor in effect writes the book from notes supplied by the author. For this level of intervention you have to get right inside the material so that you know it well enough to completely reorder and regroup headings, sections of text and individual paragraphs and sentences. There is no clear line between substantive editing and copyediting: all editors suggest structural alterations like adjusting the heading hierarchy and swapping information between the text and the captions, notes or appendixes.

On-screen substantive editing requires high levels of expertise in editing on screen, in restructuring text, and in version control. It is best to develop your skills on short publications or those that have a heading for almost every paragraph, such as textbooks and manuals.

Make sure the patient is alive

There are crucial questions to be answered before substantive editing can begin.[1] You should have a detailed project plan (Chapter 3). From this you know the proposed specifications of the publication—price, extent, format, pix, paper, print run—and the timeframe for the work. In addition, you want to know:

- the present specifications: wordcount, number of pix
- what others say about the manuscript: consult the publisher, obtain readers' reports
- what the author is like: consult your client, read the job file, talk to the author
- in what way the substance of the manuscript is to be altered
- how much time and money are available
- whether the author will be involved.

Assume you've answered all these questions and examined the manuscript. You know what you're dealing with and have a picture of what's needed to make this manuscript into a good publication. You've arranged with the author or others to supply missing material, and you have an agreement to go ahead with the substantive edit. Now you have to get stuck into it.

Analyse the structure

You use your understanding of the hierarchy of divisions (Figure 4.1) to create the guide to headings, as shown in Figure 9.4. The purpose of the guide is to reveal structural faults and enable you to assess the coverage and the proportions. For instance, the author may have:

- bitten off more than she can chew
- chewed more than she has bitten off
- remembered something she meant to say earlier and shoved it in somewhere to save reorganising or rewriting
- introduced a completely new subject into the middle of a section that she has headed with an unrelated topic name
- suddenly moved to a different form of arrangement — say, from chronological to thematic.

Where the author has provided headings, be cautious in transferring them directly to the guide to headings. First, verify that they do in fact describe the subsequent text. An author who needs substantive editing is capable of following the heading 'Tree Planting' with a discussion of salinity, wildlife corridors, land regeneration, biodiversity, or even landscape-as-process.

A guide to headings is not normally needed for copyediting, but in substantive editing it is invaluable for planning your work and for explaining proposed changes to the publisher and the author. Substantive editing consists of more than just rearranging the hierarchy, but the guide to headings is an essential tool. The headings listed in the guide will not necessarily appear in the book; they may be like scaffolding, essential during construction but distracting on the finished product.

Prepare the guide to headings

The guide to headings relates only to the editing process; it is not part of the documentation that accompanies the manuscript for design and typesetting.

The guide displays the headings and subheadings used in the manuscript with indents that show their grade in the heading hierarchy. A typical chapter ought to have no more than half a dozen main subheadings, and few of these should need more than half a dozen sub-subheadings. Once a subheading has been used, it applies to all subsequent material until a heading of equal or greater importance occurs.

The first grade of subheadings is known as *A*, the second as *B*, and so on. If there is a second sequence of headings — say, for boxed text or exercises — label them *X, Y, Z*. A third sequence — say, in the endmatter — can be labelled *AA, BB, CC*. The guide need not show every grade of heading; it is tedious to copy D-grade and below, and the guide is best kept to a manageable length of two or three pages. It's handy to show the length and location of sections by noting the page numbers on which they start.

Microsoft Word has a tool for structural editing called Outline View, which you can use after styles have been applied to the headings. In Outline View you can create the guide to headings with a mouse-click, displaying all the headings, or only the major grades, or headings plus the first line of text. You can promote or demote headings with a click on the toolbar, and drag headings, with their associated text, from one place to another. If you are less than fully confident with Outline View, copy the chapter into a test file and work on that. Outline View is also useful for copyediting the headings, enabling you to compare them and alter the wording to make it consistent or change caps to lower case.

In a typical guide to headings, as in Figure 9.4, the chapter headings are flush to the left margin, the A-heads are at the first indent and the B-heads at the second; page numbers provide an indication of length. On screen, Outline View differentiates heading grades with fonts as well as indents, but it does not show length. In Figure 9.4, note that the hierarchy is not mechanically applied but emerges from the content. For instance, the Introduction has only one grade of headings, which you would expect to be A-heads. But grading them A would exaggerate their importance and would visually overwhelm the small amount of text that follows them, so they are graded as B. In Chapters 1 and 2, the A-heads are not necessarily followed by B-heads.

Arrange the text

When you've organised the guide to headings logically, you then rework the actual manuscript to make it fit the guide, imposing or rearranging the structure and changing the presentation of information as described below. When you're restructuring, keep the guide within reach and consult it often. The rearrangement of the text and the refinement of the guide to headings are a circular process of constant interaction.

If the manuscript requires heavy language editing as well as structural editing, do it early, after you have established a rough order. In the language editing, skip (and mark as unedited) any passages that seem likely to be discarded for one reason or another, such as repetition or irrelevance. The language editing familiarises you with the content of the manuscript and the author's thought processes and habits of expression, and helps you to refine the guide to headings.

As you are working, you will delete passages and possibly whole sections. If you are using actual scissors and paste, keep all the important material on your desk and drop everything else on the floor—you know that everything that's on your desk has to be fitted in somewhere. On screen, create a file named *Dump* or *Discards* and place all deletions in it. Before you archive the rejected material, review it for relevance and reinstate it if necessary.

Having put the text in order, edit the connections, referencing and illustrations to make them fit. Read through everything on a clean printout to ensure that no substantive problems remain. After the substantive editing is complete, the manuscript may still need to undergo some or all of the twelve steps of copyediting described above.

Division	Begins on MS p.
Introduction	1
Research questions	4
Research methods	5
Ethical and political issues	5
Structure of the book	7
1 Policing in a multicultural society	9
Police racism	14
Insensitivity to language and cultural differences	18
Prejudice and stereotyping	20
Over-policing: unfair targeting and harassment	21
Abuse of power and excessive use of force	23
Attitudes of minority groups towards police	25
2 Discrimination and police work	28
Reactive policing	29
Problems with statistical evidence	30
Controlling for legal and socio-demographic factors	31
Observational studies	33
Social disadvantage, offending and over-policing	35
Institutionalised racism	38
Organisation of policing	40
Legal and management focus of police work	41
Police culture	43
Relationship with the demands of police work	45

Ⓐ Ⓑ

FIGURE 9.4   Part of a guide to headings showing two grades of subheading: monograph on police culture

Imposing a structure

Very often, structural editing consists of imposing the structure, setting up the framework. How do you do it? Manuscripts are so infinitely various that it is difficult to advise, but here is one approach.

1 Take a chunk of text—say, twenty to fifty pages. If you can discern divisions in the manuscript, take a whole chapter or section. Choose a bit that looks easy; the knowledge you gain from it will help with the more difficult parts.

2 Identify or create the main headings and label them A. Establish where each A section begins and ends.

3 Decide whether the A headings are in a logical order or should be rearranged or moved to another part of the manuscript.

4 Take one A section and identify or create the principal secondary headings within it. Label them B.

5 Decide whether some B sections should be moved into other A sections or into other parts of the manuscript.

6 You will be left with a mass of material, possibly with different kinds of division and heading, some but not all of which can be classified as C.

7 Take one C section. And so on.

The same method of imposing a structure applies to fiction. A novel works by means of narrative, possibly with devices like flashbacks, change of voice and deliberate repetition. One way to approach it is to divide the text into scenes or units and summarise each of them in a few words—'beach party', 'Tim's first quarrel with Tracey'. These summaries can be treated like headings and rearranged as above, though of course the summaries will not appear in the book.

Rearranging a structure

The structural editing of books is difficult to demonstrate. In what follows, the table of contents and number of pages stand for topics and the depth of their treatment, to give an idea of how the process works. (The contents of the contents, as it were, are discussed in Chapter 7.)

Sometimes the structure of a book is poorly thought out, as shown in Figure 9.5. The proportions of this book are faulty, with chapters varying in length from 4 pages to 80 pages. As we saw in Chapter 4, for the division 'chapter' to have any meaning the chapter lengths should be more or less equal—at least within cooee of each other. The solution that I arrived at is shown in the table, but it is not the only possibility; for instance the revised Chapters 3 and 5 could be further split.

At the opposite extreme, the author has a predetermined structure in mind and distorts the material to fit it, as shown in Figure 9.6. Again, the chapter titles and number of pages represent the coverage of the various topics; I have added the chapter numbers in the left-hand column for purposes of discussion. This book contained a lot of useful information for its readers, community development workers, but it required substantive editing on a grand scale. Here are some strategies that I used, but again, my solutions are not the only ones.

- I condensed and combined the Preface and the Introduction.
- I combined all the theoretical material into one chapter (revised Chapter 1) so that practically minded readers could skip it.
- Evaluation was a major theme in several chapters, so I combined all the discussion into one chapter (revised Chapter 7) and called it by that name to emphasise its importance.

Original table of contents	no. of pages	Revised table of contents	no. of pages
1 Mathematical Reference tables, fractions, decimals, square root	14	**1 Mathematics**	60
		Arithmetic [*all ch. 1*]	14
		Geometry [*all ch. 2*]	32
2 Geometrical Four-sided figures, three-sided figures, circular figures, miscellaneous figures	32	Rules of thumb [*all ch. 3*]	12
		Square and cube roots [*part ch. 16*]	2
		2 Workshop	25
3 Rules of Thumb Approximations, averages, percentages, various formulas	12	Concrete [*part ch. 4*]	7
		Solder [*part ch. 4*]	2
		Steel [*part ch. 4*]	2
4 Application Concrete, soldering, fixing and fastening zinc-coated steel with adhesives, galvanised and other coated steel sheets, glossary of terms	16	Wire [*all ch. 5*]	8
		Nails and rivets [*part ch. 15*]	2
		Electricity [*part ch. 16*]	3
		Speed of circular saw [*part ch. 16*]	1
5 Wire Facts Wire ropes, facts about wire	8	**3 Crops and Livestock**	79
		Pasture grasses [*part ch. 6*]	27
6 Grass Crops Pastures, legumes and pasture grasses	56	Legumes [*part ch. 6*]	25
		Silage [*part ch. 7*]	3
		Weight tables [*part ch. 7*]	2
7 Crop Reference Silage data, bushel weight, pasture and crop seeds	8	Grain and stock feed [*part ch. 15*]	2
		Orchard [*all ch. 13*]	4
		Stable [*all ch. 10, part ch. 12*]	12
8 Business and Legal The farm as a business, finance, insurance, legal matters	80	Dairy [*all ch. 14*]	4
		4 Weather and Water	36
		[*all ch. 9*]	26
9 Meteorological Weather patterns, statistics, etc., how to read synoptic charts	26	[*all ch. 11*]	10
		5 Business and Law	80
		[*all ch. 8*]	
10 Shoeing Helpful hints on horse-shoeing	10	**Glossary**	3
		[*parts ch. 4, ch. 16*]	
11 Water Use Miscellaneous tables, friction head of water, converting the pressure of water	10		
12 General Australian air routes, world times. Are you a racing fan?	6		
13 Fruit Useful conversions	4		
14 Dairy Dairy weights and measures, average composition of dairy products. Oestrus table, animal pulse, etc.	4		
15 Weight Measuring grain and stock feeds, number of nails per kg, weight of rivets	6		
16 Handy Hints Recommended speed of circular saws, electrical, origin of terms, speeding up calculations	4		

FIGURE 9.5 Faulty proportions: handbook for farmers

- Several chapters had detailed descriptions of techniques, such as personality tests and budgeting, which interrupted the flow of the exposition, so I moved them to an appendix.
- The original Chapter 6, 'Program Manager—Development', turned out to be about skills and training. I replaced the word *development* with synonyms throughout the chapter to prevent confusion with the main topic of the book, community development.
- A detailed and illuminating account of a community consultation was hidden by the imposed structure under the title 'Project Management—Implementation' (original Chapter 13). I made a feature of it by renaming the chapter as a case study (revised Chapter 6), and noted that it could be a selling point.
- References had been listed and annotated at the end of each chapter, with some titles cited in full three or four times. I converted the annotations into a brief bibliographical essay for each chapter, using author–date citations, and consolidated the full citations into a single list in the endmatter.

For this title I suggested another strategy that is not apparent in Figure 9.6. The references for each chapter included long lists of web addresses or URLs. These are better presented online, where the reader can access them with a click, than in print, where he has to copy-type long strings of characters accurately into a browser. I suggested removing the URLs from the book and setting up an associated web page with links to them. Not only is the reader better served, but also the URLs can be updated more frequently on screen than in print.

Changing the presentation

One valuable technique in substantive editing is to alter the form in which information is presented. The decision to change the presentation depends on knowledge of the readers—what would be best for them?—and the substance and context of the information. As the note to Standard C2.3 points out, tabulated material may be better presented as part of the text, number-laden text as a chart or table, a descriptive passage as a diagram, and a lengthy digression or background paper as an appendix, as in this book. When you are repurposing a document, you may condense or combine sections, or rewrite them in a different register, or convert them to lists or charts to suit the needs of the new readership.

Figure 9.7 shows information in a high-school biology textbook presented in three different ways: as a bullet list, as headings with text, and as a text table (that is, a table comprising words rather than numbers). The example is rather forced, but you can see the possibilities. The second option provides scope for more detail, if that is what is required; the table would probably be easiest for the students to understand. (Lists are discussed in Chapter 5 under Enumerations and tables in Chapter 6.)

Original table of contents	Revised table of contents
Preface [2 pp.] Introduction [10 pp.] Glossary [8 pp.]	Introduction [8 pp.] *[includes preface]*
The Ideas Units [1] Development—The Context [10 pp.] [2] Development—Ideas and Issues [15 pp.] [3] Development—The Relationships [15 pp.]	1 Context and issues [30 pp.] *[chs 1, 2, parts of chs 6, 7]* 2 The effective program manager [29 pp.] *[ch. 3, parts of chs 4, 5, 6]*
The People Units [4] Program Manager—Role [12 pp.] [5] Program Manager—Thinking [9 pp.] [6] Program Manager—Development [15 pp.]	3 Managing organisations [32 pp.] *[ch. 9, parts of chs 6, 7, 12]* 4 Managing programs [24 pp.] *[part ch. 4, chs 8, 10]*
The Management Units [7] Management of Organisations [10 pp.] [8] Management of Programs [9 pp.] [9] Management of Policy [4 pp.]	5 Defining and planning a project [23 pp.] *[ch. 11, part of ch. 13]* 6 Case study: Community consultation [24 pp.] *[most of ch 13]*

The Project Units
[10] Project Management—Levels [11 pp.]
[11] Project Management—Definition
      [21 pp.]
[12] Project Management—Planning [24 pp.]
[13] Project Management—Implementation
      [25 pp.]
[14] Project Management—Completion
      [15 pp.]
	7 Evaluation [33 pp.]
	[ch. 14, parts of chs 5, 12]
	
	Appendix: Tools and techniques [8 pp.]
	Glossary [10 pp.]
	References [5 pp.]
	Index

FIGURE 9.6   **Too much structure: textbook for community development workers**

The presentation can be changed not only within the print medium, but also from print to screen. For remarks on single-source publishing, see Chapter 4.

Ceteris paribus

Because the scale and scope of editing are contingent on many factors, you often have to weigh up difficult choices. When there are equally good arguments for and against a particular course of action, don't dither. Consult the author and publisher if necessary, and then boldly make up your mind.

BULLET LIST

Consumer organisms are grouped as follows:
*   *Herbivores* obtain energy and nutrients from producer organisms. Examples are kangaroos, rabbits, sheep and cattle.
*   *Carnivores* feed on other consumer organisms The dingo and the domestic cat are examples.
*   *Omnivores* consume both producer organisms and consumer organisms. Examples are brushtail possums, pigs and humans.
*   *Scavengers* are consumer organisms that feed on the remains of other consumers. An example is the Tasmanian devil.
*   *Parasites* derive their food, usually in a partly digested form, from another organism (the host). Ticks are parasites on many Australian mammals, and mistletoe is a parasite of eucalyptus.

HEADINGS AND TEXT

CONSUMER ORGANISMS

Consumer organisms are grouped according to their food. We will look at the various categories.

Herbivores

Herbivores obtain energy and nutrients from producer organisms. Examples are kangaroos, rabbits, sheep and cattle.

Carnivores

Commonly termed meat-eaters, these 'higher' consumers feed on other consumer organisms. The dingo and the domestic cat are examples.

Omnivores

Named from the Latin word *omni*, meaning 'everything', these consume both producer organisms and consumer organisms. Examples are brushtail possums, pigs and humans . . .

TEXT TABLE

Consumer organisms are grouped according to their food, as shown in the table.

Table: Consumer organisms by source of food

Consumer organism	Food source	Examples of consumers
herbivore	producer organisms	kangaroos, rabbits, sheep, cattle
carnivore	other consumer organisms	dingo, cat
omnivore	producer organisms and consumer organisms	brushtail possums, pigs, humans . . .

FIGURE 9.7   Three ways of presenting the same information: high-school biology textbook

There are no hard-and-fast rules in editing, but here are some guiding principles to apply when all other things are equal. They are arranged in alphabetical, not priority, order because some of them are mutually exclusive or contradictory. Don't try to apply them all at once; just pick one that justifies the decision you must make.

- Don't antagonise the author.
- Don't make work for yourself.
- Eliminate meaningless variation.
- Eschew pedantry.
- Evade responsibility and get someone else to decide.
- Get the book out.
- Get it right.
- If it's bearable, leave it.
- Make every word tell.
- Remove distractions.
- Remove unnecessary words.
- What's best for the reader?
- Will it sell more copies?

10

Working with documents and files

MANY BOOKS ABOUT editing tell you what to do, but few of them tell you how to go about it. Previous chapters have explained editorial tasks such as appraisal, substantive editing, language editing and proofreading. This chapter discusses production methods, software and hardware, and explains how to work with paper and electronic documents.

Screed or screen?

Editors agree that hard copy is easier to read than a screen and that they are more likely to detect errors in hard copy. Some jobs are still done entirely by hand, but most of the time editors work on screen using Microsoft Word. Before beginning work on screen many editors read, or at least skim, the whole manuscript in hard copy and note the editorial problems. It is inefficient, though, to fully edit on hard copy and then key in the corrections.

The screen encourages you to focus on fine detail—words and sentences—and you can lose the threads that link paragraphs and chapters to make a good book. After you've edited on screen and are reading through the printout, it may be quite plain that paragraphs are in the wrong order, or that a statement contradicts something said a few pages back, or that a connection needs to be made with some earlier mention. Books edited entirely on screen may be bitty, with the information chunked in screenfuls rather than in paragraphs, sections and chapters.

Copyediting on screen can seem faster than on paper, but if you count in the downtime for incompatible files, crashes, printer jams and oops-I-didn't-mean-to-do-that, and add the time spent explaining the technology to the author, it can work out much the same. Personally, I find it difficult to grapple with the complex themes and concepts of a scholarly book on screen, especially for substantive editing; for such jobs I prefer to edit the text on paper, occasionally referring to the e-copy to use the search function. But the notes and bibliography are better edited on screen, because search and replace helps with consistency of details like punctuation. For lighter books, especially if the language needs serious editing, the screen is preferable.

Production methods

The editor's working copy may arrive as either hard copy or e-copy. There are two possible production methods for each, as shown in Figure 10.1. The editor's and typesetter's role are different in each case, and you must find out which method is to be used. You also need to know whether the typesetter is accustomed to bookwork; a desktop publisher may not be familiar with book industry norms or traditional proof correction marks.

When the editorial brief requires a marked-up printout of work edited on screen, the freelance editor should be careful to cost it correctly. If you also proof-read the printout and make further corrections, you have actually performed five

Method	Editor's task	Typesetter's task
Hard-copy edit, then rekey	This is the traditional method, in which the editor works on hard copy that is then key-boarded by the typesetter. All editorial changes and mark-up are handwritten on the hard copy.	The typesetter keyboards all the material, incorporating editorial changes and formatting according to the mark-up.
Hard-copy edit, then set from disk	The editor works on a printout of the e-copy that is to be used for typesetting. All editorial changes and mark-up are handwritten on the hard copy.	The typesetter incorporates editorial changes in the e-copy and formats it according to the mark-up.
On-screen edit without formatting	The editor does the copy-editing on screen, and also prints and marks up a hard copy.	The typesetter removes all formatting from the e-copy and applies new formatting according to the mark-up.
On-screen edit and format	The editor does all the editing on screen, and also applies styles and other formatting, becoming a de facto typesetter.	

FIGURE 10.1 Editor's and typesetter's tasks (excluding page make-up), using different production methods

jobs—copyediting the manuscript, setting the type, pulling the proof, proofreading, and correcting the proof. You are delivering not a copyedited manuscript but a corrected first proof. This added value should be reflected in your fee.

Compiling author queries

As Chapter 3 explained, all your communications with the author must be considerate. The technique of presenting queries varies according to the author's abilities and the production process (Figure 10.1). If possible, send her the edited manuscript. This saves you the trouble of preparing a list of queries, and it is reassuring for the author because it gives her control: she can examine all the editorial changes and approve or reject or query each one.

Before you send the manuscript to the author, solve all your own queries and remove them, and check that your queries to her are legible, precise, and diplomatically phrased. The wording should be unambiguous. It is infuriating when you query an obscure initialism by asking 'sp. out?' and the author responds with 'yes' instead of telling you what it stands for. When Jim Hacker of *Yes, Minister* lifted his pen to write 'Balls' in the margin of a report, he was persuaded by his tactful secretary to substitute 'Round objects'. In due course the question came back in impeccable civil service phrasing: 'Who is Round and to what does he object?'

In a hand-edited manuscript, the editorial changes are marked in ink and the author queries are pencilled in the left margin. The author replies by writing on the manuscript, preferably in pencil, or by typing a list of replies. A manuscript edited on screen may be sent to the author as e-copy or as a printout; in either case, the editorial changes are shown with Track Changes and the queries with the Comments function (see below). The author either makes changes directly in the e-copy or writes on the printout. With the edited manuscript send the word list and any extra copy you have prepared, like captions or a list of abbreviations, so the author can approve them.

Before you send e-copy to the author, talk to her about her word-processing skills and find out what she needs to know. If she is to work on the e-copy, you may have to write a lengthy letter describing how to view changes and comments and how to accept, reject or add changes. You must be able to distinguish her changes from yours and see clearly whether your queries have been answered. There are various ways to do this:

- Ask the author to apply a particular colour to her changes and to show deletions with strikethrough, and explain the techniques for doing so.
- Alternatively, send the author a password-protected file of the edited manuscript with Track Changes turned on. The password prevents the author from inadvertently turning off Track Changes. Whatever she types in will appear in a different colour to the editorial changes. When you receive the manuscript from her, unprotect it and accept or reject the various changes.
- If you dislike working with Track Changes, ask the author to view the edited manuscript against her original using the Compare Documents function.[1]

When sending e-copy to the author, remember to fax or post items that exist only in hard copy, such as edited artwork and tables. Here are some other points to note:

- Where a manuscript has undergone extreme editing, the sheer quantity of the changes might frighten the author. Encourage her to view the manuscript, in the first instance, with Track Changes hidden.
- An author who uses an antiquated word processor should be able to read your files if they are saved in Rich Text Format.
- Microsoft Word's default style for the Comment reference in the text is small and hard to see. An author who is working on screen can use the search function to find the Comment references, but if she prefers a printout alter the default style to something large and bold.

The most time-consuming method of preparing author queries is to type a list. These 'author queries' are actually 'editor's queries', so head the list with that name—or, if you need to be especially tactful, 'editor's suggestions'. The location of the queries is shown by page numbers, so check that the author has a copy of the manuscript with the same page numbers as yours; the publisher may have had the manuscript 'cleaned up' to remove unwanted formatting, which alters the pagination. If you and the author agree on the page numbers, you don't need to locate the queries by line numbers: refer to the top, middle and bottom of the page as *a*, *b*, *c* and quote a few words. Thus *118a* signifies a query in the top third of page 118. Be sure to explain to the author that you're using this system. If the pagination differs, you will have to describe the location of the queries by referring to headings and other landmarks: 'mid 3rd para after Table 4.2'.

Software

Over the past decade, editors have added knowledge of sophisticated computer programs to their repertoire of skills.

Microsoft Word

Microsoft's word-processing program is the industry standard, and editors have to be proficient in it. You might learn the basics in a formal course, but you need to adapt your skills to the particular requirements of editing text. This is too big a subject to cover here; see the bibliography for resources.

A thorough knowledge of Microsoft Word isn't sufficient: you also have to work quickly. As a freelance, the faster you edit, the more money you make; speeding up your word processing can improve your personal bottom line. If you can't touch-type, find a tutor program and practise until you achieve a respectable speed.

Everyone develops their own ways of working, but here are some tips that I find useful. As a general rule, keyboard commands are quicker than the mouse.

I keep a list beside my screen of half-a-dozen commands that look as though they might be useful. After a few months I find that I have incorporated some of them into my editing and completely ignored others, so I prepare a new list. Word allows you to set up your own keyboard commands and also to create macros for repeated tasks.

It's worthwhile training yourself to use the mouse in your left hand because this spreads the action between both hands, thus helping to prevent RSI. For light editing where I'm making only occasional corrections, I point and select with the mouse while my right hand is at the right end of the keyboard ready to add punctuation or hit the Delete key. Thus to remove semi-colons at the end of each item in a list, I simply point with the left hand and delete with the right. A scroll-wheel on the mouse also serves to spread the load; you can move around the document with your left hand on the mouse instead of using the arrow keys and Page Up and Page Down with your right.

The Word tool called Track Changes is convenient for showing the author exactly what you have done and, as we have seen, if she can accept and reject the changes in the e-copy it saves editorial time. Turn Track Changes off when running routine global changes or macros such as removing extra paragraph returns and replacing double quotation marks with single. If you copy and paste material that is corrected with Track Changes into a new document, all changes are automatically accepted, sometimes with odd results. The command Save As will preserve them.

Experiment with different views and options in Word to find out what suits the work you are doing. The ideal time to learn is when you encounter a non-urgent problem. Alter the size of the display; display all characters to detect unwanted tabs and spaces; display or hide Track Changes; apply colours to material that needs special attention. Use Outline View for substantive editing and for copyedit-ing headings, and Page View or Page Preview to check layout.

Editors should be aware that Microsoft is progressively withdrawing sup-port for superseded versions of its software. For instance, Office 2000 will not be supported after 2006 and Office XP after 2008. You can continue to run the pro-grams—the experts acknowledge that 'some small companies will use them until the end of days'[2]—but if something goes wrong, you will have to find third-party support. Freelance editors have to stay compatible with authors and clients, so you will be obliged eventually to match their upgrades.

Typical errors

Each method of reproducing text creates its own kinds of errors. Part of the appraisal process is to find out how the document has been prepared so you can be on the watch for these characteristic mistakes.

Microsoft Word, for instance, replaces an apostrophe at the beginning of a word with an opening quote mark—'*tis* instead of '*tis*—which has to be reversed manually. In its default setting, Word applies superscript to ordinal numbers (1st, etc.), a style not popular in bookwork. Spellcheckers cannot detect errors like *expert* instead of *expect*, or one-letter mistakes in two-letter words like *it, if, of, on.* Be alert for sense in documents produced on a word processor.

The optical character recognition used in scanning software confuses similar letters and numerals, so it may read *and* as *arid*. In editing and proofreading scanned documents, you must look at each letter of every word, especially those that lend themselves to confusion, such as capital I, lower-case ell and the arabic numeral one—*I, l, 1.*

Voice recognition software faces the obvious difficulty of accommodating the many accents in which English may be spoken. Individuals can 'train' the software to interpret their idiosyncratic pronunciation and rhythm, but it is prone to errors. English is rich in homophones—*cite, sight, site; rain, rein, reign; core, corps; incidents, incidence*—which the program may not distinguish correctly. Depending on the user's pronunciation, it may confuse words that are not actually homophones but sound similar, like *formally, formerly; slither, sliver; precede, proceed; petition, partition.* It may misinterpret word division, rendering *a tax on books* as *attacks on books*, or *commercial in confidence* as *commercial incompetence*. In editing material produced with a voice recognition program you focus at the level of whole words rather than individual letters.

Allied programs

The page layout programs most widely used are Quark Xpress, PageMaker and InDesign. Web design programs include Dreamweaver, Front Page and Fireworks. As the page layout programs have been refined, they have become more compatible with word-processing programs, but they still have trouble translating symbols and special characters such as en and em rules, accented letters and fractions, so you have to watch for these in proofs. Tables and the numbering of endnotes can also go wrong (Chapters 6, 7).

Equipment maintenance

Editors who work for publishing houses or large organisations can rely on the IT department to prevent and solve problems, so this section is addressed to freelance editors, micro-businesses and laptop users who must care for their own equipment.[3]

Hardware failure

Sooner or later you will suffer a hard disk crash, virus attack or theft that leaves you without a computer for a while. Since the computer is your primary tool of trade, you are helpless without it. You have contracts to fulfil, deadlines to meet; your reputation for reliability is vital for future business. How can you maintain it if your equipment fails?

If you don't have contingency plans you might rush into an expensive purchase out of desperation. Ideally, a freelance business should keep a spare computer on hand, but most can't afford to maintain a complete redundant system. Let's look at the separate parts.

- A new keyboard or mouse can be purchased fairly cheaply at short notice.
- Small home printers are cheap and will do in a pinch, or you can manage without a printer for week or two by taking disks to a compatible friend or a printing shop.
- The crucial items are the brainbox (CPU) and the monitor, which can take a week or more to repair or replace, especially if you live outside a capital city. If possible, have spares of these—perhaps superseded models that are slow and small but will serve for a while. Alternatively, tee up a local computer supplier who can lease compatible equipment for a reasonable fee at short notice, and allow for electronic equipment insurance and emergency rental in your budget.

Backing up

Your hardware is guarded against failure, but what about your information? A large organisation should have a comprehensive backup system, but freelances have to make their own arrangements. To keep your business operating when disaster strikes, you need frequent backups of:

- the Normal template in Word, normal.dot, with your chosen settings
- relevant document files
- relevant emails
- email address book
- financial and tax records
- frequently used URLs (favorites or bookmarks, depending on your browser).

When working on screen, save your work every few minutes and back it up every few hours. The alternative, of course, is to do the work over again if the system crashes or the power fails.

If you are disinclined to back up frequently, perhaps your strategy needs upgrading. It should be swift and easy to use. A zip disk or a rewriteable CD will provide sufficient capacity; set the options in the accompanying software to cover the points above. When setting up your system, run a test backup and then, having renamed your original files in case anything goes wrong, restore the backed-up files. Then check that you can access all your information.

The process is painless if you have a program that performs an incremental backup, that is, copies only the files that have changed since the last backup. Use proprietary software or consult a manual.[4] Incremental backups, if done frequently, take only a few seconds. You can create another program to make a full backup of the files you need, which will overwrite (delete) the previous backup. Alternatively, for a modest sum you can install a second hard drive and create a complete duplicate of everything with a couple of mouse-clicks.

Information must be backed up in triplicate:

- *After each work session, or daily:* Make an incremental backup on a disk kept handy to your workspace, or copy to a duplicate hard drive.
- *Weekly:* Make a full backup to a disk that is stored separate from your workspace in a location secure against fire and theft.
- *Monthly:* Make a full backup to a disk that is stored offsite with a relative or friend.

Inspect your backups occasionally to make sure that information is being recorded correctly.

There is a horror story about a company that performed a triple backup of its data every day; one copy was placed in an office drawer, one in a fireproof safe, and one was taken home by the manager. When the company's premises suffered a catastrophic fire, the disk in the drawer burned at once. It turned out that the safe was only rated as fireproof for twenty minutes, so that disk burned as well. That left the manager's disk, but as it happened his car had electrically heated seats; the magnetic field that they generated had corrupted the data on the disk and it was unrecoverable.

In the light of this story, it's reasonable to assume that your work's not finished until it's been thoroughly backed up. Freelances should make it a habit to do the housekeeping at least once a week: update your virus checker, run a virus scan on the hard disk and then create a full backup (you can clean the office at the same time). With this regime you will have peace of mind.

Viruses

Microsoft software is particularly vulnerable to viruses, but any computer can catch one. Install virus-scanning software and run it on every file you receive—whether on disk or attached to email—before opening the file. Vendors of anti-virus programs include Vet, McAfee and Norton, and shareware programs are available.

Unfortunately, defence against viruses is not set-and-forget. New viruses appear daily: an anti-virus program that is several weeks old is no protection. Keep your virus software current by downloading the latest amendments frequently; this should only take a few mouse-clicks.

Email

Emails are no more private than a postcard. They are written business communications, and while they can be informal and friendly, take care with the wording. Do not say anything in an email that you would not say to a person's face. A lighthearted comment may be taken the wrong way; try to anticipate and prevent misinterpretation.

Don't forward email mindlessly. Consider what the recipient needs to know and remove everything else. Explain obscure references and implications in forwarded material.

The proliferation of spam is changing email habits. Some people never read emails from unknown senders, and filters may be oversensitive and screen out wanted correspondence.[5] Email seems to be instant, but the specifications require it to try to deliver a message for five days before it informs the sender that the address is unreachable. Ridiculous as it seems, you may need to phone to check that email has arrived.

To keep track of emails, set up a folder for each job in your email program, identified by author and title, and a subfolder named *Action* or *Pending*. As emails come in, store them in the subfolder until you can deal with them and transfer them to the main folder. You can quickly review what needs to be done on the job by looking at the contents of the subfolder.

Techniques

A full-time editor may have to keep track of more than a dozen jobs, so you need ample, foolproof storage for work-in-progress. Stray items such as caption copy or an author's letter trickle in while you are concentrating on other jobs; if you don't file them correctly, you'll waste hours searching for them. Adjustable shelves are the best form of storage because the required space for each title waxes and wanes as it makes its way through production.

Here are some hints for handling paperwork on both desk and desktop.

Manuscripts on paper

If you write anything by hand, make it legible: the others who handle the manuscript don't want to puzzle over your idiosyncratic calligraphy. Typesetters work very fast and only glance at the manuscript; they set what they see, and if in doubt they follow copy. English may not be their mother tongue, and they may not understand an instruction to spell out a common Australian abbreviation such as *NSW*. On both manuscript and proofs, distinguish instructions and queries from copy to be typeset by circling them. If preparing an item such as an order of book that may be mistaken for copy to be typeset, write 'do not set' clearly in a prominent place.

Paper manuscripts are easy to work with if you make them a solid block of paper, with the edges as tight as if guillotined. You stack paper like this for the photocopier and the printer; do it for yourself too. With the manuscript in a solid block, you can see the edges of the coloured sheets that separate the chapters: thus you can find any chapter quickly and see where it begins and ends, which is valuable if the notes are presented at the end of each chapter. Also, you can riffle the pages with your thumb to find either a particular author query in the left margin, or a query to yourself in the right margin. Editing requires much checking and crosschecking—was that name spelt differently last time, wasn't it 1993 when the minister resigned, and so on. If you set up your work so that it's easy to crosscheck, you're more likely to do it.

When I'm working on hard copy, I arrange the job systematically on my desk so I can put my hand on any part of it with ease. When I'm reading a manuscript and realise that I need to check something in the prelims, my hand reaches automatically to the left. If I need the captions, I know they're to my right. On screen, I use standard folder and file names that are the same for every job. This makes it easy to crosscheck and improves efficiency.

Tags or sticky notes are subject to the law of diminishing returns: large numbers are counterproductive. My heart sinks when I receive 300 pages of proofs with 299 tags. As Chapter 8 explained, when collating proofs the editor goes through every page several times and checks every correction and query. Not only is it a complete waste of time and resources for the proofreader to apply all those tags, but it also shows ignorance of the production process. Use tags to draw attention to serious, unusual problems, not to every routine query and correction. A convention is emerging in the industry for the placement of tags: at the top of the page to mark divisions of the document such as chapters, and on the right-hand side to mark queries and problems.

Before you send off manuscript or proofs, cross out or erase all queries that no longer apply. Often during editing you will query, say, the spelling of a name in five places on the manuscript. When the author sends corrections you fix the two that are wrong, but you may forget to remove the query mark against the three that are right. It's important to cross out these marks, because they slow down everyone who handles the manuscript. In traditional production, the designer, the typesetter and the proofreader will all scratch their heads over them and wonder 'Am I supposed to solve this?' Nor do they want to read a dialogue between editor and author in the margin of the proofs about some point that is now resolved. Such marks slow the process for everybody; cross them out.

Packaging

As the legendary editor Barbara Ramsden said, 'What's the bloody good of correcting a set of proofs if they all get lost in the mail when the parcel falls apart?'[6] If you have worked on hard copy, the edited manuscript is the only thing you have to show for days of work. Don't put several hundred loose pages in a manila envelope and expect it to reach its destination safely. Confine hard copy with rubber bands and enclose artwork in stiff cardboard so it cannot be bent or damaged.

Version control

The term 'version control' is used in the computer industry to refer to versions of software, but the concept has relevance in print production. Document tracking is an essential part of the editor's role. You handle the job in various forms: the author's original manuscript, and possibly one or more revisions of it by the author; the edited manuscript before and after author approval; and several sets of proofs in one or more stages. The record of editorial changes and queries, and authorial agreement, must be plain to see.

As soon as you receive any hard copy, label it on the front page with the date and the version: 'original MS' or 'author's revised MS' or 'first page proofs, proofreader's set'. In some publishing houses the production staff stack the hard copy so that all edges are flush and mark them with a felt-tip pen, one stripe for the manuscript, two for the first page proofs and so on; properly done, this shows on every page and prevents mix-ups. Every diary entry, scrap of paper and electronic file relating to a job must be labelled with the author's name and the title: it is demoralising to find an index or a record of a phone conversation and not know which job it belongs to.

On some jobs you may never see hard copy. You receive the manuscript as email attachments, edit it on screen, send author queries and receive corrections by email, and despatch the edited manuscript as e-copy ready for typesetting. It is crucial that you name files systematically, as explained below, so that you never work on a superseded version.

Electronic files

For each project, you have at least two sets of electronic files: the documents concerning the job, such as the project plan and the design brief; and copy for typesetting, such as the text, captions and cover copy. You have to devise a filing system for them.

A typical set-up has a main job folder named with the author and book title, and subfolders called *Documentation*, *Original manuscript* and *Edited manuscript*. Add further divisions as necessary: the subfolder called *Edited manuscript* might have sub-subfolders for the version sent to the author for approval, the version that shows the author's responses, and the final version ready for typesetting.[7] This provides a clear record of the editorial process in case there are later queries. For screen publications, text and graphics are placed in separate folders to facilitate linking from different locations.

There is as yet no convention in the publishing industry for naming files. Whatever your filing system, use names that describe the contents—author, title, version. Remember that you will be emailing some of your files to authors, designers and publishers, who may send them on; explanatory file names save time for everyone along the chain.

You may choose to keep each chapter in a separate file or consolidate all the text into one big file, depending on its length. When you work with separate chapter files, it's easy to miss some global changes. The only sure way is to make up a checklist—a table with the chapter numbers across the top and the global changes in the stub column—and tick off each change as you make it. The big file is more convenient for global changes but can be unwieldy to move around in.

Once you have started work on e-copy of the manuscript, the version you are working on is the top version, the only one that can be changed. While the manuscript is being edited, authors sometimes have second thoughts; they make a few alterations and send you a disk (or even a complete printout) of the new, improved version with the changes made but not identified by any marks. Proper briefing of the author can avert this disaster. Explain politely that she has three choices for making late changes: mark them on e-copy, using the Microsoft Word functions Comments or Track Changes; or highlight them on hard copy; or present them as a list. The editor then transfers these changes to the top version. When you have finished editing, save the top version under another name, perhaps with the prefix *ed* or *revised*, to distinguish it from its previous incarnations. This makes it easy to identify the version that is to be typeset.

You can also make duplicate files at intermediate stages, either to record a particular round of queries or as an extra precaution. During one heroic editing job I had chapters with file names like *2ed ch 9A - old chs 7-8*, but you don't generally need to go to such extremes. Make sure that you always know which version you're working on, especially when you have two open at once, as described below. Before you hand over your finished work, double- and triple-check that the file you send contains the complete and final version ready for typesetting, with all Track Changes accepted or rejected and all queries resolved and removed.

The pagination of the different versions of the document will vary. When citing page numbers—in author queries, say, or in the artwork or design briefs— make it clear which version you are referring to: usually the hard copy of the edited manuscript.

Techniques for keeping track of your work are described under Monitoring in Chapter 3.

Comparing two documents

The editor often has to compare two documents—notes and bibliography, author's corrections and edited manuscript, author's and proofreader's proofs— and transfer changes from one to the other. In this situation I make it a rule to place the document I'm changing—the one I will write on—directly in front of me, and turn the pages to the right. The document I'm referring to is on my left, and I turn its pages to the left. This system prevents you from inadvertently placing pages in the wrong document, which will cause you to invent new swear words.

When comparing two documents on screen, display them together on a split screen with the Window command. Again, I make it a rule to place the document I am changing at the bottom of the screen and the one I'm referring to at the top. Thus I don't make changes to the wrong document, also a cause of creative profanity.

Microsoft Word has a function called Compare Documents, which is handy if you dislike Track Changes or forget to turn it on.

Saving work on screen

Microsoft Word automatically saves your work at a predetermined interval, which can be adjusted with Tools > Options. In addition to these automatic saves, it's wise to save your work manually after completing a manoeuvre that you're particularly pleased with, such as rewriting a tricky paragraph. Make it a habit to save your work before you answer the phone, and to close Word whenever you leave your desk.

Each time you save, Word makes a temporary file, as you can see if you look at the File > Open dialog box after you've been working for a while. As a precaution against file corruption, close Word down every hour or so to consolidate all these temporary files into one. This pause in your work fits in well with the breaks that are essential for your health (Chapter 11).

Putting a job aside

While you are waiting for the arrival of proofs or responses to queries, you may not look at a job for weeks or even months. Before you put a job aside, make sure you have a complete, secure backup of the electronic files. All the hard copy for the job— manuscript, artwork, job file—should be stored in one place.

After some time has gone by, you'll forget that you were going to have another look at that awful table, or chase up a publication date in the bibliography, or do an extra check on the captions. Before you set the job aside, make a list of everything that's still to be done and place it at the front of the job file, so you can find it to answer panicky phone calls or to take up the job smoothly when the time comes.

Freelance editing

THE FREELANCE LIFESTYLE offers both the pleasures and the irritations of working at home. As a no-collar worker you wear what you like, you work when you like, you control your working environment and equipment, you don't have to commute, you avoid meetings and office politics. The disadvantages are equally obvious: you need to obtain enough work to survive, your income is uncertain, it is difficult to maintain a smooth schedule, there are no workmates down the corridor, and you need to separate your work from the demands of the household.

This chapter surveys the concerns of freelance editors. Further guidance can be found in books on freelance writing and journalism, self-employment, working from home, and small business management: look in business bookshops or under Dewey 650s in libraries. It is advisable to obtain specific professional advice on matters of finance, tax and law.

I think I'll go freelance

Some experienced editors choose freelancing as a career option; others are forced into it by retrenchment or dabble for extra income in retirement. Not everyone is suited to self-employment: being good at editing is not enough. Do not think of becoming a freelance editor unless you have the personal qualities that make editors such paragons, as listed in Chapter 1, and competence in the knowledge listed in *Australian Standards for Editing Practice* (see Appendix). In addition, you need:

- belief in yourself and your skills
- ability to plan your work and motivate yourself to do it without supervision
- skills in time management
- a liking for solitude
- a well-equipped office
- confidence to talk about money without blushing

- sufficient resources to survive a fluctuating cash flow
- contacts who will give you work.

Each year you need between twenty and thirty average-size jobs—say, copy-editing a 250-page book—to make a living. It will probably take three to five years to establish yourself in full-time work. During this period, unless you have substantial savings to draw on, a part-time job can support you through slack periods and late payments; it will also provide social contact to ease the transition to freelance life. Your business plan must make provision for income until you can rely entirely on regular freelance work. Ideally, don't go freelance until you have in-house experience and a good list of contacts.

Your office

Editing requires long periods of intense concentration, best sustained in silence and solitude. An investment in an efficient workspace will pay off. At a minimum you need:

- desk and chair
- adequate lighting, heating and cooling
- storage for work-in-progress, stationery, files and archives
- telephone services: phone, fax, answering service, internet access
- computer system and printer
- reference library (on shelf and on line).

Maintain a stationery cupboard with all the consumables that you are likely to need. You should be able to meet client requirements such as an unexpected printing of the manuscript or a request to code corrections in ink of a particular colour.

In order to live lightly on the planet (and save on bills), minimise your office requirements for energy and resources. A small under-desk heater or even a knee-rug will keep you warm. When buying equipment, choose energy-efficient models with a 'sleep' mode and low standby power use. Prefer coloured pencils to chemical highlight pens, and reuse packaging. Paper that is blank on one side can be used as scrap, but be sure to strike through the original text to prevent confusion.

If you are serious about freelancing you will set aside properly equipped office space and work regular hours just like a real job. Maintain some distance between work and family by making rules and enforcing them.

Do paid work during working hours

Because you work at home, you can get sidetracked by home duties. Some free-lances resolutely ignore all household tasks during working hours. Others find that repetitive, mindless chores provide gentle exercise and a change of pace, resulting in fresh insights on the work they've been doing. A little light house-work is permissible, but cleaning the oven is avoidance behaviour.

You can avoid work while sitting at your desk. By making unnecessary phone calls, reorganising files, tidying drawers, making lists of things to do, you can have a near-work experience. Before you begin work, especially on a new project, you may need to do a certain amount of pottering in order to tidy up loose ends and gather your forces, but don't prolong this phase.

Office manners

The telephone is your main means of projecting yourself to your client. Whenever you answer it during business hours, adopt your professional persona and have paperwork to hand. Although you work at home, you do not have to be available 24/7. Many authors have a day job and write in their spare time, so they tend to phone in the evenings or at weekends. In your initial contact with the author, state your office hours along with your phone number and remind her of the time difference if there is one. Otherwise you may find yourself taking her call in the middle of a dinner party, and it's hard to sound businesslike after several glasses of red.

It's a basic rule of good business not to be rude in writing, even in emails. Cutting remarks have a way of getting back to the person they describe. Diplomatic wording may take more time, but it pays off in goodwill all around.

Clients

In publishing houses, the person who manages outsourced work generally has a title that includes 'production' or 'manager' or 'controller'. These people are your colleagues and also your hope of future work. Often a manager who moves from one publisher to another takes his freelances with him because he knows and trusts their work.

The first transaction is critical. You must chart a course between keeping him informed, and swamping him with unnecessary detail; between asking questions when you need to, and taking responsibility for editorial decisions. You want to establish a reputation as accommodating and easy to get along with, but not as a soft touch. In your communications pay attention to the subtext as well as the words, and be creative in suggesting solutions to difficulties. Establish a climate that makes it easy for the client to raise complaints—it's better to accept criticism and modify your methods than to lose work.

Writing is not a job that can be done by a committee. If your client is a pub-lications committee or similar body, it is preferable to deal with one person who is authorised to speak for all. This can raise problems of authority and accounta-bility, which should be foreseen and clarified in the written agreement.

Health, safety and productivity

Many self-employed people are mercilessly exploited by their bosses. What follows may seem painfully obvious, but editors are by nature obsessive and excessively task-oriented.

You will be more productive if you work reasonable hours with regular breaks. Fatigue will cause you to miss errors and make poor decisions that have to be laboriously reversed. Your freelance business depends entirely on your labour, so health is a business asset that must be maintained. Editing is a sedentary occupation. Take a break of ten minutes in every hour—get up and walk away from your desk and do something active.

The major areas of vulnerability are eyes, wrists and hands, neck and back.

- Equip yourself with a good adjustable desk lamp. Buy the biggest and best monitor you can afford, position it so there is no glare on the screen, and adjust the font setting to a size large enough to read without hunching or squinting. Obviously you will have regular vision checks and keep your glasses prescription, if you have one, up to date.
- Wrists and hands are vulnerable to repetitive strain injury, also called occupational overuse syndrome. RSI creeps up on you, and a severe case can stop you working for months; it may never heal completely. To prevent RSI, position your keyboard so your forearms are horizontal; minimise your keystrokes; take a ten-minute break every hour; and don't work excessive hours.
- Your neck and back should not suffer if you sit properly. Adjust your chair and monitor so that your thighs are horizontal, using a footrest if you need one. Your head should be in a comfortable position; most work is done at the bottom of the screen, so this should be the focal point.

Coping with stress

Freelances live with unpredictable, sometimes overwhelming, flows of work, constantly shifting schedules, uncertain job prospects and irregular income. The key factor leading to stress is lack of control over your workplace and your work. Freelances have total control over the former, but the latter is sometimes a struggle. If you allow your work to be driven by the client, you might as well be an employee; learn the value of the word 'no'. In your dealings with authors and clients, it is legitimate to expect them to perform what they promise. For instance, if you receive material after the date that was agreed, you can't be expected to keep the original deadline; assert control and renegotiate the schedule.

Most people work best under some pressure and a due date is a great motivator, but you have to pace yourself. If you like to live dangerously, you will say yes to every job offer and cram your schedule full—and then somehow work the extra hours to get it all done. If you prefer a quiet life, negotiate your deadlines so you can plug along steadily with plenty of slack in your schedule to allow for unforeseen events. Scheduling is discussed further under Work Flows, below.

An essential strategy for coping with stress is physical fitness. A fit person has the stamina to get through occasional panics and late-night sessions, and is also alert to opportunities that are not apparent to one who is run-down and overwhelmed. Firmly refuse tempting jobs when you realise your workload is getting out of control. It is better to miss a couple of contracts than lose weeks of work because of RSI or stress-induced illness. Learn to recognise the signs of stress in your own body. Make the most of your freedom to set your own hours—work at night when the house is quiet, or start at dawn on summer mornings and take a siesta.

Professional development

Freelances who have a cosy relationship with a few established clients can lose touch with emerging trends in the industry. You are a knowledge worker, so thorough, current knowledge—of trends in language and writing, of changing technology and law—is a business asset. You need to devote a proportion (say, 3 or 4 per cent) of your annual income to updating and extending your skills.

Draw up a plan for your professional development over the next three years. Concentrate on any weaknesses you are conscious of, and try to cover all areas:

- language, writing, grammar
- editing, proofreading, publishing
- particular software programs
- running your business: finance, tax, record-keeping.

Short courses are offered by the societies of editors and technical communicators and through adult education and tertiary institutions and writers' centres. Conferences and seminars conducted by the societies and trade organisations enable you to network and make new contacts as well as keep your knowledge current.

Emend Editing offers an online program of interactive short courses based on *Australian Standards for Editing Practice*. The Editors' Association of Canada has published a two-volume self-teaching and self-testing package called *Meeting Editorial Standards* which is available through their website, though Australian and New Zealand editors need to adapt it to local practice.[1]

There is also a cheap and pleasurable method of professional development. This is to read constantly, widely, critically, in order to extend your general knowledge, find out about trends in writing and publishing, and increase your understanding of the possibilities of language and print. Explain to your household that lying on the couch with a book is actually high-level R&D.

Work that isn't worth it

As a freelance, you need to maintain a sense of your own worth, of professional self-esteem.[2] Don't be pressured into underselling yourself. The profession of editing selects against those who put themselves forward; if you are modest enough to defer to the author, you may tend to defer to the client as well. An editor who prepares an estimate or a tender offers the skills listed in the *Standards* that are relevant to the job, together with high levels of speed and accuracy. In the commercial world, you are only as good as your last job. If the work keeps coming, especially if it's from former clients or via personal recommendations, you must be providing a valuable service.

It's a simple rule that you don't do tasks you aren't paid for, and if extra tasks are added to the brief after agreement you expect extra money. Here we see the need for project definition and a detailed editorial brief, so that everyone knows what's expected and what is being paid for (Chapter 3).

If you have professional self-esteem, it follows that there are some jobs that just aren't worth doing, either because of the poor pay or because of the hassles. You need to have the courage to refuse such jobs. After all, what's the worst that can happen? You might have to get some other sort of work. Although many editors have a sentimental attachment to editing, they have skills that are readily marketable in other fields—administration, management, education, journalism, broadcasting, technical writing, advertising, public relations.

Once a book publisher asked me for an estimate on the structural editing of a manuscript. They sent hard copy without any brief or instructions, and it took several emails and phone calls to elicit one sentence—'We want it rewritten from the other point of view'—along with a few details about the target market and a phone number for someone who might know more. By this time two weeks had passed. With an amateur publisher I might have persevered to develop a project plan, but one expects professionals to be able to state their requirements. I took a deep breath and decided to say no. It wasn't worth working with people who didn't know what they wanted and would blame me when I didn't deliver.

If you charge cheap rates or work without a brief, you're undermining the profession and damaging yourself and your colleagues. Do a professional job, and charge professional rates.

Running a small business

As a small business operator, the freelance editor must be on top of relevant legislation, financial management, record-keeping, and so on. General advice can be found in books on small business but there is no substitute for professional advice tailored to your circumstances, especially when you are starting out.

Most freelance editors operate as sole traders or partners, but for extensive business interests you may prefer to set up a company or trust. If your partners or fellow shareholders are your spouse and relatives you might think a formal agreement is superfluous, but money matters can place great strain on personal relationships and it is best to clarify and agree on expectations at the beginning. A written agreement can go some way to protecting your livelihood from the bitterness of a divorce or a family feud.

Business plan

The usual purpose of a business plan is to support a loan application, but even if you don't need to borrow money a plan will help to clarify your ideas. General assistance in business planning is available from banks and government departments of small business, or you can consult an accountant or financial adviser.

Your business plan should be a dynamic document, updated to reflect the changes that real life imposes. Don't apply it too rigidly, but don't let it gather dust. Perhaps you find yourself moving sideways into indexing or desktop publishing, or opportunities are leading you into screen publications rather than books. In such a case you may need training, new equipment or a new marketing strategy.

Registration, tax and record-keeping

Information about administrative matters such as registering a business name, obtaining an Australian Business Number and planning for taxation is readily available. A freelance who has a low-key operation does not need an elaborate administration system; for instance, manual bookkeeping may be sufficient if you send out only a few dozen invoices a year.

Insurance

Before you hand over an insurance premium, consider to what extent your business is seriously at risk from the hazard and how much you should pay to protect it. You will need to insure against burglary and damage, particularly for the electronic equipment on which your business depends. You may also need cover for loss of gross profit, consequential loss and business interruption. Sole breadwinners may need to protect themselves against loss of income, personal accident and illness.

If you are proved negligent in your work, you may be liable to third parties for personal injury or property damage. Government agencies often require freelance editors to have professional indemnity insurance. It seems far-fetched to apply this to editors, but librarians may be liable if, for instance, they provide a book on building carports to a person who is injured while building a carport in accordance with the book's instructions. Of course the editor should make every effort to avoid negligence, especially in how-to information such as recipes and herbal remedies. Publishers often include a disclaimer in the preliminary pages, but it is not a sure defence at law. A minimum public liability cover of $5 million is recommended.

The editor as employer

Freelances sometimes employ others to help with overflows of work. Usually this is an ad hoc arrangement and the job is subcontracted. Do unto subcontractors as you would be done to: supply a detailed brief and sign a written agreement.

If your business is a roaring success and you regularly have more work than you can handle, you might toy with the idea of employing staff. This is a big step. Employers have to comply with relevant legislation and awards and provide certain minimum employment conditions. They need sophisticated financial systems to track workers' compensation insurance, superannuation, tax, and leave payments.

Whatever the employment arrangements, when other people perform work that you have contracted for, you must control the quality. Your reputation is vital to your business; if you turn in a job that's not up to standard, the client might walk. The margins on most jobs are too small to cover a realistic fee for checking the work on top of the subcontractor's fee for doing it and the administrative expenses of passing the material back and forth.

Contracts

As Chapter 1 explained, the book industry in Australia tends to operate on trust. Even though you have not signed a formal agreement, a contract usually exists between a freelance editor and a publisher. If you have proceeded on the basis of your personal relationship, the contract may be partly in writing (the editorial brief, emails), partly verbal (discussions, phone calls) and partly implied (the prevailing practices in the industry). One lawyer describes this situation as 'a bubbling cauldron from which the lawyers can produce their own prophecies to confuse the Macbeths of either side'.[3]

Friendly relations are all very well, but the freelance is vulnerable if a dispute arises. A written agreement is strongly recommended. A government department or amateur publisher may draw up elaborate terms of reference, but book publishers usually take a minimalist approach. Figure 11.1 shows an example of the latter; the checklist it mentions is the editorial brief (Figure 3.2).

Preferably the contract should identify:

- the parties: names and addresses of editor and client
- the job: author's name, working title of the publication, brief description of the manuscript
- the tasks to be done, and the responsibility, authority and accountability of each party: if the contract relies on generic terms like 'copyediting', they should be defined in an attached editorial brief or by reference to *Australian Standards for Editing Practice*
- the quality of the output
- the dates for receipt of material and handover of completed work
- the methods of communication
- the process of agreeing on variations: for instance, specify that the contract may be varied only by written agreement between the editor and the client
- remuneration: specify whether it includes GST and expenses such as phone-calls and courier fees.

Button Press
101 Any Street
Richmond, Vic. 3121

Ms A. Manuensis
PO Box 88
Woop Woop, Vic. 3999

Dear Ms Manuensis

This letter sets out the understanding between us. That is:

1. You will edit the work provisionally entitled *Great Upholsterers of Australia and New Zealand*, as marked on the attached checklist, by 30 July 2004.

2. Payment will be $2400 plus GST upon completion and supply of the finished work and receipt of a GST invoice for the agreed amount.

3. It is acknowledged that this is a contract for service and does not establish an employer–employee relationship between us.

4. You are free to engage others to perform all or part of the task, provided that the completed work is performed to Button Press's standards and is delivered on the specified date.

5. The copyright in all works created (if any) shall be the property of Button Press.

If this meets with your agreement, please sign the enclosed copy of this letter and return it to the undersigned.

Yours sincerely
J. Button
For Button Press

FIGURE 11.1 Where both parties agree on assumptions and definitions, as in the book industry, a contract with a few simple clauses may be sufficient

You may add other clauses, such as a requirement for an editorial credit line, indemnity for the editor from claims arising out of libel or copyright infringement committed by the author or the client, or a provision to terminate the contract in the event of a material change in circumstances.[4]

Freelance editors who employ subcontractors such as proofreaders should sign written agreements with them.

Costs

Your freelance business must provide sufficient income to meet four groups of costs: return on capital investment, overheads, variable costs and labour.

Capital investment, overheads, variable costs

Calculate the return you are getting on your capital investment in your office—the room itself, furniture and fittings, computer equipment and reference library—

which amounts to several thousand dollars. Consider whether you could realise a better return from this money by investing it elsewhere—shares, gold bullion, antique clocks, a piggery.

Overheads are easily overlooked, but it's not realistic to absorb the costs of running your business into your household expenses. Identify business expenses so you can deduct them from business income for tax purposes. Calculate the overheads for a home office—rent or rates, utilities, maintenance, cleaning—by apportioning a share of the household bills. The easiest way to do this is by number of rooms: if your house has six main rooms and one is your office, calculate the business share as one-sixth of the bill.

For a freelance business, the variable costs generally comprise a tiny proportion of the costs of a job. They include stationery, phone charges, postage and courier fees, travel, advertising.

Labour

Labour is, of course, the major share of costs, and freelances tend to underestimate it. Your fee should cover not only your brilliant editing, but also administration and on-costs. On a typical job, the proportion of time devoted to monitoring, liaison and management can amount to one-quarter, as we saw in Chapter 3. In addition, like any small business owner, you have to find time for marketing, filing, banking and bookkeeping.

On-costs are another aspect of labour that is often neglected. Your freelancing should pay the costs of employment: annual leave, workers' compensation insurance, provision for sick leave and long-service leave, superannuation contributions. Casual employees typically receive a loading of 25 per cent of the salary paid to full-time employees to cover these costs. For parity with your in-house colleagues under the current award, your budget should allow you paid public holidays and four weeks' paid annual leave with a 17½ per cent loading (Chapter 1 under Trade Union). If you're not achieving these figures, you have to make a sober assessment: how much income will you sacrifice in order to enjoy freelance freedom?

Another cost of labour is maintaining your skills. As a knowledge worker in a fast-changing world, you must invest in yourself as described under Professional Development, above.

Calculating your costs

Figure 11.2 lists the categories of operating costs for a freelance editing business. They do not apply in every case—established editors will spend little on advertising; you don't need workers' comp unless you employ others—but if you fill in the figures for those that apply to your business the sum is likely to be formidable. However you charge, by the hour, by the page or by the job, you have to cover all relevant costs before you're making money.

Item	$
Office	
Rent or home expenses (including council rates) Heating, lighting, cooling Cleaning	
Communications	
Telephone Answering service Fax Internet	
Insurance	
Income protection Life Office equipment Professional indemnity Public liability Workers' compensation	
Memberships, professional development	
Consumables: stationery, printing	
Travel and car expenses	
Maintenance and repair: computer, printer, etc.	
Software upgrades and updates	
Reference books, professional journals	
Advertising, marketing	
Postage, courier fees	
Holiday and sick pay	
Superannuation	
Taxes	
Other (legal and financial advice, bank fees, etc.)	

Source: Adapted from Janet Salisbury, 'Quoting Hypotheticals', workshop notes.

FIGURE 11.2 The expenses of operating a freelance editing business, excluding depreciation

Cash flows

If you can't live with a cash flow that fluctuates wildly, forget about freelancing. Most of the time you're absolutely skint; then suddenly you can pay cash for a small car. Adequate reserves will provide peace of mind.

Some freelances grade manuscripts according to their need for editing—heavy, medium and light—and charge a per-page fee for each grade that covers their overheads, labour and other costs. As it is more usual to charge an hourly rate, we will look at that method.

Hourly rate

If you are competent according to the *Australian Standards for Editing Practice*, in my opinion you're worth at least $50 an hour: anything less than that is derisory for the skills and knowledge outlined there. Many book publishers do not agree with me, but corporate and government work usually pays well above that figure. Hourly rates in the book industry in New Zealand are about $NZ35–50; in Britain they begin at about £15 and in the United States at about $US25.[5] As a rule of thumb, proofreading a publication costs about half as much as copyediting it.

As a freelance, you need to cost into your hourly rate all the expenses listed in Figure 11.2. Some editors charge different hourly rates for different services—project management, substantive editing, copyediting, proofreading. One method of determining your rate is to start with the net income you require from your business. Then fill in the numbers in Figure 11.3 to work out how much you will have to charge per hour to achieve that income.

There is no need to tell the client your hourly rate. If he presses you, say primly that your accountant has advised you not to reveal it, and you prefer to give a price for the job rather than by the hour. Clients who make decisions based solely on hourly rates are a bit silly, because some editors work much faster than others.

Fair value

When you are asked to provide an estimate or tender, it's tempting to keep the figure low because you don't want to price yourself out of the market. Builders and engineers commonly expect to lose about 10 per cent of the jobs they quote on because their price is too high, and this is a useful rule to apply. If you've successfully freelanced for some years, you must be doing something right. Having acquired some power in the marketplace, don't be afraid to exert it in order to get fair remuneration. Refusing low-budget jobs may actually enhance your reputation, and some work simply isn't worth it, as we've seen. Before you prepare an estimate for a job, it's worth asking the client what his budget is; he might not be able to afford your services.

Don't give a firm estimate unless you have seen the whole job, including illustrations and appendixes. If you must give a price based on a sample of the manuscript, state in writing to the client that it is not a firm estimate and you reserve the right to adjust it when you have inspected all the material. Generally, book publishers are willing to renegotiate the fee if you encounter some serious problem that could not reasonably have been foreseen.

On most jobs you want the relationship with your client to continue, so you have to give fair value for money. If you feel that there are too many variables to

Item	$
Net income required	
Add: Expenses (see Figure 11.2)	
Gross income required	
Hours worked per week	
Weeks worked per year	
Hours worked per year	
Billable hours per year, @ 75%	
Hourly rate to produce gross income required	

Source: Adapted from Janet Salisbury, 'Quoting Hypotheticals', workshop notes.

FIGURE 11.3 Calculation of hourly rate from net income required

give a firm estimate, provide some leeway by specifying that your price is subject to a variation of plus or minus 10 per cent. In fairness to your client, you must then bill for the lower figure if everything goes swimmingly, but don't feel guilty about charging top dollar if you strike rocks. You may want to vary your rates for the hassle factor, giving a small discount to clients who are particularly congenial and reliable and adding a surcharge for those who have shown themselves to be difficult and demanding.

Invoicing

Send your invoice at the earliest opportunity. It should include your name and address, your ABN, the words 'tax invoice' if you are registered for GST, and the name and address of the client. Identify the job with the name of the author and the title of the book (and a series or volume or edition number as needed), and state what work you have done—reader's report, copyediting, collating first proofs. State the amount payable and how you arrived at it—'agreed fee' if you are working to an estimate, or the number of hours worked and your hourly rate. You should also state your terms; thirty days is usual in the book industry, but you can ask to be paid within seven days. Government typically takes ninety days.

Progressive payments

If you are responsible for author liaison and you have to wait for the author to answer your queries before you can finish editing, there may be a long delay before you can send off the job and the invoice, even though you have done the bulk of the work. A manuscript that needs major revision may drag on for months in fits and starts as the author considers successive rounds of queries and proposals, or a project may be put on hold for some reason. In such cases most book publishers will make progressive payments for work done if you ask them, even if this was not foreseen when the contract was agreed. Maintain careful records so that both you and your client know what has been paid for. On long projects, ask to be paid monthly.

Late payment

Clients may be slow in paying. Your in-house contact is rarely responsible for this, so don't express your anger to him. In fact, try not to get angry at all, but treat it as a simple business matter. Reputable book publishers realise that free-lance editors operate on slim margins and are usually courteous about paying on time. For those that don't, some freelances send statements of monies owing with increasingly emphatic demands for payment; others cultivate a contact in the accounts department and hope for special treatment. For a client who per-sistently pays late, you might consider invoicing for a figure higher than your estimate and offering an equivalent discount for payment within thirty days.

Work flows

There are many advantages to freelancing, but a constant flow of work is not one of them. The schedule is the bugbear of freelance life. You can seldom plan with any certainty more than three weeks ahead, and you rarely know what you'll be doing in six weeks' time.

Scheduling

To secure steady work, you have to overbook, so to speak, accepting slightly more than you can manage. Material rarely arrives on the due date and occasionally it's delayed for months, so if you don't overbook you'll have periods without work. Sometimes, of course, things don't turn out as you expect; everything does arrive on time and you have to rush to meet the deadlines you've agreed to. When sched-uling, bite off a little more than you can chew, and occasionally chew like hell.

Seemingly solid schedules can crumble to nothing with alarming speed. Suppose it's April and you have work lined up for May—two manuscripts and two sets of proofs—and more jobs coming in June. Suddenly you find that all the May jobs are delayed for one reason or another. Not only are you looking at no work and no income for a month, but June will be a panic as the May jobs clash with the work you have pencilled in. In this situation, you have three possible courses of action:

- See if any of the June jobs can be brought forward.
- Phone all your contacts and see if you can scare up some work at short notice.
- Enjoy your unplanned holiday.

Figure 11.4 shows a typical schedule for work that follows the straightforward production process that was outlined in Figure 2.2; if you undertake other tasks, such as picture research, you will need to schedule extra stages. I write my schedule in pencil because it often alters.

The due date, the first main column in Figure 11.4, is rubbery: it tends to sag later and later. The second column is filled in according to your estimates of how

May	Due in	Working on	Due out
1	LESLIE pix and captions	MARTIN edit manuscript	
2			
3	VINCENZO index		MARTIN author queries
4		VINCENZO edit index	VINCENZO index
5		LESLIE check pix, edit captions	LESLIE pix and captions
6			
7			
8	HUSSEIN author cxns	HUSSEIN finalise manuscript	
9			
10	ABERFOYLE manuscript		
11		ABERFOYLE edit manuscript	HUSSEIN edited manuscript
12			
13			
14			
15	HEINZ manuscript	ABERFOYLE edit manuscript	
16			
17			
18			
19			
20			

FIGURE 11.4 A typical freelance schedule

long the work will take (Chapter 3). Unless you have a high tolerance for stress, make generous estimates of time in order to allow for the inevitable adjustments. The third column is the deadline that you have to meet. If you employ subcontractors, you need to add two columns to track work handed over and returned.

When you receive the schedule for a job, fill in all the deadlines right through to the proofs and index. Monitor your schedule to see what's coming up. Well before an item is due, phone to find out whether it's on track. If something doesn't turn up on time, find out what's happening. If there is a prolonged silence from either the client or the author, make contact to ensure that nothing has gone wrong.

Let's see how the schedule in Figure 11.4 works in practice. Suppose it's Monday morning, 1 May, and you're working away at the Martin manuscript, trying to finish it to author-query stage by Wednesday. The phone rings—a valued client has a rush job to be done. It's 300 manuscript pages, experienced author, no pix or tables or footnotes, has to be done to author-query stage in the next two weeks. What do you say?

You say yes. The job you've been offered sounds straightforward and probably requires about four or five days' work. If you examine the schedule, you'll see that it's full of promises but there's actually not much work on your desk. The Leslie pix and the Vincenzo index may or may not turn up this week; anyway, each of them should only take half a day rather than the full day you have allowed. Hussein may or may not complete her author corrections by next Monday. The Aberfoyle and Heinz manuscripts are only promises and as yet have no deadlines; even if they arrive on time, you'll have several weeks to edit them. So there's ample time to do the job you've been offered.

As a general rule in scheduling, the later in the production process, the higher the priority. Thus you put aside a manuscript to work on proofs of another title, and first proofs to work on second proofs, and so on.

Holidays

At any one time you are likely to have a dozen jobs in various stages of completion. When everything is going smoothly you can take advantage of gaps in the schedule to go away for short breaks; if you plan well, your clients and authors won't know that you were out of the office. It is not so easy, however, to take a holiday of several weeks. You have to terminate all your projects or brief someone to take over. Moreover, once your clients get hold of the idea that you're not available, it tends to stick. When you return (or even before), you'll have to make a lot of cheerful noise to let them know you're back and looking for work.

For provision of holiday pay, see Costs, above.

Getting work

A freelance editor needs a marketing campaign to build business and reputation, to keep up with changes in the industry, and to stay abreast of the competition.[6] The first step is to review your business, analysing what marketers call the four

Ps: the product, the price, the position in the market, and the methods of promotion. Having done this, you can devise strategies and draw up a marketing plan. Your promotional material should display the product you are offering—zero tolerance for errors, an eye for graphic design, and above all skill with words. Wit and wordplay can make you memorable but should be tailored to your prospective clients. Books on marketing can be found in the business section of bookshops or under Dewey 620s in libraries.

To get freelance work in book publishing you need to know people who value your work and are in a position to engage you. The Australian book industry is relatively small and its networks can be difficult to break into. As we said at the beginning of this chapter, it's best not to set up as a freelance until you have a good range of contacts. Be seen at industry functions and training courses, join the society of editors, go to writers' festivals, attend conferences, cultivate connections.

Cross-referrals can help to build your business. Develop alliances with editors whose work you know, so you can recommend them for jobs that you are too busy to accept, and they can reciprocate. You enhance your value to the client if you can recommend competent professionals for ancillary tasks such as proofreading, indexing, illustration, design and legal advice.

The societies of editors publish Freelance Registers listing members' services, which are posted on their websites and distributed to publishers and others who employ editors. The rates for this advertising are comparatively cheap, and it is tightly targeted to likely users.

As well as advertising, research the publishers that you would like to work for and approach them directly. There is scope for creativity here. A cheeky tactic, if you find a book that has obviously not been edited, is to write to the publisher explaining what is wrong with it and how you could have improved it. You have to show that you could make a genuine difference to the book, not just nitpick the punctuation, but it works: I have acquired a client by doing this.

Don't confine yourself to the book industry. Market yourself to government and corporate clients and to underdeveloped markets such as genealogical societies and other non-government organisations. Through the internet you can apply for freelance editorial work in English-language publishing worldwide.[7]

Periods without work

You are certain to have periods with no work—actors call it 'resting'. Sometimes this is only a pause between jobs; you have work lined up and you're waiting for it to arrive. Other times you have no prospect of work. This is scary. You must develop strategies to cope.

The book industry runs to an annual rhythm. Autumn and winter are usually steady, but early spring can be frantic. By November the trade books for the Christmas market and the educational books for the new academic year are being printed, and this can be a flat period for freelance editing (but a good time in the garden). In December, forward-thinking publishers begin to line up contracts for the new year. The holiday season is a convenient target date and many authors deliver their manuscripts to the publisher on Christmas Eve, so you can expect your phone to run hot in January.

As soon as you realise that your schedule is looking a bit empty, get on the phone to your contacts. There is no shame in this: everyone in publishing knows that schedules can suddenly alter and leave you high and dry. With any luck you'll get a promise or two; meanwhile, fill your time constructively. For the first few days, do work-related things during your usual working hours. Do some marketing and update your business plan. There's always filing and tax records—all that administration known as 'unbillable hours'. If you have extra time, play around with Microsoft Word to learn more short cuts, or read reference books to brush up on the finer points, so to speak, of punctuation.

Sometimes you've done all the marketing you can think of and got all your records in order but still no work arrives to rescue you—free time stretches out indefinitely ahead. This requires a huge mental adjustment, like turning an ocean liner. Working at home, you have to be blind to cobwebs, dust and weeds, so when you suddenly have time on your hands it takes an effort to realise that you can do something about them at last. But make time also to relax and treat yourself to the indulgences that your usual busy schedule doesn't allow, or go on a short holiday. When the work does arrive and you're racing against the clock, you'll kick yourself if you haven't made good use of the break.

If you are flexible, autonomous and disciplined and can adapt to the particular requirements of freelance editing, you will find your career is a real possession in the changing fortunes of time.

Appendix

Australian Standards for Editing Practice
Council of Australian Societies of Editors, 2001

Preface

Editors are central to any publishing project; they endeavour to reconcile the needs of the author, the reader and the publishing client.

Editors look at the publication as a whole as well as at the detail. They ensure that the focus, structure, language, style and format of a publication suit its purpose and readership, and prepare the final copy to a standard of quality suitable for the publication.

Australian Standards for Editing Practice covers the knowledge and skills expected of experienced editors, although editors' workplace responsibilities and the requirements of particular projects will determine the relevance of each standard. Editors also recognise when they need to find out and apply specialised knowledge from other sources or professions.

These standards have been developed for editors to use:

- as a basis for judging the comprehensiveness of their own knowledge and skills
- when promoting themselves and the editing profession generally.

They will also help publishing clients understand the range of services editors provide, and guide educational institutions in developing editing courses.

These standards were devised by the Standards Working Group of the Council of Australian Societies of Editors (CASE), approved by the members of all Australian societies of editors, and ratified by CASE. They are to be reviewed at least every three years; please address comments to the closest member society.

The working group used the Editors' Association of Canada's *Professional Editing Standards* as a starting point and the Canberra Society of Editors' *Commissioning Checklist* as a reference. Members of the Australian societies of editors also contributed valuable observations and criticisms on the draft standards.

A. The publishing process, conventions and industry practice

An editor needs to understand the steps involved in the publishing process and standard industry practices for both paper-based and screen-based publications to ensure that the editing input complements the work of the rest of the publishing team.

Editing therefore requires knowledge of the following matters:

A1 Overview

A1.1   The different types of publications, purposes and readerships, and their implications for editing and production choices.

A publication may be print-based (e.g. book, report, pamphlet) or screen-based (e.g. web site, CD-ROM).

A1.2   The implications for accessibility, cost, production processes and schedules of different types of publications and delivery modes.

A1.3   The steps in the publication process, the relationships between these, and their impact on the final publication.

The steps include publication planning, editing, designing, formatting, proofreading, navigation, indexing, print production (e.g. production checking, binding, distribution), screen-based procedures (e.g. programming, testing, uploading or replication, site maintenance) and marketing.

A1.4   The need to balance time, cost and quality to suit the purpose of a publication, and the effects that choices within each of these categories will have on the final product.

A1.5   The scope of briefing processes for the publishing team.

Depending on the specific project, the expertise required for the publishing team may include project management, editing, design, illustration, photography, electronic publishing, word-processing, typesetting, proofreading, indexing, prepress, printing, web maintenance and marketing.

A1.6   The technology and terminology used in the industry, and emerging trends.

A2 Editing and proofreading

A2.1   The various roles that an editor may take in a publication project, and the need to have responsibilities, authorities and accountabilities properly defined.

A2.2   The extent of editorial intervention appropriate to a particular publication project, and the need for this level of intervention to be agreed.

A2.3   Standard reference materials for editors.

A2.4   The ways in which readers access and absorb information.

A2.5   The principles of clear writing.

A2.6   The principles of structuring material for print and on-screen use.

A2.7   Accepted spelling, punctuation, grammar and usage in Australia, and evolving trends in language use nationally and internationally.

A2.8   The stages in the editing and proofreading processes, and when stages should be repeated in order to ensure editorial integrity.

A2.9   The conventional parts of a publication and their usual arrangement.

A2.10   The conventions for citing sources.

A2.11   The standard symbols for text mark-up and proof correction.

A2.12   The range of fee rates for professional editorial work.

A3 Legal and ethical concerns

A3.1   Current definitions of libel, defamation, obscenity, discriminatory language, intellectual property, plagiarism, moral rights and copyright, and their implications for a publication.

A3.2   The implications for publishing of legislation relating to trade practices and trademarks; privacy and freedom of information; social justice, access and equity; and subjudice matters and parliamentary privilege.

A3.3   Legal deposit requirements and registration practices.
> Registration practices include cataloguing-in-publication (CIP) data, international standard book number (ISBN) and international standard serial number (ISSN).

A3.4   The information required by law to appear in a publication.
> Information required by law includes publisher's name and address, acknowledgments and copyright notices.

A3.5   Material that may need permission for reproduction, and the procedures and responsibilities for obtaining permission.

A3.6   When to suggest that legal advice may be necessary.
> Legal advice may be required on libel, plagiarism, moral rights and reproduction of materials from other sources.

A3.7   Ethical concerns in editing practice.
> Professional objectivity and confidentiality are two examples of ethical issues.

A3.8   Cultural sensitivities.

A4 Design, typography and formatting

A4.1   The value of professional design input.

A4.2   The use of design elements to convey meaning and enhance readability.
> Design elements include fonts, layout, colour and illustrations.

A4.3 Typographical characteristics and their effects on readability in different media.

Typographical characteristics include serif and sans serif fonts, kerning, leading, font weights, capitalisation, and line and column widths.

A4.4 Requirements associated with illustrations in different media, including techniques for adapting them to fit a given space and for ensuring their correct placement in the final publication.

'Illustrations' is used in the widest sense and includes drawings, cartoons, diagrams, charts, graphs, maps, photographs, computer-generated graphics and moving images.

A4.5 Technical requirements associated with different reproduction processes.

Technical requirements include colour systems, paper sizes, screen resolution and file size.

A4.6 Requirements for sample setting and estimating the length of a publication.

Sample setting is material selected as representative of the design elements of a publication and prepared as a proof so the design can be reviewed and modified if necessary.

A5 Technology relevant to editing practice

A5.1 The use of word-processing software for editing.

Features relevant to editing include styles; revision marking; finding and replacing items; reviewing headings; and checking spelling, grammar and language level.

A5.2 Techniques for handling electronic files.

Techniques include backing up, use of virus scans, transmitting and receiving files, and converting and saving files.

A5.3 The basic principles and requirements of software for design, formatting and web authoring, and the interaction of word-processing software with these programs.

A5.4 Typical errors that may arise with scanned material, text derived from voice-recognition software, and material transferred from word-processing software to formatting software.

A6 Reproduction

A6.1 Prepress, print production and proof-checking processes.

A6.2 The characteristics of different types of printing, embellishment, paper and binding styles.

A6.3 Production requirements of the different options for screen-based dissemination.

Current screen-based options include disks, CD-ROMs and the Internet; evolving technology is likely to produce further options.

A6.4 The production options available for enabling people with disabilities to access printed and on-screen material.

A6.5 The procedures for web site and document maintenance.

Maintenance includes handling responses, updating and authorisation procedures.

B. Management and liaison

An editor might be expected to undertake a range of tasks from managing the entire publication process to performing one very specific part of it. Regardless of the size of the publication or the extent of the editor's role, all editors need to manage their own (and sometimes others') time and resources. They also need good communication skills, initiative, tact, perseverance, flexibility and respect for others' points of view.

Editing therefore requires knowledge of the following matters:

B1 Project definition

B1.1   How to define exactly what the project is: its purpose, readership and delivery mode.

B1.2   How to clarify who the client is and the lines of authority.

> A client is the entity to which an editor is answerable for a publishing project. The client may be an individual, group of individuals or an organisation; the client may or may not be the author.

B1.3   The components of the publication, the standard of quality required, and the resources that may be needed:
(a) the different publishing skills and services
(b) the time
(c) the budget
(d) the materials, equipment and facilities.

B1.4   How to negotiate an acceptable and achievable result from the available resources.

B1.5   How to find and engage the necessary publishing team members, and define their accountability, responsibility and authority.

> The publishing team may include project manager, editor, designer, illustrator, photographer, electronic publishing specialists, word-processing operator, typesetter, proofreader, indexer, prepress operator, printer and marketing personnel.

B1.6   How to establish review and approval processes.

B2 Project documentation

B2.1   How to prepare a project plan including:
(a) the work required
(b) the equipment and facilities required
(c) a detailed, realistic timetable
(d) the budget and payment schedule
(e) approval processes
(f) a document management system.

> A document management system controls drafts, filenaming, the tracking and marking of changes, the archiving of text and original illustrations, and back-up files.

B2.2 How to prepare briefs for members of the publishing team.

B2.3 How to establish guidelines for writing, editing, design and screen-based publishing.

B2.4 The need for formal agreements that detail at least:
(a) the responsibility, authority and accountability of each party
(b) the services and final output required
(c) the schedule for receipt of material and handover of completed work
(d) methods of communication
(e) the process for agreeing on variations
(f) remuneration.

There should be an agreement between the editor and the client, as well as between the editor (in whatever role) and any subcontractors.

B3 Monitoring

B3.1 How to track and record a project's progress against budget, schedule, scope of work and required standard.

B3.2 The need to liaise with the client and team members regularly to meet deadlines, contain costs and prevent major problems.

B3.3 How to keep copies of successive drafts and proofs identifying the sources of changes; see also B2.1(f).

C. Substance and structure

Editors ensure that the form, arrangement, focus and length of a publication are suitable for its purpose, taking into consideration the needs of the readership, the author's intention, the available resources and the type of publication.

Editing the substance and structure of a document requires knowledge of the following matters:

C1 Appraisal

C1.1 How to appraise the suitability and quality of the original material.

C1.2 The length, structure and focus appropriate for the purpose of the publication, the intended readership and the medium.

C1.3 The ways that readers may find their way around the publication.

C1.4 The types of material from the publication that could be used in promotion and marketing.

An editor may be required to draft a blurb or select representative sections of the publication for use in promotional material.

C2 Techniques

C2.1 The need to liaise closely with the author and/or client in making all significant substantive editing decisions.

C2.2   How to produce a complete, coherent and balanced publication by restructuring and rewording where necessary, and by adding and deleting material.

C2.3   When material would be better presented in another form.

Material in tabular form may sometimes be better presented as part of the text, number-laden text as a chart or table, a descriptive passage as a diagram, and a lengthy digression as an appendix.

C2.4   The use of paragraphing, emphasis and lists to help readers scan the text.

C2.5   The use of cross-references or electronic links to guide the reader through the publication.

C2.6   The need for headings and other labelling devices that are relevant, logically graded, consistent and appropriate to the publication, and that accurately reflect the contents to which they apply.

Labelling devices include menus, buttons, hyperlinks, headers and footers.

C2.7   When supplementary material is required.

Supplementary material may include a map, chronological table, glossary, genealogical table and a list of further reading.

C2.8   Whether referencing is needed and, if so, what form is appropriate, given the nature of the publication and the brief.

Referencing includes citations, bibliography, list of references, endnotes, footnotes, margin notes, cross-references, glossary and index.

C2.9   The use of lists, abstracts and metatags to identify the content for potential readers.

D. Language and illustrations

Editors ensure that the 'building blocks' of a publication—the language and illustrations—are suitable for its purpose, taking into consideration the needs of the readership, the author's intention, the available resources and the type of publication.

Editing the language and illustrations of a publication requires knowledge of the following matters:

D1 Clarity

D1.1   The principles of clear language.

D1.2   How to avoid ambiguity, repetition and verbosity.

D1.3   The use of clear and logical connections between phrases, clauses, sentences, paragraphs and sections.

D1.4   The use of punctuation to ensure clarity of meaning and ease of reading.

D2 Voice and tone

D2.1   The type of authorial voice or voices appropriate to the publication.

The author may be one or more individuals, a committee or an organisation. The author may or may not be the client (see B1.2).

D2.2   The reading level, formality and terminology appropriate to the publication, and the principles of tailoring language to a specific readership.

D2.3   When and how to maintain consistency of tone.

D2.4   The need to monitor the text for non-inclusive or potentially offensive language.

D3 Grammar and usage

D3.1   The conventions of grammar and syntax in written English.

D3.2   Words and their meanings.

D3.3   The various conventions governing the expression of numbers, dates, percentages, measurements and statistical data.

D3.4   The various conventions governing the use of italics, capitalisation, hyphenation, symbols and shortened forms.

D3.5   The various conventions governing quoted material and the display of lists and quotations.

D4 Spelling and punctuation

D4.1   Australian spelling and punctuation conventions.

D4.2   Alternative spelling and punctuation conventions (including UK and US forms) and when to use them.

D5 Specialised and foreign material

D5.1   Requirements relating to the language and display of specialised material. Specialised material includes poetry, music, mathematics and scientific notation.

D5.2   When and how to replace or explain technical and specialised terms.

D5.3   Conventions for expressing foreign and historical currencies and units of measurement, and the conversion of these figures where necessary.

D5.4   The use of diacritics and conventions for foreign words and names.

D6 Illustrations and tables

'Illustrations' is used in the widest sense and includes drawings, cartoons, diagrams, charts, graphs, maps, photographs, computer-generated graphics and moving images.

D6.1   The principles of presenting information in visual form.

D6.2   The style of illustration appropriate to the publication.

D6.3   When additional illustrations might be necessary.

D6.4   The appropriate placement of illustrations in the text.

D6.5   Where captions are required, and how to write or obtain appropriate caption copy.

D6.6   The different types of graphs and charts and their uses.

D6.7   The various elements of graphs and the conventions governing their use.
Elements of graphs include axes, scales and labels.

D6.8   The various types of maps and their elements.
Elements of maps include labels, boundaries, contours, scale, legend and orientation.

D6.9   The parts of a table and the principles of clear, logical and effective structure and layout.

D6.10   How to assess whether the technical quality of illustrations is appropriate for the medium.
Technical quality refers to resolution, clarity, file size and tonal contrast.

D6.11   Accessibility requirements relating to illustrations and tables for screen-based publications.

E. Completeness and consistency

Editors minimise unnecessary distractions for the reader by ensuring that elements within the publication are complete and consistent.

Editing for completeness and consistency requires knowledge of the following matters:

E1 Integrity

E1.1   The parts of the publication, including as needed:
(a) preliminary matter or entry sequence
Preliminary matter may include cover, title page, publishing details, table of contents, acknowledgments, abstract and summary. Entry sequence may include splash screen and home page.
(b) body
The body includes text, tables, illustrations, captions, labels and notes.
(c) endmatter.
Endmatter includes appendixes, glossary, references, bibliography and index.

E1.2   The need for accuracy and completeness of cross-references and links:
(a) within the text
(b) between the text and the illustrations and tables in the body of the publication
(c) between the table of contents and the headings, text and page numbers in the body of the publication
(d) between the lists of illustrations and tables in the preliminary matter and the illustrations and tables in the body of the publication.

E1.3   The need to test screen-based publications for:
(a) performance, including links, buttons, menu selection, navigation routes, download time and interactivity
Interactivity refers to aspects of a screen-based publication designed to elicit responses from the user.

(b) functionality using different platforms and browsers, and site integrity and accessibility

(c) usability.

Usability refers to the efficiency with which users can locate information to their satisfaction.

E2 Tools and procedures

E2.1   How to use an established style guide or manual.

E2.2   How to develop and apply an editing style sheet specific to the publication, establishing a consistent and appropriate approach to:
(a) terminology
(b) spelling and capitalisation
(c) punctuation
(d) use of fonts such as bold and italic
(e) shortened forms
(f) expression of numbers, dates, units of measurement and statistical data
(g) citations, bibliographies and reference lists.

E3 Text

E3.1   The need to detect and correct errors and inconsistencies in, for example:
(a) spelling, grammar, punctuation, capitalisation, hyphenation, symbols and shortened forms, and italics
(b) style of numbers, dates, percentages, symbols and equations
(c) heading hierarchies
(d) alphabetical and numerical sequences

Alphabetical sequences apply to bibliographies, glossaries and indexes; numerical sequences apply to chapters, paragraphs, sections, pages, illustrations and tables.

(e) chronology, descriptions, names and terms.

E3.2   When explanations of symbols, terms and shortened forms are required, and the most appropriate place for them.

E3.3   When statements seem, from general knowledge, to require checking.

E3.4   The need for completeness and internal consistency in all referencing.

Referencing includes citations, bibliography, list of references, endnotes, footnotes, margin notes, cross-references, glossary and index.

E3.5   How to prepare copy for preliminary material, headers or footers, and covers.

E3.6   The need for lists to help readers find information efficiently.

Lists may be compiled for contents, shortened forms, illustrations, tables and dramatis personae.

E3.7   How to assess the length and content of an index and the conformity of its style.

E4 Illustrations and tables

E4.1   The need for completeness, relevance and consistency of non-text elements, including their captions, labels and legends.

E4.2   The elements that need to be checked in tables, graphs, charts, maps and diagrams (see D6.7 and D6.8).

E4.3   The need to identify any discrepancies between statements in the text and information in illustrations and tables.

E5   Format, layout and reproduction

E5.1   The need to check format and layout against design specifications.

Format and layout considerations include type sizes and style, line lengths, alignment, leading, heading hierarchy, weights of rules and design features.

E5.2   How to correct layout problems.

Layout problems may include widows and orphans; rivers of space; awkward breaks in words, lines, tables and lists; and placement of design features and illustrations.

E5.3   The need to check page numbers, headers and footers.

E5.4   What to check at different production proofing stages and during binding.

Proofing stages for print may include galleys, page proofs, dyelines, colour proofs, machine proofs and press checks; see E1.3 for testing of screen-based documents.

Council of Australian Societies of Editors (CASE) member societies

The Council of Australian Societies of Editors (CASE) comprises the presidents of the following societies or their nominees.

Canberra Society of Editors
PO Box 3222, Manuka ACT 2603
www.editorscanberra.org

Society of Editors (New South Wales), Inc.
PO Box 254, Broadway NSW 2007
www.users.bigpond.com/socednsw

Society of Editors (Northern Territory)
GPO Box 2255, Darwin NT 0801

Society of Editors (Queensland), Inc.
PO Box 1524, Toowoong Qld 4066
www.editorsqld.com

Society of Editors, South Australia
PO Box 2328, Kent Town SA 5071
www.editors-sa.org.au

Society of Editors (Tasmania), Inc.
PO Box 32, Sandy Bay Tas 7005
www.tas-editors.org.au

Society of Editors (Victoria), Inc.
PO Box 176, Carlton South Vic 3053
www.socedvic.org

Society of Editors (Western Australia), Inc.
PO Box 99, Subiaco WA 6904
www.editorswa.iinet.net.au

Copies of the *Standards* are available from the above organisations.

CASE Standards Working Group, 1998–2001
Kathie Stove, convenor (South Australia)
Catherine Gray, secretary (New South Wales)
Catherine Bruce (Tasmania)
Amanda Curtin (Western Australia)
Janet Mackenzie (Victoria)
Rhana Pike (New South Wales)
Loma Snooks (Canberra)
Janette Whelan, Mary-Jane Bosch (Queensland)

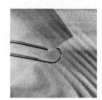

Notes

1 The editor in context

1 Peter Ryan, long-time director of Melbourne University Press, quoted in Louise Poland, 'Out of Type: Women in publishing in Australia, 1931–1973', MA (Publishing) thesis, Monash University, 2002, p. 116.

2 David Crystal, *The Cambridge Encyclopaedia of the English Language*, 2nd edn, p. 377.

3 See Judith Brett, 'Publishing, Censorship and Writers' Incomes', in Laurie Hergenhan (ed.), *New Literary History of Australia* (Penguin, Melbourne, 1988), pp. 454–66; Hilary McPhee, *Other People's Words* (Pan Macmillan, Sydney, 2001).

4 *Book Publishers, Australia, 2001–02*, Cat no. 1363.0, September 2003. All ABS figures in this chapter are taken from this report.

5 Poland, 'Out of Type', p. 10.

6 Ibid., p. 20.

7 Michelle Harmer, 'Children's books finally get to come of age', *Age*, 16 August 2003.

8 Several organisational models of publishing are presented in Diane Brown, 'Publishing Culture: Commissioning books in Australia, 1970–2000', PhD thesis, Victoria University, 2003, pp. 82–126.

9 Speaking at the CASE national conference, Brisbane, July 2003.

10 Some of the papers presented at the conference are on the website of the Queensland society of editors.

11 For current information, see <www.case-editors.org>. An online discussion forum called Editalk is hosted by the South Australian society.

12 Renée Otmar, personal communication. The *Standards* are also available on the websites of the societies of editors.

13 Kathie Stove, 'Launch of *Australian Standards for Editing Practice*', at the Partnerships in Knowledge Conference, Canberra, April 2001: Canberra Society of Editors website, Conference Papers, Day 1.

14 Haya Husseini, '*Australian Standards for Editing Practice*: A comparative critique', essay for MA (Publishing), Monash University, 2003, pp. 15, 16.

15 The Alliance website <www.alliance.org.au> has a summary of the award: go to My Rights, and select Journalists (Book Industry).

16 <www.thorpe.com.au>.

17 'Industry News', <www.electriceditors.net>.

18 'Books and Libraries' in 'Quick Facts—Communications, Arts and Sciences', <www.stats.govt.nz>.

[19] <www.lpf.org.nz>; <www.bookcouncil.org.nz>.

[20] Renée Otmar, 'All Dressed Up ... Editors stake out their future in the knowledge economy', paper presented at the Book Conference, Cairns, April 2003.

[21] The complete results of Pamela Hewitt's survey are available on the website of the Canberra Society of Editors under Conference Papers. The survey was run again two years later at the Brisbane conference, with similar results (personal communication). See also Ann Milligan, 'National Notes', *The Canberra Editor*, vol. 11, no. 2, February 2002.

[22] 'Careers in Publishing', <www.publishers.asn.au>.

[23] CREATE Australia, *Final Report: Writing, publishing and journalism scoping study*, vol. 1, p. 31, 2002, available on <www.createaust.com.au> under Training Programs: Writing, publishing, journalism.

[24] Pamela Hewitt provides a self-paced, modular training course based on *Australian Standards for Editing Practice* on <www.emendediting.com>. The Australian Society of Technical Communication, which has branches in New South Wales, Victoria and Queensland, runs relevant short courses; see, for instance, <www.astcnsw.org.au>.

[25] See the websites of the Local Publishers Forum <www.lpf.org.nz> and the Technical Communicators Association of New Zealand <www.nztechwriters.co.nz>.

[26] CREATE Australia, *Final Report*, vol. 1, pp. 16–20.

2 The publishing process

[1] *Timequake* (Jonathan Cape, London, 1997), p. 157.

[2] Trischa Baker, 'Word Surgery: Delivering the kindest cut to corporate publications', paper presented at the CASE national conference, Brisbane, July 2003. Don Watson demolishes management-speak in *Death Sentence: The decay of public language* (Random House, Sydney, 2003).

[3] But Trischa Baker argues that editors (and designers and indexers) own copyright in the creative content that they produce, and technically the publisher cannot use it unless the right is assigned by the creator: 'Copyright for Editors: The bits that count', paper presented at the CASE national conference, Brisbane, July 2003.

[4] See Trischa Mann, *Essentials of Business Law* (Tertiary Press, Melbourne, 2001), ch. 8.

[5] <www.copyright.org.au>; <www.copyright.org.nz>.

[6] The Law School of Deakin University provides links to sites on Australian defamation law at <www.law.deakin.edu.au/research/subject/defamat.htm>. Media Libel, a project of the College of Humanities, Fine Arts and Communication at the University of Houston, briefly summarises defamation law in various countries in plain English: <www.hfac.uh.edu/comm/media_libel/index.html>.

[7] <www.privacy.gov.au>.

[8] Their website, <www.thorpe.com.au> has information and application forms. There is a proposal to increase the number of digits in ISBNs and ISSNs from 10 to 13 in 2007.

[9] National Library services are explained at <www.nla.gov.au> under the curious heading For.

[10] See 'Specialist Advice and Services', <www.natlib.govt.nz>.

[11] Michiko Kakutani, review of Diane Ravitch, *The Language Police: How pressure groups restrict what students learn* (Knopf, New York, 2003), in *New York Times*, July 2003.

[12] Douglas R. Hofstadter, 'Metamagical Themas: "Default assumptions" and their effects on writing and thinking', *Scientific American*, November 1982.

[13] Stephen Murray-Smith, *Right Words*, rev. edn, p. 71.

[14] See Margaret McDonell, 'What's the Difference? Cross-cultural editing in Australia today', paper presented at the CASE national conference of editors, Brisbane, July 2003. The Australian Society of Authors provides guidelines for writing about indigenous Australians and explains indigenous rights to intellectual and cultural property: see 'Publications', <www.asauthors.org>. On commissioning indigenous writing, see Diane Brown, 'Publishing

Culture: Commissioning books in Australia, 1970–2000', PhD thesis, Victoria University, 2003, ch. 6.

15 Cathie Dunsford, *Getting Published: The inside story* (Dunsford Publishing Consultants, Auckland, 2003), p. 2.

16 R. Dixon and W. Ransom, *Australian Aboriginal Words in English* (Oxford University Press, Melbourne, 1992); Nick Thieberger and William McGregor (eds), *Macquarie Aboriginal Words* (Macquarie Library, Macquarie University, Sydney, 1994). The Aboriginal Languages of Australia Virtual Library <www.dnathan.com/VL/austLang.htm>, devised and maintained by David Nathan, has annotated links to resources for about sixty languages.

17 A handy online list, '100 Maori Words Every NZer Should Know', is at <www.nzhistory.net.nz/Gallery/tereo/words.htm>.

18 <www.tetaurawhiri.govt.nz/>. A general dictionary is Maori Language Commission, *Te Matatiki: Contemporary Maori words* (Oxford University Press, Auckland, 1996).

3 Management and liaison

1 David Whitbread, 'The Impact of the Net on Print: A future for design', paper presented at the CASE national conference, Brisbane, July 2003; available on the Queensland society of editors website.

2 This description is based on the commissioning checklist prepared by Loma Snooks for the Canberra Society of Editors.

3 From a handout at a workshop of the Victorian society of editors, 1970s.

4 Substance and structure

1 I am indebted to John Bangsund for this example.

2 This section draws on Patrick J. Lynch and Sarah Horton, *Web Style Guide* (Yale Center for Advanced Instructional Media, 2002), <www.webstyleguide.com>, which exemplifies the principles of effective structure as well as explaining them; and Victoria Richardson, 'Digital Inspiration: Techniques for editing screen-based documents', paper presented at the CASE national conference, Brisbane, July 2003.

3 <www.w3.org>.

4 Personal communication. An earlier version of the paper, 'Repurposing Texts: Morphing for other media', was presented at the CASE national conference, Brisbane, July 2003.

5 Language

1 Paul Brian, 'Common Errors in English', Washington State University <www.wsu.edu:8080/~brians/errors/index.html>.

2 'Burnt Norton', *Four Quartets* (Faber & Faber, London, 1959), p. 19.

3 David Crystal, *The Cambridge Encyclopedia of the English Language*, 2nd edn, ch. 20, examines regional Englishes.

4 Ibid., p. 438.

5 *The Shorter Oxford English Dictionary* gives the date of first usage for each entry.

6 2nd edn, p. 17.

7 *Modern English Usage*, 2nd edn, p. 359.

8 See Sue Pechey, 'From Tape to Paper', paper presented at the CASE national conference, Brisbane, July 2003.

9 Crystal analyses two illuminating examples in *The Cambridge Encyclopedia of the English Language*, pp. 372–3.

10 See ibid., pp. 374–7; Peter Butt and Richard Castle, *Modern Legal Drafting: A guide to using clearer language* (Cambridge University Press, Melbourne, 2001).

11 Verna Reischild, 'Words Between Languages and Cultures', *Australian Style*, vol. 11, no. 1 (June 2003), pp. 1–2, comments on the connotations of Arabic words adopted in English.

6 Illustrations and tables

1 *Modern Australian Usage*, p. 281.

7 Completeness and consistency

1 <www.nla.gov.au>; <www.natlib.govt.nz>; <www.electriceditors.org>.
2 Max McMaster, workshop notes, Society of Editors (Vic.), 1988.

8 Proofs

1 See Jacqueline Kent, *A Certain Style: Beatrice Davis, a literary life* (Penguin, Melbourne, 2001).
2 'Muphry's Law', John Bangsund's Threepenny Planet <users.pipeline.com.au/bangsund/muphry.htm>.

9 Editing methods

1 Parts of this section are taken from a presentation by Jane Arms at a Victorian society of editors workshop, on a date now forgotten.

10 Working with documents and files

1 For these suggestions I am indebted to Michele Sabto, *The On-screen Editing Handbook*, and to Gail Warman and Kathie Stove, Editalk, 9, 10 December 2003. Sabto, pp. 64–6, provides a sample letter to the author explaining procedures.
2 Adam Turner, 'Software's Twilight', Next, p. 5, *Age*, 12 August 2003.
3 I am grateful to Sam Mackenzie for technical advice.
4 For instance, George Skarbek, *Computer Guide*, 3rd edn (Skarbek Consulting, Melbourne, 2002), p. 104.
5 The shareware program Mailwasher enables you to review email before downloading it, thus cutting spam and providing some protection against viruses; see <mailwasher.com>.
6 Quoted in Louise Poland, 'Out of Type: Women in publishing in Australia, 1931–1973', MA (Publishing) thesis, Monash University, 2002, p. 126.
7 'Versions' here refers to documents created in Word with Save As, not to the Version feature on the File menu.

11 Freelance editing

1 <www.emendediting.com>; <www.editors.ca>.
2 This section draws on a paper by Pamela Hewitt, 'Valuing Your Services, Having Your Services Valued', presented at the Partnerships in Knowledge Conference, Canberra, October 2001: Canberra Society of Editors website, Conference Papers, Day 2.
3 Jim McCarthy, 'Bullet-proofing for Self-employed Editors', workshop notes for the Society of Editors (Vic.), April 2003, p. 12.
4 The Editors' Association of Canada has a Standard Freelance Editorial Agreement, downloadable from <www.editors.ca>, which may be adapted to Australian requirements.
5 Cathie Dunsford, personal communication; Carole Pearce, 'World Freelance Rates: How do they compare?', *Society of Editors (Victoria) Newsletter*, vol. 32, no. 8, February 2003, p. 9.
6 This paragraph draws on Renée Otmar, 'Marketing Your Freelance Editing Business', workshop presented at the CASE national conference, Brisbane, July 2003.
7 For instance, the NewsJobs Network <www.newsjobs.net/usa/default.asp> lists jobs in Britain, Canada and the United States.

Select bibliography

There are so many good books on relevant topics that only a few can be mentioned here. For more titles, see the catalogue of the Canberra-based bookseller Writer's Bookcase, <www.writersbookcase.com.au>.

The *Style Manual*, 6th edn (Commonwealth of Australia, revised by Snooks & Co., John Wiley, Brisbane, 2002) is an essential reference for Australian editors; it covers most of the matters below.

Editing

Australian Standards for Editing Practice is available from the societies of editors (listed at the end of the Appendix) and you can download it from their websites.

A good basic textbook is Elizabeth Flann and Beryl Hill, *The Australian Editing Handbook*, 3rd edn (John Wiley, Brisbane, forthcoming). The bible for British practice is Judith Butcher, *Copy-editing: The Cambridge handbook for editors, authors and publishers*, 3rd edn (Cambridge University Press, 1992). The American bible is the *Chicago Manual of Style*, now in its fourteenth edition; its editors answer questions of style at the website of the University of Chicago Press <www.press.uchicago.edu>, under Chicago Manual of Style FAQs.

Robin Derricourt, *Ideas into Books* (Penguin, Melbourne, 1996) is an entertaining and practical guide to non-fiction publishing by the founder of the Cambridge University Press Australian publishing program.

The requirements of screen publications are explained in Patrick J. Lynch and Sarah Horton, *Web Style Guide* (Yale Center for Advanced Instructional Media, 2002), downloadable from <www.webstyleguide.com>; and Constance Hale and Jessie Scanlon, *Wired Style: Principles of English usage in the digital age* (Broadway Books, New York, 1999) and <hotwired.wired.com/hardwired/wiredstyle/>.

The South Australian society of editors hosts Editalk, an online discussion forum; to subscribe, see the society's website. A quarterly Australian ezine on matters of professional interest, *The Word*, is at <www.emendediting.com>. The Technical Editors' Eyrie, <www.jeanweber.com>, provides tips, techniques and checklists. The Electric Editors <www.electriceditors.net>, based in the United States, have links to dictionaries and grammars and to the British Library and the Library of Congress, as well as mailing lists on editing, computer topics and translating. The websites of libraries and publishing companies provide information about publishing practice and links to further sites.

Dictionaries

The most widely used Australian dictionaries are *The Macquarie Dictionary* and *The Australian Concise Oxford Dictionary*. Freelances must own both so they can meet client requests to follow one or the other. You should also have dictionaries of British and American English and at least one thesaurus. The New Zealand Dictionary Centre publishes *The Dictionary of New Zealand English*.

The handy size and format of Shirley Purchase, *Australian Writers' Dictionary* (Oxford University Press, Melbourne, 1997) make it the first book to consult for difficult spellings of names and words. Other specialist dictionaries are David J. Jones, *The Australian Dictionary of Acronyms and Abbreviations*, 5th edn (Australian Library and Information Association, ALIA Press, Canberra, 2000); *Collins Gem Dictionary of English Spelling* (HarperCollins, Glasgow, 1994), which includes a complete hyphenation guide for word breaks; and Adrian Room, *Cassell's Dictionary of Foreign Words and Phrases* (Cassell, London, 2002). Oxford University Press publishes dictionaries for mathematics, computing and scientific specialties from astronomy to zoology.

Writing, grammar and usage

A feast for language lovers is David Crystal, *The Cambridge Encyclopaedia of the English Language* (Cambridge University Press, 2003), packed with information and addictively browsable.

The two classic works on good writing are H. W. Fowler, *A Dictionary of Modern English Usage* (Oxford University Press, 1926) and William Strunk Jr and E. B. White, *The Elements of Style* (Macmillan, New York, 1959); both are available in several later editions revised by other hands.

Formal grammar textbooks include Rodney Huddleston and Geoffrey K. Pullum, *The Cambridge Grammar of the English Language* (Cambridge University Press, 2002), which takes account of the latest theoretical advances in linguistics; and R. L. Trask, *The Penguin Dictionary of English Grammar* (Penguin, London, 2001). A small guide to the essentials is *Quickfix: The Edward Arnold guide to check and edit your writing* (Edward Arnold, Melbourne, 1993). Lynne Truss, *Eats, Shoots and Leaves: The zero tolerance approach to punctuation* (Profile Books, London, 2003) approaches the subject with humour but encourages a sense of superiority that is inappropriate in editing.

For current Australian usage, two distinguished bookmen provide genial and occasionally idiosyncratic guidance in the tradition of Fowler: Nicholas Hudson, *Modern Australian Usage*, 2nd edn (Oxford University Press, Melbourne, 1997) and Stephen Murray-Smith, *Right Words: A guide to English usage in Australia*, rev. edn (Viking, Melbourne, 1989). In contrast, Pam Peters, *The Cambridge Australian English Style Guide* (Cambridge University Press, Melbourne, 1995), takes a descriptive approach, drawing on the database of the Australian Corpus of English at Macquarie University.

Two free periodicals discuss current Australian usage: *Australian Style*, published by the Dictionary Research Centre at Macquarie University, New South Wales, available through the National Office for the Information Economy; and *Ozwords*, published by Oxford University Press in partnership with the Australian National Dictionary Centre at the Australian National University.

British usage is described by R. M. Ritter, *The Oxford Guide to Style: The style bible for all writers, editors and publishers* (Oxford University Press, 2002), a modern descendant of *Hart's Rules for Compositors and Readers at the University Press, Oxford* (1893); it is strong on transliteration, spelling and typography in foreign languages. Entertaining advice on matters of usage and style is dispensed by Michael Quinion, a British lexicologist, at *World Wide Words* <www.quinion.com/words>, and Bill Walsh, an American newspaperman, at *The Slot: A spot for copy-editors* <www.theslot.com>.

Word processing for editors

If you find the Help function in Microsoft Word insufficient, many third-party manuals are available. For the specialised use of Word for editing for publication, a good guide for beginners is Michele Sabto, *The On-screen Editing Handbook* (Tertiary Press, Melbourne, 2003). A more detailed treatment is Brett Lockwood, *On-Screen Editing for PC and Mac: Styles and style templates* (Brett Lockwood, Melbourne, 2004); for news of further titles in this series see <www.wordbytes.com.au>. You can purchase editing macros for use with Word from Editorium, <www.editorium.com>.

Societies of Editors

The website of the Council of Australian Societies of Editors is <www.case-editors.org>. The postal and web addresses of the member societies of CASE are listed at the end of the Appendix. The societies' websites have links to other professional organisations and sites of interest to editors.

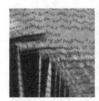

Index